# THE
# HIDDEN CRISIS
# IN AMERICAN
# POLITICS

## *POSTSCRIPT*

As this book was going to press the nomination of Judge G. Harrold Carswell to the Supreme Court was rejected by the Senate. President Nixon denounced the Senate action as evidence of prejudice against the South, which led to heated political exchanges. Many persons may assume that what followed was touched off by Judge Carswell's rejection.

This would not be accurate history. The lure of changing the Supreme Court has been the key to Nixon's southern strategy, around which is being woven perhaps the most astonishing political gamble in American history—that a President elected by 43.7 per cent of the popular vote might by capturing the South split the Democratic Party irrevocably; in the process, gain effective control of both Houses of Congress and the Supreme Court; and, as the head of a business-oriented coalition in a managed economy, emerge with the greatest concentration of political and economic power that any peacetime President has held.

*Books by Samuel Lubell*

THE HIDDEN CRISIS IN AMERICAN POLITICS

WHITE AND BLACK: TEST OF A NATION

REVOLT OF THE MODERATES

THE REVOLUTION IN WORLD TRADE

THE FUTURE OF AMERICAN POLITICS

# THE
# HIDDEN CRISIS
# IN AMERICAN
# POLITICS

BY

*SAMUEL LUBELL*

W · W · NORTON & COMPANY · INC ·
NEW YORK

SBN 393 05370 9 *Cloth Edition*
SBN 393 09886 9 *Paper Edition*

**FIRST EDITION**

Copyright © 1970 by W. W. Norton & Company, Inc. All rights reserved.
Published simultaneously in Canada by George J. McLeod Limited, Toronto.
*Library of Congress Catalog Card No. 69-17630.* Printed in the United States
of America.

1 2 3 4 5 6 7 8 9 0

*Dedicated to our granddaughter,*
*Courtney Lubell,*
*who brings new hope into the world.*

# CONTENTS

# FOREWORD

## How This Book Came To Be Written

THE THOUGHT that rapid social change was becoming a disrupting political force in this country first crept into my mind in the early 1960's. In looking back over my earlier election surveys, I was struck by how much more complex my questions to voters had become in just a few years.

This set me to thinking, as I wrote in the Spring 1962 issue of the *Columbia University Forum,* how little we knew about change as a process in itself. As a journalist I decided we had to try to master the systematic reporting of change, along with its effects on American life.

From my election reporting I had learned that to understand change one must be able to follow the time-flow of the past to the present and into the future.

My first testing of varied means of how this could be done was undertaken in the fall of 1965 when the anti-draft demonstrations began. The interviewing I did of college students across the country was structured around the central query, "How do you differ in your thinking from your parents?"

This proved a sensitive means of determining what parts of the past (as represented by the parent) students were rejecting and what parts they were holding onto. Two later surveys, done with a Ford Foundation grant, in 1967 and 1968, confirmed that the struggle of the young was not with their parents but over their inability to enter into society.

I moved on in 1966 to examine other changes reshaping the nation, particularly our urban-racial troubles. My general working method has always been to immerse myself in a detailed analysis of the nature of a problem and then go out to talk with people about it. My interviewing is done in areas selected with the utmost care on the basis of past voting returns, which enables one to judge how the people being interviewed relate to the whole electorate.

Always in the past, I have been optimistic about this country's political system. But as my research and interviewing went from one conflict to another, I became alarmed. These first findings suggested that too rapid and uncontrolled a rate of change was being injected into our society for the people and our political institutions to stand, and that this was beginning to tear the nation apart. I felt that the critical issue in the 1968 election, and the task that would face whoever became president, would be to reunite a nation more deeply divided than people sensed.

Governor Nelson Rockefeller was an old friend with whom I had worked in the past, and I took my findings to him. He arranged the financing that enabled me to continue my studies.

At that time it wasn't easy to convince people that the nation was in peril. In early December of 1967 I voiced my feelings before a group of city editors at a luncheon session of the American Press Institute. They listened politely, but as I walked out, one remarked, "What are we supposed to do, hang ourselves?"

In April of 1968, I met with another group of political and government reporters. This time their questioning seemed endless, as they pressed for some understanding of what was happening. By then, of course, President Johnson had been forced out of running for re-election, Martin Luther King, Jr., had been murdered, news of upheaval was being headlined almost daily.

When Rockefeller decided to run for the Republican nomination I worked for him, reporting the results of voter interviewing, and submitting ideas and drafts of speeches. I did no writing publicly on the primary campaign. After the Republican convention in Miami, I decided to interview the voters around the country in a novel way. At the outset I told the editors of the newspapers running my stories that I would not predict the election outcome, as I had each election since 1952. Instead, to me the really important candidates were continued disruption or national unity. Which was coming out on top?

My net conclusion was that the dominant desire of the voters was for unity but that no candidate and no party knew how to reconcile our conflicts.

Writing about the impact of uncontrolled change on American political life turned out to be almost as hectic as change itself. Twice the publishers advertised the appearance of this book in their catalogues, only to be informed that I wanted additional time to probe more deeply into the implications of my findings through further interviewing around the country.

This practice of going back to the people has always characterized my political writing.

The gravest weakness of election reporting in this country remains the degree to which it concentrates on the candidates and their campaigning, leaving voter feeling to statistical polls which, however accurate, cannot do the reporting job that is needed. This tendency to picture elections as a contest of image-staging, of actor-heroes against actor-villains, has been strengthened by the mounting use of television and the Kennedy influence. It comes as a shock to have so able a political reporter as Theodore White declare flatly in his account of the 1968 election that "It is the choice of leaders that creates the personality of a political community."

This has never been true, let alone in such agonizing times as these. Little that President Nixon does can escape being influenced by his efforts to pull down what is left of the old Roosevelt coalition and to fashion a new Republican majority. Only twice before in our history—in the Civil War period and during the Great Depression—have we experienced the breakup of the majority party. It is a nation-shaking, historical process which sweeps far beyond the personality of any political leader.

We should also realize that public opinion is playing a drastically different role from that described by Walter Lippmann in his classic study, when he wrote that direct public action is limited to "for all practical purposes the power to say yes and no," a view he reiterated late in 1969 when interviewed by a group of journalism students at Columbia.

This is precisely what so many voters of clashing viewpoints are revolting against. They are unwilling to be limited to "yes" or "no"; nor are they content to channel all their interests and emotions through the parties. Instead there has developed a sharp struggle for political visibility—by the voters to make themselves seen and felt, and by presidents and other managers of society to control or shape what should become visible.

One of the more fearful aspects of our whole crisis is that the relationship of government and the governed is becoming a psychological contest, in which manipulation tends to eat away the principles on which men must agree if they are to be able to govern themselves.

One part of this book deals with that struggle, which began before the Vietnam War. My article in the 1962 issue of the *Columbia University Forum* pointed out that the complexities of our age were propelling us toward a managed society; and yet "too many highly placed persons now think of the American people as gullible fools whose emotions or opinions are to be manipulated—for the public's own good, of course."

Democracy rests upon a decent respect for the opinions and judgment of others. If our democracy is to survive, we will have to restore a justifiable faith in the good sense—not the perfection—of the public. As you read this narrative I hope you will come to understand why I believe this faith in the American people is justified.

*Washington, D.C., March 1970*

# ONE

# THE POLITICS OF CHANGE

## 1. Lo, the Coalition-Makers

THIS BOOK is an effort to bring into focus the strange new politics of impatience which seized hold of this nation and has transformed the tempo and character of American politics.

The nature of this transformation is not easily labeled. One might begin by captioning it as a near-revolutionary quickening of the whole of American political life, as if time itself had been abruptly shortened.

But then one would have to hasten to note that this speedup in our political reflexes has plunged us into disruptive conflict over the reshaping of our society; it has also brought the beginnings, at least, of both a voter revolution and a realignment of our parties unlike any experienced in our history.

To the politicians creating a new majority coalition seems mainly an exercise in reshuffling the party loyalties of key voting blocs. But the compulsive force twisting our political insides and restructuring both parties is the fact that rapid change has become the prime political disturber of our time.

In its first turbulent stage, the reeling impacts of un-controlled change pushed us off balance as a nation, wrench-ing much of society out of control and leaving us more divided than we dared admit. During the last years of the Johnson Administration, we were making decisions like a giant Gulliver hopping on one foot.

In struggling to regain our national balance, we naturally tend to pull back toward more "normal" times. But we are carried into the 1970's on a whole train of unresolved crises which we have been unable—or unwilling—to reconcile. Much of our society is being reshaped to continue battling these conflicts indefinitely.

It is these unresolved conflicts which President Richard Nixon is trying to ride and guide so they will bring into existence a new Republican majority.

Virtually the whole of our society is caught up in the "crises" around which this book is structured—the deepening hostilities between whites and blacks; air-polluted, crime-stalked cities; the "generation gap" which has been trans-formed into a crisis of our universities; the resistances to the Vietnam war and how they have projected into a new iso-lation which pressures for far-reaching changes in foreign policy; the battle to reorder our priorities and to reallocate our economic resources, a struggle made all the more bitter by the slowness in checking inflation.

Each of these conflicts has been headlined repeatedly. Still, what remains elusive is a sense of their lasting impacts, how they have locked together to form what might be termed the politics of a polarized nation that has chopped away so much of the past, now irrevocably gone, has shaken psychological attitudes through the country and still runs on uncontrolled. It is our inability to reconcile these con-flicts that divide us that I see as the hidden crisis in Ameri-can politics today.

Eight points of departure from the old politics of stability stand out:

1. How quickly an unresolved crisis becomes a conflict on the run which can hardly be caught up with.

All the conflicts examined in this study share a common proliferating quality, generating their own momentum and taking on new forms as they rush along. In the process, old choices of action that are being debated get foreclosed, usually leaving only harsher options.

With our racial crisis most of us can still remember when gradual desegregation would have been acceptable to Negroes generally. Currently, though, a new form of territorial racial conflict is taking over our cities, with whites and blacks separated into expanses of "turf" so large that effective school and residential integregation is pushed out of reach. Gary, Cleveland, and Newark have already been split into polarized halves, with more such polarizations on the way.

We often argue as if prejudice and bigotry were the only enemies. Yet the main force structuring this new racial crisis is residential mobility, which continues unchecked.

When the white exodus to the suburbs began after World War II, it had little to do with race. But the suburban migration soon found itself linked up with two other happenings of the 1950's—the northward drift of Negroes displaced by the mechanization of cotton, and the surging racial militancy stirred by the Supreme Court's desegregation decision. All three time-locked together to transform our cities, break down urban government, and now threaten to nullify the Supreme Court's school-desegregation decision.

Who would have thought when William Levitt put up the first of his Cape Cod houses on Long Island that he would become part of a process which would enable Mississippi Senator John C. Stennis to demand equal enforcement of desegregation in the North, hoping that this would provide an out for the South?

Other conflicts of more recent origin display the same proliferating quality. The youth crisis, which might have been eased by sensible draft reform, radicalized much of a whole student generation, pushing our universities into deeper turmoil that became further aggravated by black-studies agitation. At stake now is nothing less than what kind of intellectual legacy will our colleges and universities be able to transmit to further generations.

The Vietnam battling between "doves" and "hawks" is also being perpetuated, as colleges and universities are turned into anti-war shelters and opposition to military spending is pressed as a crusade to "regain civilian control of our society" and release funds for social spending.

2. These conflicts on the run have plunged us into zealous combat to remake American thinking, pressed with an intensity not known in this nation since the pre-Civil War period.

Reasoned argument and orderly debate have been shoved aside by efforts to impose beliefs through force, by violence, control of government, and other uses of power.

Black power, student power, George Wallace power—all the varied demands for power—seek to rearrange other people. In fighting back, many of the people who were being rearranged have dug in to resist all change.

That may be the real meaning of "polarization"—to take shelter in hardened silos, to create a situation that others will be forced to accept because they cannot change it.

3. This battling has been targeted largely at our institutions, with the public schools, universities, the draft, the police, churches, the welfare system, perhaps in the future whole cities serving as successive staging areas.

Partly this reflects the fact that these agitations have sought lasting changes in basic social relationships; in our zeal to get at each other, we have been ready to break down institutions that stood in the way.

But rapid change also turns society's points of entry into special fronts of vulnerability, and at least two of the raging conflicts have been basically entry assaults.

Negroes, banging at every door they can reach, are demanding entry en masse in place of the old pattern of each individual making it on his own.

Less clearly recognized, the so-called "generation gap" has been primarily concerned with how to find a meaningful place in society for greatly enlarged numbers of young people.

In a single year—1965—the count of young people reaching eighteen leaped from 2,769,000 to 3,739,000. By 1970 the number between eighteen and twenty-four was half again as high as in the 1950's.

Certainly, from at least 1965 on, every policy of government should have sought to speed the absorption into society of these youthful millions. Instead, the escalation of the Vietnam war and a failure to change the draft caged those millions back onto the campuses. Much of a whole generation has been left at odds with a society that has stared in bewilderment at the on-goings in the university zoos.[*]

Revealingly, some students in our highest institutions of learning and blacks on the streets reacted with similar, near-revolutionary violences. Both tried to sieze and transform whatever part of society they could reach, the blacks by asserting "black nationalism" in the ghettos, the college students by occupying buildings and demanding that universities be "restructured."

It may be one of the "laws" of unreconciled conflict that it lunges at whatever can be reached, without plan or rationality.

4. No longer can we be sure which of the self-correcting

---

[*] My manuscript included this term before Vice President Agnew's reference to "a whole zoo of dissidents." Mr. Agnew does not sense the caged off feeling of so many collegians.

strengths of American democracy still prevail.

We have been accustomed to believe that economic progress overcomes or eases social ills. The unprecedented boom of recent years has yielded remarkable benefits, quadrupling in a single decade the number of families with incomes over $10,000 and reducing by nearly half the proportion of families at the statistical "poverty" level. However, this prosperity has also quickened racial frictions in our cities and is eroding the effective power of all government, aggravating political conflict generally.

In the process, loyalty to all political parties has been loosened, which in turn is changing voter psychology.

Virtually all elements in society appear to have been strengthened so they are better able to fight one another politically, to be more assertive of their rights and self-interests, readier to press their claims upon each other and against the government. It is as much our strengths as our weaknesses that divide the nation.

5. The crisis has been one of management, that is, of a managed society—call it mismanaged if the results seem displeasing.

Through its 1954 desegregation decision, the Supreme Court, without quite realizing it, put the government into the business of managing racial relations in much of the country. The enterprise brought the most dramatic racial advances in our history, but it also backlogged desires for political revenge that are now being cashed in.

With the tax reduction of 1964, the nation moved officially into a managed economy. For one spectacular year, the performance of the "Keynesian revolution" seemed miraculous, as economic growth soared and tax revenues increased even though federal tax rates had been lowered. Economists became the newest of our high priests.

But the "model" by which the economy was being managed proved inadequate. It never was programed for the pressures of even a limited war. Booming the economy also unloosed great economic and social demands too costly for local governments to support. Burdening local government further were inflationary rises in costs and the high interest rates used to curb inflation.

"Economic stability" was the ideal talked of by both the new economists and the old money managers, but structural changes in our economy seem to be transforming us into a claimant society in which we fight one another for tax cuts and favored government programs, over what share of the tax dollars are to go to missiles, schools, space, or the wider distribution of food stamps. Once the most bitter economic warring was waged by business and labor; today it seems to be the military-industrial complex against the health-education-research complex.

Nor have we been content to leave the driving to Washington. A managed society, as will be seen, generates new compulsions upon the citizenry to take an active hand in the managing.

Southerners battle to end the government's efforts to enforce desegregation, while civil rights advocates would intensify them. Some would extend economic controls; others would throw them off; still others would take them over and charge a commission for the greasing job. In the universities, economists still teach of the wondrous promises of Keynesian economics, while the marketplaces pull back toward McKinleysim.

6. A new structure of political bargaining has come into being in the struggle for political visibility, to make oneself seen and heard.

The great peace and civil rights marches on Washington have been the TV spectaculars which illustrate the huge scale on which attention-getting is being organized.

But the proddings for voter recognition also come from how our society is being reorganized. The greater the powers exercised by government the harsher become the costs of being neglected or overlooked.

Visibility is also a means of protesting against the selection and rejection processes by which our society is run, against the draft, against racial discrimination, against inflationary price rises. As its structure of political bargaining is extended through the country, the unorganized are spurred to organize; political activity has become less orderly, spilling into the streets.

For their part the managers of society try to control who and what is to become visible. Where Presidents Kennedy and Johnson pushed the "war on poverty" before the cameras, President Nixon tends to ease it out of the picture, and to up-front his "war on crime."

As one by-product effect, the relationship between the government and the people is becoming something of a psychological contest, which is changing the arts of government in many subtle ways. It is a feedback contest; while the politicians try to manipulate the voters, the people try to manipulate their politicians.

7. We seem to be losing the ability to moderate and compromise the conflicts that divide us.

The question must be asked whether we really want to come to terms among ourselves? Certainly during the Johnson and Nixon years dissension has been pushed to the surface and made more visible than areas of agreement.

What has happened to the fabled "middle ground" in American politics? Is it still there?

President Nixon has pictured himself as a "centrist" politically; yet the near-fatal weakness that almost lost him the 1968 election lay in his effort to hold the middle ground without any policies or programs that could bring compromise. The same riddle dominates his presidency. Can he really "bring us together again" or is he improvising his own partisan patch-work of disunity?

8. For the first time since the Civil War the effectiveness of our foreign policy has come to hinge on domestic conciliation.

In his Guam doctrine, Nixon began the hazardous process of reducing our military commitments abroad to use more of our resources at home. Done well, this process could prove highly beneficial, but how long will it take? And while we turn inward, what will happen in the rest of the world? How long can we stay divided without inviting troubles abroad and without impairing our ability to act on behalf of peace?

At some point in this process the adjustments made abroad will have to be balanced by domestic reconciliation. But there is no party coalition in command of a sufficiently stable majority to be able to advance a unifying set of policies. The coalition-makers in both parties are organizing to intensify political competition.

Taken together, these eight departures add up to a drastically different kind of politics than we have ever known. My emphasis on conflict should not be interpreted as meaning that it is bad in itself. Quite the opposite. Conflict is indispensable for needed change and for continued progress.

What is deeply troubling is that we seem simultaneously to be intensifying conflict and to be weakening our powers of reconciliation. Unless this spiral is broken we risk being torn apart as a nation, with catastrophic consequences for the whole world.

The choice is not quiet against change. No matter who sits in the White House—and who pickets it—drastic and far-reaching changes will continue to rock our society. The choice, as I see it, is whether hasty "solutions" will be imposed by whoever happens to be in power, or whether we can bring these conflicts under manageable control and, in doing so, learn how to manage the fresh changes that are certain to come tumbling in upon us.

Accelerated change quickens political passions and tends to make people impatient of facts that do not support the cause they favor. Probably I haven't escaped this contagion completely. Still, in examining what rapid change is doing to American life, I have followed the processes of change wherever they have led, reporting my findings whether they were pleasing or not, and trying to label my biases as the narrative runs along.

In analyzing these conflicts I combined intensive research into the nature of the problems with systematic interviewing of people caught up in these conflicts. Through these interviews I sought particularly to trace what effects these conflicts are having on the competition between our major parties to build a new majority coalition. How are old voter loyalties being altered? Are these changes moving us closer or farther apart as a nation?

One could look on this book as a sequel to *The Future of American Politics,* which told the story of how the famed Roosevelt coalition was brought together into a new Democratic majority that dominated American politics for so long. Has that coalition been broken for good? Can it still be revitalized? What sort of new majority coalition is Richard Nixon trying to put together and how would it transform American politics if he succeeds?

## 2. Time As a Political Force

Although staggering problems confronted both presidents, Nixon can be said to have come into office in circumstances almost exactly opposite to those which prevailed when Franklin Roosevelt became president.

In 1933 the whole American economy had come to a halt; when Nixon was inaugurated nothing seemed to be standing still. Yet in both eras the American people gave evidence that they had not lost that personal ingenuity which enabled many of them to go about their affairs regardless of the government's doings.

When Roosevelt, as his first official act, closed all the banks in the country, a million Americans were not inconvenienced. They had learned during the Depression years to live without money by bartering their services for food and shelter.

For Nixon, of course, the great economic battle has been billboarded as inflation. Still, after more than a year of his efforts, an unrevealed number of Americans were using credit cards to pay taxes, which had been levied supposedly to curtail credit and spending.

From barter to credit cards represents quite a social leap. Writing about such prodigious changes and conflicts on the run requires new ways of organizing our thinking, with new concepts especially adapted to change.

One such concept that proved particularly helpful to me was the realization that rapid change makes time itself a political force.

Political time leaves virtually nothing untouched. As a result, sensitivity to time lights up obscure corners, yielding a keener sense of the deeper dimensions of all our problems.

Why, for example, has the battle to shape public opinion been pressed with such fierce, even fanatical tenacity? From my interviewing it was not surprising to discover that the views held by many voters reflected their upbringing, how they had been brought up to think about war, race, and money.

Digging more deeply, though, revealed that we are also divided by clashing visions of what the future should be like.

We might find it easier to compromise if we were not so conscious that the future is being molded by our daily actions and what is done *now* will have lasting effects.

At times, our capacity to overload the future is staggering. Take the much-advertised "fiscal dividend" that is supposed to become available as the economy grows and federal tax collections jump. One might suppose that the prospect of such a bonanza—as much as $15 billion year after year—would encourage greater flexibility in handling economic problems. Actually, it appears to have made our economy more rigid. Programs for spending the "dividend" are organized by competing claimants, and often the money is committed long before it becomes available.

When President Nixon came into office he had the politician's natural desire to launch a new program or two that could be headlined "Nixon did it." But Johnson had put a down payment on every political promise in sight. In a budget of more than $190 billion, Nixon's aides had trouble scraping together a few loose billions.

Another blinder on our political vision has been the practice of organizing our thinking of most public problems in terms of money. This remains the frame within which the debate over "reordering our priorities" rages, of how to shift tax dollars from one use to another.

But an effective sense of priorities requires time tags, which spell out what is to be done into units of time, as well as price tags.

Actually, much of the turmoil that divides us so furiously is over the use of time rather than money. Since all of our more critical conflicts are carriers of past neglects, each comes up at us as a double crisis, at two differing time-dimensions.

At one time-level—always on stage and highly visible—are all the clamorous pressures for "action now," with the varied tactics of impatience wheeled into belligerent display—marches and strikes, sit-in demonstrations and staged confrontations, northern and southern style.

But at another time-level, with each major conflict we find submerged, even hidden, neglects which have gone

unrepaired for too long. Altering these long-range under-
lying forces is unavoidably a slow process, but if they are
not dealt with, much that is attempted at the visible time-
level could be nullified.

Basic to our whole crisis is that we have lost the proper
balance between these two time-levels, between what is
made visible and acted on and the deeper neglects we
cannot seem to reach. Confrontations try to quicken the use
of time, but often the actions taken are poorly thought
through; simultaneously, evasions hold back long-overdue
changes. As a result, orderly evolutionary change has been
forced to yield to disruptive, spasmodic change.

Thinking in terms of time also provides a more sensitive
basis for appraising Nixon's political strategy.

His first, current time-stage might be captioned: "To
finish dividing the Democrats." One tactical problem Nixon
faces is that the forces of realignment have been running
most rapidly in the South, and yet to form a nationally
spread majority Nixon needs to gain additional strength in
the North and West.

This problem reflects the fact that the New Deal coalition
has not collapsed in one heap, in the manner of the one-
horse shay, but broke down at one enormously important
point, that of racial conflict.

In fashioning his coalition, Franklin Roosevelt transformed the Democrats into a party whose main appeal was
economic. By suppressing racial and religious prejudices
beneath a stronger, Depression-born sense of economic interest, he was able to bring into a new majority both white
and black workers, southerners and northerners, the children
of immigrants and of the native-born.

In the South, this coalition of white workers and Negroes
collapsed completely in 1968, Hubert Humphrey doing
worse than any Democratic presidential candidate since
Reconstruction. But in the North, the New Deal alliance,

although suffering heavier losses than generally realized, held together with sufficient strength so Humphrey was almost able to win the presidency.

Since 1952 the Republicans have gained two U.S. senators and twenty-four congressional seats in the South, which remains the one region where large numbers of new Republican supporters can be recruited quite quickly. Nixon's problem has not been whether to pursue a southern strategy —he did that all through 1968—but how to do so, and more crucial, with what timing?

My own reading of Nixon's disposition is that he is seeking the broadest possible coalition, with political living space for both Strom Thurmond and Jacob Javits, Barry Goldwater and Nelson Rockefeller, John Tower and Charles Percy, plus, if possible, some Negroes.

But realignments are often shaped by the voters they attract. When Roosevelt was elected in 1932 there was a wide array of voting groups which had been looking for a party that could serve their economic interests. To the one-time supporters of Al Smith, former socialists, frustrated trade unionists, hard-pressed farmers, the varied minority elements in the cities—to all of them—the New Deal Democratic Party was exactly what they had dreamed of to realize long-held aims.

With the realignment that Nixon has been pressing, voters generally have been waiting to see how his economic policies and Vietnam turn out. But one voting element—the white southerners—has been itching to lay its hands on a new party. The Supreme Court's ultimatum to desegregate "at once" quickened its desires to use the Republican Party to fight the Court and hold back desegregation.

As political forces are running in the South, the decisive issue in 1972 is likely to be headlined:

NIXON CAN CHANGE THE COURT

This lure of a sympathetic "Nixon Court," I see as the

key to his southern strategy. Handled effectively, it could lock up the South's 128 electoral votes, perhaps for good. That would be the political equivalent of Sherman's march to the sea, cutting the Confederacy in two. The Democrats would be divided so that the New Deal coalition could not be restored in its old form.

But it is possible that these gains could come too rapidly in relation to Nixon's strength outside of the South. Pro-civil-rights senators have had the votes to block his court nominations.

At stake in the 1970 Senate elections is whether enough liberal Democrats are beaten to give Nixon clear confirming power. A White House strategist examining the list of Democratic senators coming up for re-election would mark for defeat with double checks at least five names: Albert Gore in Tennessee, Ralph Yarborough in Texas, Harrison A. Williams, Jr. in New Jersey, Vance Hartke in Indiana, and Quentin N. Burdick in North Dakota.

A premature Nixon confrontation with the present Court would risk splitting the liberal Republicans in the North. Without being planned that way, New York City's 1969 mayoralty election turned into a test run of such a conservative strategy, when John Lindsay, rejected by the Republicans as their candidate, went on to be re-elected with liberal Republican and overwhelming Negro and Puerto Rican support. In that election, much of the voter following of both parties was reshuffled in a manner reminiscent of the Civil War period.

In its first time-stage, in short, the Nixon presidency has sought not political reconciliation, but a sharpening of divisions in the nation. The demolition of the old New Deal structure had to come first, to clear the ground for the erection of the new shining Republican edifice. The Democrats, for their part, have been equally intent upon sharpening prevailing dissensions. No pattern of possible victory for either party in 1972 can resolve our unreconciled conflicts. Even if Nixon were to win by a landslide, many of the voters supporting him would be doing so primarily to give him more time to deal with what are generally recognized as enormously difficult problems. Nor would he have brought into existence a stable and lasting Republican majority. After 1972 there would still lie ahead the testing of whether Nixon would be able to shift into the second time-stage of really bringing the nation together into a new unity.

### 3. The Quest for Unity

In plotting their strategies both the Republicans and Democrats have come to rely heavily on public opinion polls and computer analysis. But at least one crucial influence will remain unpredictable for several years, no matter what questions are asked by the pollsters or what data is fed into the computers.

This influence is the weakening of party loyalty generally, stimulated, as will be seen later, by prosperity, the changed role of government, and the emergence of a new generation of voters. As a result, dramatic voter swings from one election to the next have become almost a regular occurence; but that is very different from gaining the sustained voter support which is essential to build and hold a stable and lasting party majority.

These ready-to-shift voters may refrain from giving either party a lasting majority until one of the parties manages to demonstrate that it can unite this sorely divided country.

This emphasis on unifying ability as a test of our political parties, readers should be warned, reflects a bias I have held to in all my political writings. The real drama of American politics, as I have seen it, has always lain in the ceaseless struggle for national unification, in our constant striving for that "more perfect union." This has always been a dis-

tinctively American problem because of our immense geo-
graphical expanse and the astonishing variety of people
drawn to our shores.

Unifying a great nation like ours once it has become
divided has never been an exercise in image-making or
public relations. Always the unifying process has been one
of conflict and reconciliation, touching virtually everything
that was happening, as broad as the sweep of American
history.

The label pinned onto the majority party has been relatively unimportant, whether it was considered "liberal" or
"conservative," whether the party's leaders were politically
clever or virtuous. The decisive factor has been the party's
capacity to serve as the means through which the nation's
needs for unification could be met.

During the era of Republican dominance after the Civil
War, unification had to be achieved through physical expansion across the continent; the "impatient ones" were
the robber barons, the railroad builders, and assorted
monopolists.

The formation of the New Deal coalition was essentially
an "adventure in social unification" which brought together
into a new majority all of the once-despised "minority"
elements—the unemployed, both white and black, along
with the children and grandchildren of the former immigrant elements, debt-burdened farmers, and other victims of
the Depression.

Today the American need remains one of social unification, but on the basis of a far more intimate involvement
and under more perilous conditions than any which have
ever prevailed in our history.

We are not a sick society. We have become an under-
governed and overmanipulated one. Part of our troubles
reflects, I suspect, the fact that we have become perhaps
the most demanding people in all history, asking more of

each other than human imperfections enable us to deliver. Our productive wealth and technological skills sharpen this dilemma, since we cannot plead scarcity or ignorance as an alibi. It is largely to be able to demand more of each other that we exaggerate some of our dissensions and difficulties.

Another aspect of our troubles is a deeply rooted habit of letting conflicts "work themselves out" or to "let time cure all ills." But the sweep of uncontrolled change during recent years has generated new disunities and vulnerabilities in the country.

Two distortions that have developed and which clash fiercely for the allocation of tax resources, are also giving a strange sectional twist to party realignment. Looking to the Democrats are the northern cities, overburdened with lopsided concentrations of Negro populations. In the South and Southwest, where Republicans are gaining strength, is concentrated much of our defense technology, whose costs in missile and nuclear development unbalance the rest of the economy.

Both of these distortions are national problems, requiring national solutions, but since each is centered in a different area, they tend to give our parties conflicting geographic orientations.

Age has become another new force for disunity. Each year between now and 1984, the eligible voting population will be enlarged by nearly four million new twenty-one-year-olds. For many of these youths entry into society must still be reconciled with the protective walls that have been erected by older people.

Wherever one looks at American society today, high potential is confronted by high tension; full employment by inflation; vast expectations of what government can do by vast fears of what government may do.

It is at this screamingly high pitch of conflict that the

American nation must be unified, not in tune with the slow time of accepted tradition, but in terms of acute self-awareness and impatience.

Where all of it will come out remains uncertain. Still, I am reasonably optimistic and feel that some years from now we will be able to look back upon these impatient years as part of a larger drama of a great nation adjusting its political habits and institutions in a time-shortened world.

Profound adjustments will have to be made. Our parties, if they are to succeed in performing their customary unifying role, are likely to be transformed.

Three new sensitivities which both parties will have to acquire can be discerned:

1. Both parties will be adjusting to the many novel political relationships that arise from our having become so highly managed a society. As our first president-manager, Lyndon Johnson undertook to manage the economy, racial relations, and a war, all at once. He left behind a legacy, impressive in its accomplishments but equally impressive in the demands that were stirred for safeguards against the excesses of too much White House management.

Nixon has been brewing a different managerial mix— what he hopes will be a "strict constructionist" Supreme Court, more power for the states, more concern for balanced budgets—all of which are designed to be visibly different from the Johnsonian memories.

But the test of unity comes through performance, not rhetoric. Will the Nixon mix sustain economic prosperity, bring racial peace and freedom from war?

2. The parties will also be struggling to adapt to the quickened pace of time. Here again the example of Lyndon Johnson has been serving as a point of departure. Under Johnson, the Democratic majority was given a push toward becoming an impatient coalition, which whipped itself on to undertake too much, too quickly. This spurring urge may

have reflected Johnson's own restless energies and prodigious ability to manipulate everything his hands could reach. There was also the competing and goading presence of Robert Kennedy, who had pitched his political appeal to the most impatient voting elements.

It would be a nice literary touch to depict Nixon as building a "patient coalition" in contrast with the Johnson-Kennedy effort. But that would not be accurate despite Nixon's emphasis on lowered voices.

His major actions, all deliberately timed, vary strangely in their pacing. Efforts to slacken the enforcement of school desegregation in the South suggest a slower tempo but they also risk ending the whole integration effort, which would represent a new kind of impatience. Similarly, the spacing of troop withdrawals from Vietnam suggests slower action but they seem also to reflect a determination to stay in Asia whose implications are uncertain.

Nixon's new family assistance plan is a fine example of careful progress; he seems to have moved quite quickly to commit us to a long-range expansion of the ABM missile program.

My overall impression is of a president testing public opinion and congressional roll calls to determine how fast he can move toward goals he has not fully revealed to the people. Also it may be that the only coalitions possible these days are impatient ones.

3. Both parties will also have to come up with a workable answer to the question of what the voters can expect from the processes of politics and what should be considered beyond the reach of politics.

These decisions—what is left in, what is dropped out—could prove the most revealing political actions to watch, since they reflect so closely how a managed society operates. The computer can be taken as a symbol. Computer experts have a favorite wisecrack—"garbage in garbage out," which is their way of saying that what is programed into the machine determines what comes out on the printout.

If something is left out, it is as if it does not exist. The struggle to be included in the programing could become among the most crucial of all our conflicts.

This suggests another concept that might be helpful in judging change: to pay special attention to the acts of selection that are going on around us—by our leaders, by ourselves, by other people. These decisions will point to how the future is being shaped.

Every president, of course, feels that he must do many things he does not relish to gain and consolidate his power, but that once the rough battling is over, he will be able to "rise above politics," be more statesmanlike, and put his ideals to work.

This is certainly true for Richard Nixon as it was for Franklin Roosevelt and other presidents; and should be kept in mind as one weighs the Nixon actions and policies. But a managed society brings one difference which our political leaders have not yet learned. Thus far the programing of a managed society has proven far more rigid than one less subject to management. Once something is left out of the computers it is not easily gotten in.

The stubbornness of inflation and the extent of dissension in the nation suggest that we have been overloading our government.

But whose expectations are to be dropped out of the government computers and whose are to be left in? Pressures for government action will vary enormously if the Supreme Court's desegregation decisions are obeyed, defied or sidetracked; if employment and prices run high or low, if we really reduce our commitments abroad or plunge in somewhere because of some "communist" happening.

More than one election, perhaps more than one presidency will probably be required to develop the unifying balance of what controls are to be applied and where permissive policies should run free, what time tempo is best for the nation, what government should not try to do.

If our entanglements were simply domestic there might be little need to worry over how long this process would take. But at stake in our struggle for social unification is also our own and world survival.

The domestic troubles of Soviet Russia and Red China yield us an uncertain span of time to complete this process of reducing our foreign commitments and coming to terms among ourselves. Will we make it? Or will the spectacle of a divided, distracted America encourage the kind of adventurism abroad that could bring on the war we dread to think about? Or will the urgencies of foreign affairs be used to justify over-quick "solutions" at home?

That, in essence, is the ordeal of national unification that I have tried to describe in this book. Where do we stand in this race between unity and disruption? What is it we are witnessing today—the breakdown of this country, or the self-conflict of a nation determined to preserve its freedoms as it takes the measure of what unity requires?

Let us begin with the voters themselves and why the failure of image-making in the election of 1968 was a portent of so much to come.

# TWO

# REVOLT OF THE
# VOTERS

### 1. Upsetting Big Brother

ONCE ONE OF THE more sluggish and slow-changing of American habits, voting in recent years has become volatile and excitable. The "happenings" of both 1968 and 1969 suggest that something akin to a voter revolution is brewing, with a sizable part of the electorate demanding a more direct political role than our parties have ever given the American people.

These pressures for a more activist and demanding politics have been coming from voters generally and not simply from youthful militants. The basic factors are that party tradition and loyalty have become so much weaker than in the past and yet, simultaneously, people seem driven to make politics do much more than it ever has before.

One manifestation of this is the extent of political activity being pressed outside of the parties, and not just at elections but all year round. The targets of protests have been as varied as rising rents, birth-control pills, and pollution; white citizens' councils and black militants have both defied the law; the police themselves have become political activists, on the losing side for mayor in New York and

Cleveland, on the winning side in Detroit, Los Angeles, Minneapolis, and Waterbury, Connecticut.

Some Democratic strategists have drawn up schemes of "participatory democracy" as the answer to voter restlessness. While "participation" may appease the cravings of some young activists for psychological visibility at the presidential conventions, it is not likely to remove the deeper frustrations with the party system shared by voters generally.

The "solution" toward which most voters appear to be moving is a double one—to continue activity outside of the party structure but also to use both parties much as a sheriff might wear two guns rather than just one.

The 1969 elections provided several examples of such two-gun voting. In New York, Cleveland, and Virginia, even loyal party followers bolted to the opposition rather than see their own party's candidate win.

Normally Democratic, the mass of Cleveland's white voters went Republican for mayor in 1969, as they had in 1967, in a vain effort to defeat Carl Stokes.

In New York City, the Negro assembly districts voted almost as heavily for John Lindsay, against the Democratic candidate for mayor, as they did for Humphrey in 1968.

Nor was this the first time that Negroes have deserted the Democrats when they felt "betrayed" by the party's selection. When George Mahoney won the Democratic nomination for Governor of Maryland in 1966 with the slogan "Your home is your castle—protect it," the Negroes in Baltimore, along with white liberals, broke from their party to elect a then-obscure Republican named Spiro Agnew. That Agnew won because of Negro support seems to have been forgotten when he was selected to serve as Nixon's special father confessor for the South.

What is happening is that in this period of intense conflict, party identification is often shelved so voters will be able to use any and every piece of political machinery in sight to fight for their vital interests.

The Ides of 1969 also marked the election of the first Republican governor in Virginia in a century. But this truly historic event was not accomplished according to the "southern strategy" of merging the Nixon voters with the Wallaceites.

Linwood Holton won because the clashing Democratic factions used both parties to fight each other not once but twice in the same year. In the contest for the Democratic nomination, the more conservative Democrats, most of whom had voted for Nixon, beat the liberal supporters of Henry Howell, mainly Negroes and labor unionists. To keep the Democrats from winning in November, labor and a sizable majority of Richmond's Negroes swung for Holton, but so did many pro-Nixon conservatives. William Battle, the defeated Democratic candidate, wound up running best in strong Dixiecrat localities and, outside of Richmond, in Negro areas through the state—an unlikely combination indeed.

This same kind of free-wheeling shifting in and out of the parties was evident in 1968 as well, in the early support for Nixon that broke abruptly in October and in the splitting of Wallace's following toward the end of the campaign. The 1968 vote-switching was generally attributed to the emotional unrest of that strange election year, but the tendency toward party-swapping has been building up since 1948.

A few statistics reveal the extent to which the hold of tradition and party loyalty has been crumbling.

A generation ago most voters felt that they could protect their political interests best by sticking steadfastly with one party. In the five presidential elections from 1932 through 1948, just over half—51 per cent—of the counties in the country, including nearly all of the most populous cities and many of their suburbs, cast a majority of their vote for the same party's presidential candidate each time.

But in the five elections that followed, spanning 1952 through 1968, only a fifth—22 per cent—of the counties stuck with the same party's nominees. During these years a decisive proportion of the electorate abandoned one-party regularity to protect themselves politically by using both parties.

No other period in American history has been marked by such wild trapeze swinging between the major parties. All five elections were either landslides—two for Eisenhower and one for Johnson—or cliffhangers, settled by less than 1 per cent of the vote. None of the five could be considered a "normal" party showing.

This trend toward the use of both parties has been fed by numerous changes in American life: better education; the weakening of hometown tradition as millions of families moved from one part of the country to another; the declining importance of religion in shaping people's vote; the growth of industry in so many sections of the country. Because of these and other changes, different parts of the nation have become ever more alike, and have tended to shift together.

But my interviews since 1952 indicate that the most important single influence has been the steady expansion of government power.

As the impact on the people of Big Brother government has grown more intimate, the voters have kicked free of one-party regularity. Through varied attention-getting stratagems they have used both parties to make certain they would not be taken for granted by the party leaders; to overreact against even moderate economic setbacks; and to bolt from and defeat national leaders of their own party, as was done twice by Democrats with Adlai Stevenson and by Republicans with Barry Goldwater.

In short, the voters' response to big government has

been to make Big Brother uncertain of where the voters stand to give our party politicians a rough time.

This could prove a strange portent of the future. What restraints and safeguards are needed to keep a highly managed society responsive to the public will, to stabilize race relations, balance the costs of inflation and unemployment, domestic needs with our role abroad?

Until some of these problems are worked out, the voters may not be prepared to give either party a stable majority.

Some of the skills which the voters have acquired in how to "upset" our party politicians are worth noting, since they are likely to be developed on a larger scale in the future.

The deliberate and widespread use of both parties first flourished during Eisenhower's stay in the White House. In that period of political transition, a majority of voters preferred to have a Republican President and a Democratic Congress "so neither party has too much to say."

This balancing off of one party against the other went further than Democrats hedging that Eisenhower would keep the peace while a Democratic Congress kept up the benefits. One striking feature of the Eisenhower years was what Republican voters did to make certain that they would not be forgotten.

At a time when Eisenhower was cracking the "one-party" South twice, the Democrats scored upset victories for governor in such Republican citadels as Kansas, Nebraska, South Dakota, and Maine, where Edmund Muskie became the first Democratic governor to be elected in twenty years. At least twenty congressional districts which had stayed Republican through the whole New Deal period were lost, Vermont sending its first Democratic congressman to Washington in more than a hundred years.

After each of these "upset" elections, I visited some of these staunchly Republican counties. Always, part of the explanation given me ran, "The Republican politicians think we have to vote for anyone they put up" or "This county got on the Republican bandwagon after the Civil War and it's time we got off."

The Republican chairman of one Iowa county said: "Farmers have been too Republican for their own good. We should work on both parties to get the program we need."

The speed with which Republican farmers broke from their party was evidence of another new voter characteristic which still persists—a tendency to overreact against even mild economic setbacks. During the 1920's, farmers in the Midwest stuck with the GOP through ten trying years of low farm prices. Under Eisenhower, one bad year brought a political shift; in 1954 the dairy counties boiled over like overheated milk; in 1956 the crop rotation of revolt shifted to the wheat and corn-hog growers.

If any serious economic setback occurs in the future, we can expect sharp political shifts. The Spartan tradition of tightening one's belt through hard times has been replaced by a new economic impatience. If they are in trouble, the voters want Big Brother to get busy.

This tendency to overreact was demonstrated across the nation during the recession of 1958, when a relatively moderate increase in unemployment and rising prices brought a Democratic landslide for Congress almost as strong as that of 1936, the peak of Roosevelt's voting strength.

Fred Crow, a middle-aged carpenter from Muncie, Indiana, provided a perfect illustration of how drastically voter thinking had changed since the Depression.

The 1930's had been tough years for Crow. Bouncing between jobs, he unloaded banana boats in Florida, tried installing furnaces, drove a truck at eighteen dollars a week. But he stayed off relief, which to him was important.

"I'd been brought up to think it was terrible if someone in your family went to the poorhouse," he recalled. "Roosevelt made people expect relief. It was pride with me to vote against him every time."

In the spring of 1958, though, Crow was laid off for five weeks. During that time he drew unemployment checks, which tided him over. But now, he felt, "the Republicans are out to choke labor," and that November voted the straight Democratic ticket "for the first time in my life."

All the hammerings of the harsh Depression had failed to shake Fred Crow's Republicanism; but twenty-odd years later the slap of five weeks of unemployment did.

The 1950's also brought the emergence of a "generation gap." It was among the younger voters that the heaviest political shifting took place, since they were more vulnerable economically. In the cities and suburbs they had plunged into debt to buy new homes. As a Delco-Remy worker in Olathe, Kansas, demanded, "How can I meet payments on my house if I'm working only four days a week?"

Younger farmers starting out on their own were also heavily in debt and needed higher returns to meet expenses. Often the father who had paid off the mortgage on his farm voted Republican, while his son turned Democrat and signed up with one of the more militant farmer organizations.

Still another characteristic of the new quick-free voting has been the steady weakening of the hold of tradition. It always seems surprising to read of a party shift in a locality that has voted for one party for half a century or more. But often such areas are overripe for political change. In these localities, the traditional party attachments reflect conflicts and events of long ago. When tradition collides with a new vital interest, tradition bites the dust.

With time as well, some of the old rigidities of both parties have broken down. In the North the Catholic-Protestant cleavage which locked many Protestants into the Republican Party has lost much of its force; in the South the desire to maintain a one-party monopoly to prevent Negroes from voting has become irrelevant in the face of rising Negro voting.

The ease and calculation with which voters have been swinging between the parties warns against regarding these shifts as lasting changes in party loyalty. In days of old when landslides stood out so bold, such shifts did indicate decisive changes in political allegiance. Today many voters are going for whichever party happens to be available to serve their need, perhaps for only one or two elections.

Landslides, no longer rarities, can be reversed abruptly in the very next election. Lyndon Johnson, in his election sweep, actually carried 133 counties that Roosevelt had never been able to win; all swung back to Nixon in 1968 except eight in New England, where a long-time Democratic trend is at work. Johnson also won more than 460 New England towns which had not voted for a Democratic president since at least 1896; Humphrey held seventy-seven of them.

In the South, Goldwater swept 235 counties which had never voted Republican for president. Wallace won 221 of them. What is striking was how low Nixon's vote fell in these pro-Goldwater counties. In Alabama, twenty-two counties had gone for Goldwater with at least 80 per cent of the vote. All but one gave Nixon less than 10 per cent, which dropped him below his 1960 showing. Wilcox County, which had been 91 per cent for Goldwater, left Nixon a bare 5 per cent bone. In this case, the Deep South was signaling that it would realign with astonishing white pluralities for any party that championed their racial cause.

Against this backdrop, the turbulence of 1968 seems somewhat less erratic than generally pictured. In fact, one might say that 1968 marked the beginning of a new, second stage in this voter revolution that had begun twenty years earlier.

In Stage One, we have seen, the American voter wanted more from politics than could be achieved through one-party regularity, so he turned to using both parties. In 1968, many voters wanted even more from politics, much more than could be realized by simply choosing between the two parties. This brought many of them into revolt against the whole party system.

This turn in voter feeling raises questions rarely asked about American politics.

What can the people reasonably expect from political action? What if the goals being pressed cannot be achieved through political action?

Is it possible to continue to have coalition politics, which require compromise by clashing interests, if impatience becomes the prevailing ideology?

Is the middle ground, so long the marketplace of American politicians, being torn apart, or does it still exist as a meeting place for men of moderate temper?

None of these questions were openly debated in the campaign, yet they were implicit in how the election looked not to the candidates, but to the people themselves.

## 2. The Image-Makers Fail

Probably the most important single fact about the voters in 1968 was their intense emotional involvement in issues, an impatience that exceeded anything I have encountered in any previous presidential election.

This altered mood was expressed rather well by an airline inspector at the Detroit airport early that spring who complained, "I've never had so much trouble deciding who I want elected president."

Asked why that was so, he replied, "You see, there are so many different things I want to do with my one vote."

That response expressed how most people felt. They

wanted something done, not about just one, but about so many different and often conflicting things—to end the war, "make the streets safe to walk on," stop the rise in taxes and prices, halt student uprisings, "stop telling us what school we can send our children to," "get back the *Pueblo,*" "give those hippies one good bath," and so on.

Along with this voter impatience went a surprising readiness to break with party loyalty.

In every election since 1952 I have asked a standard question—"What do you see as the big difference between the parties, in what the Democrats and Republicans stand for?"

During the months before the 1968 presidential conventions as many as half of the persons interviewed replied, "There is no difference."

When I probed into why they thought so, it developed that nearly all of these voters were impatient for action on issues that troubled them and were ready to vote for any candidate, regardless of his party, who would give it to them.

Another source of impatience was the fact that these intense feelings on issues were held by the voters *before* any of the candidates were named, before even the first presidential primary in New Hampshire.

The fact is worth special emphasis. As the political impact of television has grown, we have heard more and more about the powers of "image-making" and "personality" politics. Candidates are elected, we are told, through the manipulative skills of advertising experts who merchandise a candidate as they do soaps and automobiles.

But one distinguishing characteristic of the 1968 campaign was the virtually complete failure of all image-making techniques. In no previous election had so much money and time been devoted to the use of television. But to millions of voters no candidate projected an "image" with which they could identify satisfactorily.

For much of the electorate the whole election year was devoted to an intense, often bitterly frustrating search for a candidate into whom they could project their own strong feelings on the issues.

Through the primaries right up to election day they tried on candidate after candidate, only to find that the man who fit their war feelings might not fit their racial emotions or if he satisfied their racial concerns might not their economic or war interests.

While President Johnson was thought of as seeking re-election, these emotions were structured for or against him with simple directness. In New Hampshire a waitress explained her vote for Senator McCarthy by saying, "I have a son in Vietnam. I want him home."

A shoe worker in Derry said, "I voted for that new man, what's his name. We've got to end this war."

A retired factory worker emphasized, "I'll still go for Johnson in November, but I wanted to tell him to stop the war before my grandson is taken."

But when Johnson withdrew on March 31, the voters were left holding handfuls of darts but with no targets for their angers, fears or hopes.

In this situation the preconvention campaign was almost bound to turn into something of a war of the voters against the party system. Traditionally, our parties operate to narrow the choices before the electorate and to blur rather than sharpen differences on issues. This was exactly what most voters did not want. To sort out their clashing emotions they needed a wider choice of candidates. They also wanted the candidates to speak out and talk directly about what they intended to do about the issues that concerned the country so deeply.

In the past, voter interest has usually waited on the naming of the candidates, and even then the campaigners have had to expend much of their energies whipping up voter attention. In 1968, though, the people were whipping up the feelings of the candidates. Through the whole campaign the arguments that raged inside people's homes, on the streets, and over backyard fences were more impassioned than the oratory of the candidates.

Some voters never did find a candidate who satisfied them. During the last weeks of the campaign housewives or their husbands would grumble, "I've changed my mind so often I'm not sure how I'll vote" or "I just won't vote" —and many did not vote.

Other voters did latch on to "my man" in Senator Eugene McCarthy or Robert Kennedy or, to a much lesser degree, Nelson Rockefeller, only to lose him at the conventions or to an assassin.

For some, Robert Kennedy's assassination left an emptiness which was never filled. "The election doesn't mean the same thing any more," was a common response in Negro neighborhoods. Vowed one metal polisher in New York City, "I won't vote. It's just like killing the man; every good man we get they kill."

Well into October other voters were to remark sadly, "They shot down the election for me when they shot down Kennedy" or "After you've put your faith in one man, it's hard to shift to someone else."

It is idle speculation, of course, to ask what would have happened if Kennedy had not been shot and had gone on to become the Democratic candidate. Still, the question is worth exploring since it helps illuminate one of the more puzzling and important aspects of both Nixon's campaign and his presidency—his reliance on a "centrist" strategy and whether moderation is losing strength in American politics.

A Nixon-Kennedy contest would probably have been one of the most bitterly fought in American history. Few persons reacted neutrally to Bobby personally. Beyond that, he had made himself the voice of the more impatient political elements—of the blacks, the poor, and the young, as the chant went.

In doing so, Kennedy had deliberately turned away from the middle ground, which American politicians have long considered the most profitable ground to occupy, where one can do political business with all sides and employ the techniques of trade-off to the greatest advantage.

Kennedy, by positioning himself well to the left of the center of compromise, seemed to be saying that swifter, more radical, and more far-reaching actions were needed.

Some election analysts have declared flatly that Kennedy's personal popularity was so great he would have beaten Nixon handily. But the alignment of voter feeling on the key issues does not support this thesis.

The war would probably have been Kennedy's strongest appeal, and on this issue I think he would have been a more convincing candidate than Nixon was. But a Kennedy campaign would more certainly have polarized the country around the racial conflict, which, I believe, would have defeated him. George Wallace would not have splashed so far beyond the Deep South puddle, and perhaps not even there. Rather than bring on a possible Kennedy victory, most of the voters who backed Wallace would have swung to Nixon.

With Bobby's death, any such confrontation was postponed for at least four years. The way the nominations worked out, Nixon was left in command of the middle ground, between Wallace and Humphrey, whom most voters identified as meaning "four more years of Johnson."

At first this must have pleased Nixon. Within the Republican Party, he had long been rated the most skilled practitioner of middle-of-the-road politics and later tried to make "moderation" the stamp of his presidency.

Nixon probably reasoned that standing between Wallace and Humphrey positioned him perfectly to draw strength from both sides and sweep the country. The grievances against the Johnson Administration were so clamorous, the desire for change seemingly so general, where were the voters to turn except to Nixon?

But as the campaign developed, this middle ground proved to be political quicksand. On no important issue was Nixon able to articulate a middle-ground policy. None of the brilliant maneuverings—a thrust to this side, a parry to the other side—were forthcoming. Even when his own polls must have shown him losing voter support, Nixon stood immobile, as if in a trap.

Why?

Was it simply that as front-runner in the public opinion polls Nixon was playing it safe, saying as little as possible in hopes of offending no one?

Or had he and his aides tried to develop a moderate approach to the major issues but failed?

For compromise to be possible, the extremes must be willing to seek agreement. But this was not the temper of the country in 1968. Divisions over the war and racial policy were probably too wide to be bridged by anyone.

Whether Nixon sensed this is not clear from the public record. Some of his campaign advisers have been quoted by Joe McGinnis as saying that Nixon's election chances would be hurt if he advanced specific programs to deal with the critical issues. What is clear is that, first, he had no thought-out policies to propose around which a divided country could unite, and, second, his campaign finally reduced itself to a gamble that the public wanted "a change" in the White House. The fact that he went no further than that almost defeated him.

### 3. Blind Date in the White House

In all respects but one Nixon's was perhaps the most efficiently organized presidential campaign in modern political history.

Every possible detail had been meticulously planned in advance. More than $29 million was officially accounted for as having been spent on his behalf; his experiments with regional television broadcasts worked out well; in key states polls were taken almost regularly.

Mindful of Nixon's difficulties with the press in other campaigns, his aides saw to it that the newsmen traveling with him had bigger, faster planes and had all their creature comforts tucked in.

At headquarters a battery of computers were installed with a memory bank of "66 Key Nixon Positions" from which a trained staff punched out replies to voters who wrote in.

Notwithstanding all this technical efficiency, one thing was lacking: the campaign had little effect on the voters.

At no time after the Miami convention did Nixon's campaign gain momentum with the public. From the start of my interviewing I found sizable numbers of one-time Democrats who said they intended to shift to Nixon, but only rarely was there any lift in their voices when they talked of it.

They saw Nixon as little more than a convenient collection basket, the only one available, into which they were depositing their numerous discontents with the Johnson Administration.

In fact, the campaign began almost as a competition of distrusts. Neither Nixon nor Humphrey was an easy figure for the voters to identify with.

The primary battles and conventions had left many

people bitterly resentful of the whole party system, which they felt "didn't give the people a chance to name the candidates."

Since both Nixon and Humphrey were considered "strong party men," both were hurt by these resentments.

Many voters, in fact, wanted to give both Nixon and Humphrey a hard time of it before settling down to make their choices.

With Humphrey, this was conspicuously true of the anti-war Democrats who had backed Senator McCarthy. Particularly in Jewish neighborhoods and among the more liberal Democrats, those interviewed would often begin by declaring flatly, "I won't vote for Nixon, that's for sure!" Then they might go on to say, "Maybe I won't vote at all" or "I won't vote Republican, but I won't vote unless Humphrey breaks with Johnson."

In his 1969 interview with Walter Cronkite, President Johnson contended that Humphrey would have been elected if he had not swerved from Johnson's Vietnam policy. Had he stuck with Johnson to the end, Humphrey would have been swamped.

In Nixon's case, a more exacting question was being asked. Possibly because he was being headlined and advertised as a sure winner, people wanted to know, "What will Nixon do after he gets elected?"

This, of course, was the question Nixon never answered, even to the satisfaction of Republicans. It also troubled many one-time Democrats who were ready to shift to him.

In Huntington Park, California, a bakery salesman grumbled: "I have a son in Vietnam and three more who may be drafted in the next three years. I guess I'll vote for Nixon but I wish he wasn't so vague about what he'd do."

Similarly, in Rockford, Illinois, a bookkeeper's wife, always a Democrat before, said, "I lean toward Nixon mostly because I think he'll try to settle the war, but he hasn't been saying much."

But if some Democrats were ready to accept Nixon on a "blind date" basis, for others the impact of issues like the war and racial conflict was too intimate and personal for them to be satisfied with generalities.

By early October the weight of my interviews was clear and I sent out a story stating: "Perhaps the key fact about the presidential campaign at this point is that Richard Nixon has thus far failed to achieve any real emotional identification with the mass of voters in the country."

The article went on to say that in such emotional times "no candidate can hope to create the image of a leader who inspires trust and confidence unless he discusses the more critical issues in specific detail."

At that time I did not know that my emphasis on the importance of discussing issues in specific detail ran counter to the advice Nixon had been receiving from his campaign experts. In studying the 1960 contest, they had concluded that the key to a victorious campaign was the skillful use of television, which may have been a sound judgment. But they also decided that TV was not the appropriate medium for discussing issues.

Within the Nixon staff, memoranda were circulated quoting typical passages from Marshall McLuhan which included statements such as "policies and issues are useless for election purposes since they are too specialized and hot to TV."

But in elections the medium is not the message. The emphasis of the Nixon staff on techniques of presentation overlooked one critical fact about voter psychology—the content of a message, whether short or long, must be pitched to the emotional involvement of the voter.

My interviewing through the years has taught me that when people are only moderately concerned about something they will accept superficial generalities. But when their emotions and self-interests are deeply engaged, they demand meaningful detail and feel cheated if it is not given them.

In 1964, I found relatively few voters who were worked up over Vietnam, since their personal involvement was still remote. But by 1968 several million voters felt that how they marked their ballot might mean life or death for their sons. They shared the frustrations of a Milwaukee fireman who protested, "We've been given an eeny-meeny-miney-mo choice. Humphrey means four more years of LBJ and Nixon is backing the same war policy."

Some millions of voters with teen-age sons refused to or couldn't sleep with so vague a choice. They became unwilling players in an agonizing guessing game, a grim form of American roulette in which they tried to guess from Nixon's or Humphrey's actions who could really be counted on to try to make peace.

A few examples will illustrate how intense was the vigil so many parents kept.

In Guthrie County, Iowa, I visited one couple—the John Menefees—whom I have interviewed in every presidential election since 1952. They had always been among the staunchest Democrats in the county, but that summer they were wavering.

"We hoped Rockefeller would get the Republican nomination and were for McCarthy at Chicago," John explained.

His wife interjected, "They assassinated the man I wanted. If only there was someone who could be trusted to tell us what to do."

She then talked of a family dinner at Christmas, "shortly before our younger son left for Vietnam. My older boy is in the National Guard, with only one more year to go. The two boys started to argue over the dinner table. The older one wanted us to just get out of the war. Our younger son felt we have a duty to help these smaller countries keep their freedom. They argued so violently the younger boy had tears running down his cheeks.

"You can see why it's not easy for us to decide what we should do," she continued. If peace negotiations collapsed, the younger son would stay in Vietnam. If the war were escalated the older son might be drawn in.

The husband tried to sum up his position. "It's too late to try to win military victory there. We ought to swallow our pride and arrange for a gradual withdrawal. It's too late for just saving face."

Asked who would be most likely to follow this course, the Menefees shook their heads and replied, "We don't know."

"I'm going to watch the men Nixon and Humphrey have around them," said Mrs. Menefee. "That's the best way to tell what a man will do—to find out who's backing him."

"I'm waiting for the TV debate," said John. "Those cameras bring the men right in front of you. I want to study their faces when they're asked the question, 'How will you end the war?' "

The next Guthrie County farmer I talked with had no sons. He said, "Let's use the A-bomb if that's what it takes to get it over with."

Near Blairsburg, one Iowa farm-wife gave only half-hearted answers on how she would vote until asked how long the war would last.

"Too long," she replied with a kind of sleepless weariness. Then her agony broke through.

"It's not right to be fighting so far from home!" she protested. "You read that those people there don't want to fight for their own country. Why should my two sons be sacrificed for a country like that? It's not right!"

We were talking by the back door and seven or eight kittens were crawling where we stood. When one kitten jumped on my back the farm wife called out, "David, come and get your kittens! Mix them some milk; they're hungry."

David and his older brother came up to gather in their kittens. "David is twelve and the older boy is fourteen," remarked the mother. "I don't want them to die in that place, but I don't want them to live under communism either.

"You ask how I'm going to vote. I'm sitting on a fence and I don't know which way to fall."

Rarely had so many voters felt so lonely with their fears and hopes, trying to guess what the candidates meant.

Less than a month before election day, in Huntington Park, California, a young man of twenty-four answered the door. Asked whom he wanted as president, he shook his head and replied, "I don't feel any candidate is a real leader."

He invited me in and his mother and aunt joined us. They were Catholics and "working people." As they talked, it developed that the issue burdening this family was the Vietnam war.

"I'm in the reserves," the son remarked. "I'm ready to go if I'm called, but this war should be ended quickly."

He had decided to cast his first presidential ballot, along with his father, for Humphrey, explaining, "The Republicans have never been for people like us."

He denounced Nixon, declaring, "If Nixon gets in he'll just make it a bigger war."

The aunt agreed but the mother didn't fully accept her son's arguments. In a low, tired voice, like someone who has repeated the same words to herself endlessly, she said, "Wallace is a racist, Nixon is a Republican. I know I'll have to vote for Humphrey."

"But I still can't decide finally," she added wearily. "I've felt this way for months. I keep asking myself who can we trust to really end the war. I still don't know."

Nor was this torment confined to Democrats. In New Jersey, the wife of an engineer (both were lifelong Republicans) had been so upset when the draft notice came for her only son that she hid it from him for several days.

She tried to reconcile herself to Nixon's nomination, explaining, "I think he's just disguising his hawkishness, but my husband reminds me that there has never been a war under the Republicans."

Still, this argument didn't really quiet her fears. On election eve she was listening to Humphrey's telethon, and told her daughter,

"I hope your father never finds out what I do tomorrow but in my heart and in my true conscience I have to vote for Humphrey. He sounds like he'll do more for peace. I can't vote for Nixon, not with a son in the service. Nixon hasn't ruled out a military victory, you know.

"I've been listening to Humphrey more and more this week, and he sounds to sincere. Nixon's so ambiguous. He answers questions, but when he's finished you don't know what he meant. At least Humphrey says I *will* do this."

After the campaign I was told by Herbert Klein, Nixon's director of communications, that the entire Nixon campaign had been designed to project a single image of Nixon as a strong leader, the cool, confident winner to whom the public could turn in trust.

This has been much the image that Nixon has sought to project as president. He has done better at it because of the advantages of being in office, but during the 1968 campaign the strategy was impossible image-making.

Given the emotional involvement of the voters, a failure to discuss the issues in detail could only appear as evasive.

It is difficult, in fact, to believe that Nixon, Klein, and other Republican strategists really believed that a candidate could project a strong "image" without discussing issues. The probable explanation is that there was not much that Nixon felt it safe politically to say about the war.

During the presidential primaries Nixon had talked of

having a "plan to end the war" which he didn't think it wise to reveal prematurely. But few voters I interviewed took this claim seriously. At first Nixon profited from the feeling that "Johnson isn't doing anything about the war" and a change of parties might speed the war's end. In Milwaukee, for example, nearly half the Democrats interviewed in early August urged, "Why not give Nixon a chance?"

But this advantage ebbed after Nixon endorsed Johnson's war policy and the differences between him and Humphrey on the war issue were minimized. Nixon gained some one-time Democratic votes because of the war, but these gains were not decisive.

Nixon's failure to speak out on our racial conflicts probably cost him more politically than the war issue. As the vote-pulling effect of the war declined, the desire for a change in racial policies became Nixon's strongest single vote-getting issue. More of the Democrats who were switching to him cited *racial trouble* as their reason than any other issue.

Here, as with the war, rioting and violence had had too emotional an impact for vague statements to be satisfactory. Nixon did make one speech on "law and order"; also, in a talk directed to the South he criticized the cutting off of federal funds as "going too far" and implied he would end the busing of schoolchildren as a means of bringing about desegregation. Beyond that people were left to guess what he would do.

This silence offended even his sympathizers. In North Philadelphia a forty-seven-year-old programmer for the Reading Railroad, a Democrat, talked enthusiastically about voting for Nixon when first interviewed in August.

"I have a feeling that Nixon would bring more harmony to the races," he explained. "He'll control the riots and see that these Negroes get the education they need."

But by October, he was angry that "Nixon has kept his mouth shut since he was nominated. Humphrey hasn't said anything either.

"This racial thing is the biggest trouble we've got and neither has any program to make things better.

"Maybe I won't vote—both of them saying nothing."

On a nearby street, a house painter's wife had talked in the summer of casting her first vote for Wallace. Re-interviewed in late October, she explained: "I wanted to vote for Wallace, just so the politicians will wake up and realize that people won't go along with what we have now. But I've found out a lot about him and I'm afraid he might win.

"Still," she added, "I don't know what Nixon will do about our racial troubles. You don't hear much about what he thinks. I'm not happy about voting for the quiet one."

In Raleigh, North Carolina, a salesman who was supporting Nixon couldn't bring his wife around. Her complaint? "Nixon is so cocksure, he seems to think he doesn't have to tell us what he's going to do."

Similarly, many Wallace sympathizers who were moderate in their racial views talked of voting for Nixon if "he'll say what he'll do."

In Elm City, North Carolina, a cooperative employee started the interview by declaring, "I'm from the country and I'm proud of it."

"Right now Wallace would get my vote," he went on. "But I ask myself: what could Wallace get done if he were elected and had no party backing in Congress? I'd go for Nixon, if he made clear where he stood."

Generally, throughout the country, Wallace's campaigning had spurred a desire for a middle-ground racial policy, strong on law and order but not carried to the point of repression.

But what sort of policy could Nixon have spelled out?

The actions taken by the administration after Nixon became President have revealed what he was trying to do during the campaign. Counting heavily on getting the South's electoral votes, he wanted southerners to feel that he intended to slow the pace of school desegregation. But it would have been impossible to voice such sentiments openly without inviting violent attacks that he was adopting racist policies.

Whatever Nixon said along these lines would also have been topped by Wallace, and Nixon could not seem to be in open competition with the Alabama governor.

A policy of saying as little as possible could be justified by his campaign aides as a means of keeping Nixon free of commitments so that he could preserve some balance between both Negroes and the white South after he got elected.

But Nixon's silence was politically dangerous in view of the gains that Humphrey was making beginning in early September. These gains did not reflect any major change in how Humphrey was regarded personally, but he did have two assets. Many anti-war Democrats were searching eagerly for some sign that would justify their voting Democratic. Even more important, the economic appeal of the Democratic Party was steadily reasserting its strength week by week. More and more voters, when asked whom they were going to vote for, were replying, "I'm a Democrat" or "I'm for labor." Often these voters expressed strong racial feelings or resentments about the war, but they still were holding for the Democrats.

This new partisan turn was a sharp reversal from my interviews earlier in the campaign, when half of the voters were saying they saw no difference between the parties. Then their responses had reflected a readiness to break party lines. Their September and October replies indicated they were settling back to vote as they had traditionally.

Some of these dissidents were probably bound to return to the Democratic Party. Still one should note how small were the considerations that settled the vote of some wavering Democrats. In New York City, a fifty-nine-year-old furrier, a lifelong Democrat, had decided in the spring to switch to Nixon after his factory was robbed.

As the campaign dragged on, though, this furrier became less certain that Nixon would provide the "strong hand" to deal with racial troubles. On election morning when he reached his polling place he could not decide whom to go for and left in disgust, without voting. At five-thirty that afternoon he returned, but still could not bring himself to choose either Nixon or Hubert Humphrey.

In the final week, however, the public opinion polls came to Nixon's rescue—in the South, that is. During the last campaigning days in some southern cities radio and TV spots paid for by Republicans drummed home one message: "A vote for Wallace is a vote for Humphrey." In one Richmond suburb, at least a third of the Wallace supporters switched over during that final pre-election weekend.

After the election a Nixon sympathizer who sold beauty products door to door recalled: "All summer almost every house I went to was for Wallace. But somebody got to 'em and they got scared. That last week almost every house I went to was going for Nixon. They'd tell me, a vote for Wallace is a vote for Humphrey."

Two young housewives had registered for the first time to vote for Wallace because "he'll stand up against everybody for what he believes in." But all through the final weekend, they said, "we just didn't know what do do." They argued with their husbands, who hadn't registered, and finally decided to shift for Nixon. "I really wanted Wallace," explained one after the election, "but I got too scared 'cause I didn't want Humphrey to get in."

### 4. Beyond Two Parties

"The next president will have to be oh, oh, so much."

That comment of a housewife in Raleigh, North Carolina, midway during the campaign helps sum up much of what the 1968 election revealed.

Above all else, I believe, it showed that the chain of crises burdening the country was far heavier than generally sensed, much too heavy for our party system or for any of the candidates to lift and handle.

In their exultation over how close to victory Humphrey came, some of the more partisan Democrats may have overlooked the fact that a shift of a few percentage points in the vote would still have left the country sorely divided. The conflicts were too deep to be reconciled in the campaign, to permit a unifying surge for any candidate.

Nor would other nominees have been more successful in generating such a unifying surge. Both Humphrey and Nixon were fairly representative of their party followings. Senator McCarthy would have commanded legions of enthusiastic workers but for every voter who declared "it's a senseless war—pull out" there was at least one other voter who felt, "you can't just walk out and say all those lives were wasted."

If Robert Kennedy was idolized by the blacks, he was feared for just that reason by many white voters. A Kennedy candidacy would have split the country sectionally—the North against the South—which, of course, was pretty much the pattern of Humphrey's vote.

The fact is that in 1968 the party system was called upon to do more than could be done through the processes of politics, with any leadership.

Looking into the future, Nixon's re-election will be settled less on the basis of party feeling than by what the voters think of his record in office. If he has been successful as president-manager in handling the war, race relations, and prosperity, he could win by a landslide.

Beyond that, the level of voter activism will fluctuate, of course, with the intensity of the issues. Still, I doubt that our two parties will be able to steer into orderly channels anything like the full emotional concerns of the voters.

Our political parties have been organized to serve as insulators that ground the electricity of conflict; but sizable voting elements would convert them into live conductors, or strip away the insulation.

Many voters also want to be able to influence the government's policies and public opinion all year round, not simply at election time.

These desires have found expression in what I have described as the struggle for political visibility that really began in John F. Kennedy's administration. I have pictured political visibility as a new structure of political bargaining in that it enables individuals and groups to gain attention for their views and interests.

At times it has seemed that almost anyone, anywhere, can come alive politically; all that was necessary was to get in sight of a TV camera. These demonstrations and protests do not have to filter through the clogged channels of bureaucracy or the committees of Congress. They reach government officials directly through the newspapers and TV, often with dramatic impact.

If oil escapes from offshore drilling rigs near Santa Barbara, pictures of polluted beaches and of dying fish and birds are seen, and protesting voices are heard across the nation.

The civil rights struggle was spurred, perhaps even shaped, by the fact that so many of its battles were visible on television and press photographs. The new anti-pollution crusade seems to be profiting from the fact that its abuses are also so photogenic.

This competition for visibility can clash sharply with

what we regard as representative government and raises some serious problems for a democracy like ours. Is what becomes visible truly representative of the whole? Who, for example, speaks for the Negroes—the angry black militants or the officials of the NAACP? Who do the disruptive Chicago Seven represent—anyone but themselves? So much of what is made visible comes to us as only a distorted fragment. Almost never do we see it whole.

Other threats to our democracy arise from the fact that the President has undertaken to compete directly with dissident groups in deciding who and what is to be made visible. It is of course the right and responsibility of the President to defend his policies; but *how* this is done has become perhaps as important as what is said. A new theatrical quality has been added to, or has replaced, what was once described as "debate." Demonstrators and the President in his response are apt to make an issue appear as a staging of uproar against quiet.

"The silent majority" is an advertising creation which does not exist, my interviewing shows, in the way it has been repeatedly invoked, no more than the demonstrators and their marches speak for the nation. How are the mass of citizens, well-mannered on both sides of the issue, to be heard and seen?

Also, in a managed society politics takes on a near-totalitarian flavor. Thus we find the president trying to shape public thinking about an unpopular war, on racial relations and the Supreme Court, inflation and unemployment, while simultaneously trying to realign the party loyalties of millions of voters. Around his as well are men who believe in employing every known trick to manipulate public emotion.

Previous presidents have been just as thorough in employing every available means to gain and solidify voter support for themselves and their party. But the potential for manipulation is greater today than ever before. As yet, there are no good answers to questions on what should be done about this.

The ordinary voter's ability to gain visibility can serve as a release for people caught up in the pressures of a changing society and who may want to try to influence the shape of the future. It could also provide a valuable democratic safeguard for the individual against an overmanaged, over-manipulated society.

Each new president will bring in with him a new style and tempo in the contest for visibility. Under President Kennedy, the thrust was simple, to get speedier action. Largely this reflected Martin Luther King's determination, in taking to the streets with his "nonviolent" demonstrations, to force quicker change on behalf of civil rights.

Kennedy had been rather slow in pushing the civil rights cause until the 1963 spectacle of Bull Connor using fire hoses and dogs on black children in Birmingham. After that Kennedy assumed leadership to press impatiently for civil rights action.

Under Nixon the competition to be seen and heard has become much more an effort to quiet rather than to encourage dissent. Both Johnson and Kennedy wanted to make discontent more visible, and tended to exaggerate it; under Nixon the image effect sought is that everything's under control when little really is.

New twists and tricks in this contest for visibility will be developed endlessly, of course. Still, the net effect is likely to be a greater public distrust of politics and our political leaders.

Increasingly voters have come to believe that things happen because they are made to happen, which often encourages further voter activism and make-happenings.

In stimulating self-awareness, visibility tends to politicalize what it touches. It is more likely to increase rather than reduce the public's expectations of what politics and government should do.

One other running conflict should be touched on briefly
—that of determining what direction each party should
follow on major issues. Here again, the embattled factions
are not likely to be entirely satisfied with what the boys
in the air-conditioned rooms decide.

One possible development might be four-party politics
such as exist in the state of New York. There the Conservative Party tries to put pressure on Republican policy and
the choice of candidates; the Liberal Party puts the squeeze
on the Democrats. This arrangement permits each group to
demonstrate how large a following it can command and to
bargain with the party leaders, which was how Wallace's
candidacy was used by many voters.

Canadian voters have developed considerable skill in
using their four-party system. In three successive elections
the two minority parties won sufficient seats in Parliament
to prevent the Liberals from forming a majority government.
Not until both the Liberals and Conservatives retired their
leaders—Lester Pearson and John Diefenbaker—were the
voters ready to give the government a majority.

How the 1968 voting broke across the country left an
unusual semi-sectional alignment of the parties, with the
Democratic support anchored in the big city northern states,
while the Republicans gained new strength in the South and
Southwest. Neither of these alignments forms an adequate
base of support for a truly national majority coalition. The
uncertainty over where the parties stand should sharpen the
competitive bidding by both parties for the voters and force
each party to give less emphasis to old issues and more attention to the newer conflicts that divide the country.

To judge the likely outcome of the realignment, we will
need to examine why it has been so difficult even to ease
these conflicts. A good place to start is with our racial crisis and the political legacy left by George Wallace.

# THREE

# THE MANY USES OF GEORGE WALLACE

## 1. A Live-Talking Candidate

IN ITS IMPACT ON THE VOTERS George Wallace's candidacy could be likened to a two-stage rocket. On launching it burst upward in a spectacular explosion of support for "law and order" and, for a time, trailed as he was by student and black hecklers, it dominated the campaign skies.

But with each circling of the political orbit more Americans were frightened into settling for a less extreme racial action. Toward the end a third or more of Wallace's supporters decided it would be wiser to use either the Democratic or Republican vehicles for re-entry to political earth.

Despite this anti-climatic ending, Wallace's journey through political space makes for intriguing analysis, particularly if one searches beyond his demagogic skills to the following he attracted.

What is the real significance of those 9,893,952 Wallace votes? Do they actually constitute the balance of voting power in the nation? Were they a one-shot protest or do they represent a foundation on which Wallace or other segregationists can build an even larger vote in a future try? What would the Republicans or Democrats have to do to win over these Wallaceites?

The Wallace campaign is also instructive for at least two other reasons—it gives us insights into the new manipulative skills being developed by the American voter, and it demonstrates the value to a democratic society of a real live talking-out candidate.

Racial reconciliation was hardly Wallace's purpose in running for the White House. Still, by speaking out in blunt backwoods language while Nixon remained silent, Wallace did make it possible for the voters to register their opposition to an extremist racial policy. The "somewhere down the middle" mood of the majority of voters was expressed by a thirty-one-year-old lab technician in Cicero, Illinois, a Democrat who was shifting to Nixon. Asked why, he explained, "I want some action."

"What about Wallace?" he was asked.

"That's too much action," he replied.

The strength of this desire for a middle-ground racial policy has never been generally appreciated, even though it has been the majority feeling in the nation.

Partly this reflects how campaigns are reported, with conflict personalized in the candidates, as if the "bad guy" is the cause and beating him will settle the issue favorably. Where racial conflict is involved the candidates have usually been personalized in extremes, as if the only choice for the voter is to be pro-Negro or anti-Negro.

In that fashion, early in the 1968 campaign, demands for "law and order" were quickly labeled as "code words" for racism and made synonomous with support for Wallace and racial repression, all being jumbled together under the term "backlash."

Whatever trickery the candidates may have had in mind, this was not an accurate description of how the voters felt. Wallace drew 13.5 per cent of the nation's vote. Yet four of every five persons interviewed were prepared to use "force if necessary" to end racial riots and violence. Included were voters favorably disposed toward civil rights.

To cite just one example, in Pittsburgh, a thirty-seven-year-old teacher of high school math said, "Negroes are finally getting enough sense to know they must organize if they want something."

But he felt, "When things reach riot proportions, they must be handled with force. Once quelled, we should look into what started it."

This desire to halt racial violence was the strongest single sentiment voiced by the voters through the whole campaign. But most of those advocating stiffer law enforcement did not want to stop Negro advances.

Each person interviewed was asked, "Of the civil rights laws enacted over the last fifteen years, which would you keep, which would you repeal?" The overwhelming majority expressed no desire to turn back the civil rights clock.

One particularly striking example is worth noting. In Greensboro, North Carolina, a sixty-year-old textile mill supervisor had difficulty expressing his fury at the thought of Negroes rioting and destroying property.

"Wallace says he would shoot the looters but I'd go further," he declared. "If anyone tried to put fire to my house, why—I'd tie them up in the street and burn them!"

Asked about the varied civil rights programs, he studied the list and then replied, "I'd keep them all. I ain't for holding the colored down."

The mixed feelings of this textile supervisor indicate how inaccurate it is to apply the term "backlash" to every critical reaction toward Negroes. The feeling of many voters was closer to that of a pendulum swing against "going too far." "Backlash" connotes a resurgence of racial hatred and a turn against Negroes because of prejudice. The pendulum suggests a protest against excesses, which if corrected would bring a pendulum swing back in the other direction.

Nor have the shifts in racial views from one election to the next been as erratic as many persons believe.

Over the years I have found considerable consistency in the racial thinking of white people. A Negro I once interviewed remarked, "To the white man the solution of the racial crisis means the absence of tension. To me it is getting my rights."

That remains a pretty good description of white racial feeling. In all my interviewing since 1950, I have found that the main concern of most white voters has never been racial justice. Always the balance of sentiment has swung to the course of action that seemed to them to offer the best prospect for racial peace.

Early in the 1964 presidential campaign, sizable numbers of voters talked of going for Barry Goldwater because of the riots disrupting some cities, only to switch later in the campaign because, they feared, "he'd make things worse."

In Rochester, New York, one house I stopped at turned out to be the home of the Republican precinct captain.

"When that rioting started," he recalled, "I took down my baseball bat and sat down on the doorsteps. If any colored came up I was going to let him have it. They weren't going to hurt my kids."

Asked whom he would be voting for, he replied, "Johnson."

"How come," I pressed him, "since you're the Republican precinct captain?"

He answered, "Goldwater would only make them madder than hell."

By 1968, however, the swing of voter sentiment was against leniency. Both pendulum and backlash feeling was reflected in two oft-repeated protests, "The more they get the more they want" and "The coloreds get away with stuff I'd be put in jail for."

In Dumont, New Jersey, a fifty-eight-year-old cashier

for Pepsi-Cola supported open housing, saying, "Negroes are better than some whites." Nevertheless he felt, "Police have been too soft on rioters. What's the use of having police if they can't take any action?"

Wallace, of course, was doing his best to manipulate voter emotions for his own ends, and it was as victims of his demagoguery that most Wallaceites were usually pictured. Some newsmen simply dismissed Wallace's supporters as "bigots" and "racists" or even as "mentally sick" or "frustrated outcasts" of society. Indignant articles were written analyzing in depth what was wrong with a country in which so many Americans, young as well as old, could be led to even think of supporting someone like Wallace and what he stood for.

Much that same reasoning has governed most speculations about Wallace's political future, as if the decisive factors were his personality and demagogic skills.

But the racial potential for any third party shapes up differently if one examines the varied uses to which Wallace was put in 1968. Some of these uses are being taken care of by Spiro Agnew, others by President Nixon, which leads to the conclusion that Wallace would not draw as much support in a second presidential run.

For southerners Wallace served as a means of releasing all the pent-up resentments and desires for political revenge that had accumulated in the fourteen years since the Supreme Court's decision on school desegregation.

Much more than his "standing in the schoolhouse door," it was the march from Selma to Montgomery that really made Wallace the spokesman for so many southerners. At that time, in the spring of 1965, I was interviewing through the South, and was impressed by how many southerners thought that Goldwater's defeat meant that the battle against desegregation had been lost. This feeling produced a greater readiness to accept further desegregation than I had ever found before. Typifying this new mood, a South Carolina grocer who had voted for Goldwater remarked, "It doesn't matter what I think. When the whole country is for it we might as well get used to it."

But the battling at Selma changed the tone of southern comment. In every southern state people would ask, "Did you hear Wallace say how he would obey the courts if Martin Luther King did?" or they would volunteer, "I wish we had a governor like Wallace who would stand up against Washington."

On one street corner in Clanton, Alabama, a well-dressed merchant drew obvious pleasure from praising Wallace for refusing to call out the National Guard and telling how he "slickered Johnson into making the federal government pay the cost of guarding that march."

For many southerners the march itself was humiliating and embittering—like a show of force by an occupying foreign power.

Wallace spurred southerners to vote in 1968 who had had no interest in politics. In Richmond, an elderly woman confided, "The first time I voted was when I was a young girl. Somebody paid me five dollars to vote for a justice of the peace. After that I always figured I wouldn't vote unless somebody paid me. But crime in this country has gone far enough. This year, I'm going to vote without being paid for it."

The Supreme Court's decision to desegregate "at once" was used by Wallace to reveal his intention to run for Governor of Alabama, with intimations that it was a first step to another presidential try. But President Nixon holds a vastly different position in the thinking of southerners than in 1968.

His nomination to the Supreme Court of two southerners, Clement Haynsworth and G. Harrold Carswell has dramatized one crucial political fact—Nixon is the man who can

change the makeup of the Supreme Court so its views will
be closer to those of the South.

In 1972, I believe, most southerners will vote for the
man who can change the Court rather than for any third-
party candidate, even if he puts on a truly terrific demagogic
show.

The role of Wallace and other segregationists in the
South, I would judge, has been reduced to that of a double
agent, pressuring Nixon to move closer to their views, and
keeping the Democrats divided in voting areas where the
Republicans have few followers. Both these strategies are
discussed more fully in a later chapter on the South.

In the northern states, where Wallace drew 4,820,543
votes, his potential is more uncertain, since racial tensions
are still on the rise there. "He speaks flat out like us," was
how Wallace was described by an Akron garage mechanic
who termed himself "a West Virginia mountain boy." That
remark pointed to one main source of Wallace strength in
the North: the communities which have been settled by
hillbillies and white southerners.

If one plots on a map the places where these work-
seeking families came from, it becomes a picture of the migration routes they followed—to Akron from Blue Ridge,
Georgia, and Letter Gap and White Water, West Virginia;
to Detroit's factory suburbs from Sparta, Tennessee, and
Pine Bluff, Arkansas; to Columbus, Ohio, from Hazard and
Harlan, Kentucky.

We are conscious of how the northward migration of
southern Negroes transformed our cities and politics, but
we are still dimly aware of the political impact of the out-
pouring of white southerners and Appalachian hilljacks.

In other parts of the North, the high Wallace vote provides a thermometer reading of mounting racial friction.
His top Maryland percentage was recorded in Cambridge,
subjected to martial law in 1963, and where H. Rap Brown

was indicted for inflammatory oratory in 1967. Wallace also drew 30 per cent of the vote in the white precincts of Cairo, Illinois, where racial violence broke out in the summer of 1969. In most northern cities the strongest Wallace percentages were found in neighborhoods which border on the edge of expanding Negro areas.

During the 1964 presidential primary in Indiana, a South Bend factory worker declared: "I'm not for Wallace. He's against the Constitution." When I reinterviewed him in 1968 he said, "I'm going for Wallace."

What had changed him in four years? "The coloreds live just a block away," he explained. "Last night they firebombed the tavern on the corner."

Again, a young Philadelphia policeman was interviewed during the tense pre-election days when the schools were shut down because of troubles in South Philadelphia.

"A lot of people say Wallace is extreme," this policeman said. "I've been on twelve-hour shifts with this school trouble. I saw a colored guy come up to a policeman with a big club and smack him across the face with it. Well, I'll tell you I got extreme. I chased that nigger for three blocks and when I caught up with him I beat his ass off.

"Maybe I've talked too much, but if there's any more trouble here I'll vote for Wallace," the policeman went on. "If things would quiet down I'd vote for Nixon."

Wallace was also listened to intently across the whole country by many more millions who felt, "Some of the things he says make sense."

Rarely during the entire campaign did one encounter a voter who remarked, "Nixon said . . ." and then repeated some point made in Nixon's campaigning. This held equally true for Humphrey.

But any number of voters played back such Wallaceisms as:

"There isn't a dime's difference between the parties."

"If any demonstrator lay down in front of my car I'd run him over."

"When I get to Washington I'll throw all these phonies and their briefcases into the Potomac."

Often, what Wallace said divided husbands and wives in angry argument—the only bit of campaigning that did. Usually it was the husband who supported Wallace, perhaps because there was a thump of masculinity in saying, "Wallace doesn't pull punches," and also because much of the Wallace organizing effort came from the factories.

But their wives would dismiss the former Alabama governor with "too radical," "a nut," or "send him back to the trees."

Others shared the feelings of a mail clerk in Philadelphia who said, "I listen to Wallace to let off steam. He gets rid of my antagonisms when I hear him."

Still others employed Wallace as a means of "talking back to the politicians" in hopes of influencing their views.

However the fact that people listened to Wallace did not mean that they intended to vote for him. For many voters Wallace served as the means through which they worked out their own emotional ups and downs on the racial conflict.

This was not easily done. A majority of voters felt quite strongly about the need for action to end racial violence, but, as has been pointed out, they did not want Negro repression. No candidate, though, really spelled out such a position.

Humphrey, it was generally felt, meant "more of the same"; with Nixon, no one was sure if he would do anything; as for Wallace, most voters said, "you know where he stands," but that frightened them.

Many, in rejecting Wallace's extremism, volunteered that they were turning to Nixon as a middle-road choice.

In Levittown, Long Island, the wife of a sixty-four-year-old engineer, and a lifelong Democrat, explained, "My daughter's a pianist. She works late at night and has to go home to Brooklyn. I can't sleep at night for worrying. I don't relax until she telephones me the next morning."

Asked which candidate would be best for handling racial problems, she replied, "I was for Humphrey until he started shooting his mouth off about the coloreds, saying how much he's going to give them. I don't think we should give them any more."

As for Wallace, she said, "I'm afraid to vote for him. If he were elected there'd be a real revolution. I think Nixon would do the best job on the racial thing."

From my interviews I was struck by how high a buildup of personal fears had taken place in the years of rioting and violence.

The wife of a real estate broker in Siler City, North Carolina, confided. "It's gotten so I'm afraid to let my child out of sight. TV has done this to me—the things you see. We have no trouble here, but I dread her going to school."

A twenty-eight-year-old truck driver recalled, "When we had the riots in Akron, a couple of guys jumped in front of my truck and started stealing things. I tried to fight the looters; then these two young fellows jumped on the back of my truck and helped me out. I don't know what I would have done without them.

"That's why I'm so confused in this voting," he went on. "I believe the police should have more authority. But I wouldn't want to see innocent people hurt, like those fellows who helped me."

A Miami secretary, who was sticking with Hubert Humphrey, thought, "You must keep school desegregation. Education is the only hope that Negroes will become more like us in the future."

A bit later she remarked, "When I get into my car I always lock the door. If any of them tried to stop me I'd just as soon run them down."

Another major irritant was that looting had been openly tolerated during the riots. In Wheaton, Maryland, the wife of a printer, who was shifting to Republican, recalled, "When Negroes were rioting in Washington our car was stopped by a traffic cop so a looter could cross the street. That really put me off."

Rather large numbers of voters had also come to feel that Negroes were being treated with favoritism. In city after city, one complaint was repeated: "There should be one law for all alike" or "If I broke into a store they'd shoot me."

In the fall of 1969 Wallace made a tour of Vietnam, suggesting that he was testing the use of the war as an issue. Later, in February of 1970 he was photographed with Lieutenant William Calley, whom Wallace defended by criticizing his favorite target—"the press"—for its handling of the alleged massacre at Songmy. Still, I doubt that Vietnam would bring Wallace or any racial party many votes. The war was not a vote-getting issue for him in 1968.

In some communities, people who had rooted for Senator Eugene McCarthy or Governor Nelson Rockefeller did talk of going for Wallace, but these were voters who felt strongly about war and wanted to protest against the Tweedlenam-Tweedleviet choice which they felt Nixon and Humphrey gave them.

They did not care what Wallace thought about the war; they were using him to voice their own views, not endorse his.

The bulk of Wallace's supporters, drawn to him for racial reasons, didn't really care what Wallace said about the war. About as many wanted to "pull out" as urged "step up the fighting." Most of them attributed their own views to Wallace.

In one Richmond neighborhood a forty-seven-year-old

electrical contractor, after talking at length about the many guns he kept in his home, urged, "Level Hanoi and Haiphong. I'm for using nuclear weapons."

He went on to say, "I don't know how, but I'm sure Wallace would end the war faster than anyone."

Down the street another Wallace backer, a bricklayer's wife, said, "Bring the boys home—just plain pull out."

Asked what Wallace would do about the war, she replied, "It's hard to say, but I feel he'd definitely pull out."

Nor did the selection of General Curtis LeMay as Wallace's vice presidential running mate have much effect on the voting. By early October, when LeMay's candidacy was announced, the "bargaining" stage of the campaign was almost over. The people who had been holding out to worry Nixon and Humphrey into speaking out more forthrightly were about ready to make their final choice for president.


## 2. Rumpus Basement Politics

Perhaps the most intriguing use that Wallace's candidacy was put to was as a temporary landing platform on which several million voters waited until the likely election outcome became clearer.

Two sharply conflicting political elements employed Wallace for this same purpose.

Through most of the South, voters would confess, "I think like George Wallace," only to add, "but I'm afraid Humphrey will win, and he would be worse than Johnson."

While public opinion polls showed Nixon way out front, some southerners shared the pleasure of a South Carolina milkman who grinned as he said: "This is a great election. Nixon is sure to win and that will take care of Humphrey. I can help run up a big protest vote for Wallace."

A similar conflict was raging among factory workers in Detroit, Cleveland, Pittsburgh, and other northern industrial areas. They were vehement in urging, "Untie the police so they can end these riots" or "You can't coax any more—crack down on the first outbreak."

But they were also bitterly opposed to voting for a Republican president. Asked "Why don't you turn to Nixon for a change in racial policy?" the invariable answer was "Republicans are no good for workers" or "All our improvements were given to us by the Democrats."

And so there they were, on both sides—4 to 6 million pro-Wallace voters who were eager to overhaul our racial policies but sharply divided over who they wanted to run the nation's economy.

In searching for a phrase that would describe this odd situation, I wrote that, in effect, Wallace's candidacy had been turned into a gigantic rumpus basement where his sympathizers could kick up enough bargaining noises to trouble and influence the party leaders upstairs. That October the big question was how many would remain in the rumpus basement, loyal to Wallace, and how many would troop upstairs on election day to vote for their second choice.

Sometime during the final two weeks of the campaign, as best one can judge, the movement up from the rumpus basement turned into quite a rush.

Early in September, six of every ten Democrats interviewed in several worker precincts of Akron and Barberton, Ohio, had talked of voting for Wallace. Reinterviewed the Saturday before election day, half of these one-time Wallaceites had decided—mostly a week or two earlier—to switch, mainly to Humphrey.

Particularly striking was the abrupt change in the mood of these voters compared with early September. Then the "I'm for Wallace" surge seemed so irresistible that even staunch Democrats were wavering in his favor. One municipal employee who took care of petunias in the Barberton park had only nice things to say about Humphrey. Still, he thought, "There's so much Wallace talk at work, maybe I'll vote for him."

At the time there was a good deal of speculation that the public opinion polls might be understating Wallace's real strength. Since newsmen regarded voting for Wallace as a shameful act, they reasoned that goodly numbers of Wallace supporters might not admit openly how they were going to vote.

But this reasoning misunderstood the motivations behind the Wallace upsurge. As I wrote at the time. "I doubt that there is any 'silent' vote still to be heard from. If anything, the Wallace strength is being deliberately exaggerated to increase its bargaining power."

In every heavy Wallace area where I interviewed, in both the North and South, the Wallace supporters wanted to make their strength visible and known. Often they boasted of having signed petitions to put Wallace on the ballot. They talked openly of how "we hope to make an impression so the other candidates will have to do something" or "maybe Wallace can scare the other parties into accepting his policies." At the close of an interview, workers would point out house after house on the street and urge, "Talk to that fellow."

Nor was there any evidence, in September, that the labor unions were really fighting Wallace. More than half of the pro-Wallace workers described themselves as "strong" union members.

Pressed as to how they would vote "if the election outcome looks real close" most of them replied, "I'd swing to Humphrey."

Still, none of them reported any strong union effort to switch their vote. In fact, it seemed that a two-stage political strategy was at work: first, to sidetrack the racial angers of these unionists to Wallace and away from Nixon; then, in the closing campaign days to make the real pitch that "a vote for Wallace means a vote for labor's real enemy, Nixon."

By late October the real pitch was on and it seemed like a different election. Barberton's petunia man was standing fast for Humphrey and the Wallace sympathizers were on the defensive, with most of the waverers resolving their doubts *against* the Alabama governor.

A thirty-year-old divorcee remarked, "My boyfriend said he'd break off with me if I didn't vote for Wallace, but you know, my boyfriend didn't even register. I told him, 'too bad.'

"Lots of people talk for Wallace," she continued, "but when it comes right down to it, they don't vote for him. My brother was talkin' Wallace all along, but he voted absentee for Humphrey. I guess he figured like I do, there was too much hate in Wallace. There'd be a civil war."

Others of those shifting to Humphrey in those last days had voted for Goldwater in 1964. One forty-eight-year-old foreman in an aluminum factory, with a sixteen-year-old son, was pleased with the bombing halt in Vietnam.

"When McCarthy endorsed Humphrey that made it definite with me," he explained.

"If South Vietnam doesn't want to even talk peace let 'em fight the war themselves and bring our boys back home."

But the most frequently given reason for the switch to Humphrey was an intense distrust of the Republican Party and a desire to keep Nixon out of the White House.

In September, the wife of a sixty-year-old tire cureman at Firestone had said that she and her husband would vote for Wallace because "he'll go down to Washington and clean out all the phonies there."

Late in October she felt that "Wallace doesn't have a chance and Humphrey's ways are better than Nixon's. I don't want to help Nixon by voting for Wallace."

Similarly, the twenty-three-year-old wife of a Pittsburgh

glassworker had said in September, "I'll probably vote for Wallace. There couldn't be any more racial trouble than now."

Four days before the election, though, she felt that "Wallace has some good points, but he's too strong on some issues. Then there'd be too much of a split with Congress. He wouldn't have anybody of his party in there. I decided to vote for Humphrey a week ago. I just didn't want Nixon in."

On the same pre-election weekend, in Warren, Michigan, North of Detroit, a third of the Democrats interviewed admitted they had been for Wallace in the beginning, but no longer were.

In one house a "UAW Workers for Wallace" sticker was still in the window. The resident, a twenty-six-year-old salvage worker for Ford, from Tulsa, Oklahoma, kept muttering, "The three of them are no damn good. I don't think I'll vote."

His wife, who happened to walk into the cluttered living room in time to hear him, interrupted, "You're not gonna vote for Wallace? Really? You mean I can take your Wallace sticker down?"

She ran for the window and ripped away the sticker.

"I've wanted to do that all week," she explained. "I've heard that if Wallace doesn't win, he'll turn his support to Nixon.

"You go down to Republican headquarters here," she went on, "and they'll give you Wallace literature. You can pick up all this stuff at Republican headquarters. It kinda scares you—like they're working together."

Even with this late-show drop in his support, Wallace held a fifth of the vote in these Warren and Akron-Barberton precincts.

Those who stuck with him were usually quite intense in their hostility against both Negroes and Republicans.

### 3. In the Southern Image

Why the Wallace voters were described by so many writers as "conservative" and "right wing" remains a puzzle. His backers are reported to have included John Birchers and oil-depletion messiahs like H. L. Hunt, but economically the tie that bound most of his following to Wallace was the feeling "he knows how a poor man feels."

In the South, Wallace did draw support from varied economic groups, but in the northern industrial areas his vote was concentrated in worker precincts. Generally, his followers were rather loyal Democrats. Of those interviewed, a sizable majority had not voted for Eisenhower in 1952 or 1956, but had stuck with Adlai Stevenson. They also held strong working-class views, which prevented them from voting Republican.

A thirty-two-year-old Goodyear worker in Akron who supported Wallace protested, "Negroes want more than equal rights, and they're getting it, too."

But he also felt that "if the Republicans win we'll be so bad off my wife will have to go to work."

Most of Wallace's northern supporters maintained: "Wallace is for the working man. He couldn't be for anyone else." When they talked of his political future they usually saw him leading "a real labor party."

The real significance of the Wallace movement will be found, I believe, in this conflict between racial and economic interest that agitated so many of his supporters. Politics in the South have always revolved around this struggle of race and economics, over whether the workers and poorer farmers would find common economic interests with the blacks or be divided by race.

The vote Wallace drew among northern workers must be read as evidence of a new nationalizing force that is operating to make the politics of the North and South more alike. Always in the past the assumption has been that the South, as it changed, would come to resemble the North more and more. Wallace raised the prospect that the North, as it changes, may become southernized.

How far-reaching a political departure this would be can perhaps be appreciated best by thinking back to one of the New Deal's truly historic accomplishments. Prior to Franklin Roosevelt, most Negroes had voted Republican and had been anti-labor, often serving as strikebreakers. In 1935, with the formation of the CIO as the "one big industrial union," Negroes and white workers were brought together into the New Deal coalition which was to win five successive presidential elections.

After that the great dream of most Negro and labor leaders in the North was to "remake the South in the image of northern liberalism" by forging a similar union there of white and black workers.

By 1950 "Operation Dixie," as the CIO's drive to organize southern labor was named, had turned into "Operation Fizzle." The dominant economic craving of most white southerners was to get new factories, and it was toward business, not the unions, that the South was turning. In 1968 Wallace took the next step into history by trying to remake northern politics in the southern image.

In all the northern cities the 1968 campaign was a test of whether that New Deal coalition of white and black workers, formed thirty-three years earlier, could endure.

A retired printer in Rochester, New York, declared, "I'd shoot all those rioters," but he also recalled that "during the Depression I lost everything" and held firm for Humphrey.

In Bell Gardens, where Wallace drew his heaviest vote in the Los Angeles area, a plant guard contended, "They shouldn't send a colored mailman or a colored garbageman into a white neighborhood." Still, he felt that "a working man has to vote Democratic."

My interview notebooks contain scores of equally anti-Negro comments voiced by Humphrey supporters. The vote Wallace drew in the North was not the measure of the racial anger that prevailed; it was a measure of the anger that could not be repressed or restrained by Medicare, Social Security, high employment, and other economic appeals of the Democratic Party.

This struggle between race and economics will rage on, apart from any third-party move. In all elections to come, until our racial conflict is resolved, a sizable segment of the voters will be torn between racial antipathies and the economic pull of the Democratic Party. Which of these emotions wrestles to the top will shift from election to election, as racial tensions ease or intensify, as economic satisfactions fall or rise.

That same conflict will be dividing the Republicans as well as the Democrats. Through the southern following they have attracted, the Republicans have become sensitized to the same clash of economic and racial feeling. In talking of Nixon during the fall of 1969, many southerners would praise his stand on desegregation, but then express fear that "Nixon is pulling stuff that will hurt the working people —cutting back construction and helping out business with their taxes."

Between the North and South, the political stakes of racial conflict differ in one important respect. The key issue in the South has become how much closer to the segregationist view can Nixon be pushed? In the North, the main target remains the political alliance of labor and Negroes, and whether it can be broken apart fully and finally.

In following these developments, one should not make the mistake of attributing all this to Wallace personally, as if he were the maker rather than just the carrier of political history. In truth he is the caboose on a whole train of change that stretches back to the formation of the New Deal, the failure to project the labor-Negro coalition into the South, the southern hunger for new industry, the militant battling of the Negroes to implement the school desegregation decision, and now the effort to southernize the North.

The key to Wallace's potential remains less his demagogic skills than how racial feeling in the country changes. That the vote he got in the North was evidence of a new trend in public opinion, rather than any reassertion of old prejudices was clear in the answers people gave when asked which of the civil rights laws they would keep and which they would end.

In previous years those questions had always brought wide variations in the responses of northerners and southerners. On some items these differences still persisted, as with the public-accommodation laws, which stirred little opposition in the North but were attacked by nearly half of Wallace's southern supporters. But in both the North and South sizable majorities were agreed on two desires—wanting to repeal the open housing law and to end school busing.

Never before in my interviewing had I found northerners and southerners in agreement on civil rights issues. But on school busing and open housing a line of national, rather than sectional, opposition had been drawn. Some new nationalizing forces are at work which suggest that something new and important has been happening in our northern cities.

# FOUR

# BLACK CITIES ON THE MOVE

## 1. *The Wallace Thermometer*

ON THAT SUMMER WEEKEND in South Philadelphia, American flags and banners stretched across the streets, proclaiming, "Welcome home Pete, John, and Paul."

A stranger strolling through the neighborhood might have wondered who Pete, Paul, and John were, but everyone interviewed knew they were "neighbors' boys" who had returned from Vietnam and were being honored with an Italo-American block hero's welcome.

Still, those cheery welcoming banners had their darker side. For it is in just such neighborhoods across the country, where community ties are so strong, that the battle for meaningful integration has been just about lost and one can see the new trend of territorial racial conflict that is taking hold in our cities.

How that conflict moves could determine whether the big-city coalition that made the Democrats the normal majority party in the nation can be re-established, or whether it will be torn apart by the new southern efforts to stir northern whites into racial revolt.

The seriousness of the urban political threat confronting

the Democrats has been obscured by Humphrey's sensational photo finish in 1968 and by the early election reports, which stressed how poorly George Wallace fared in the northern cities.

Citywide totals did yield relatively low Wallace percentages, but these included the nine-to-one Negro majorities for Humphrey. A quite different picture emerges if one examines the election returns for white neighborhoods separately. In some industrial cities close to half of the known white precincts gave Wallace at least 15 per cent of their vote; in Cleveland, Gary, and Newark, two-thirds of the white precincts did.

Table 1, discloses a somber picture of how much more widely the polarization of racial tensions has spread through our cities than generally appreciated.

TABLE 1

*In the Southern Image: Wallace Vote
in Northern White Precincts*

| CITY | % GIVING WALLACE 15% OR MORE | CITY | % GIVING WALLACE 15% OR MORE |
|---|---|---|---|
| Gary | 78% | Akron | 44% |
| Cleveland | 71 | Cincinnati | 43 |
| Newark | 65 | Indianapolis | 42 |
| Baltimore | 55 | Flint | 41 |
| Columbus | 48 | Detroit | 35 |
| Pittsburgh | 45 | | |

Fifteen per cent for Wallace—one in every six to seven votes—may not seem alarmingly high. But in three of these cities the presidential count can be matched against mayoral elections which pitted white and black candidates against each other.

In Cleveland the white precincts where Wallace drew 15 per cent or better voted 84 per cent against Carl Stokes in his 1967 bid for mayor and 85 per cent against him in

1969; in Gary they voted 83 per cent against Richard Hatcher in 1967; in Detroit 87 per cent against Richard Austin, in his close 1969 defeat.

Presidential voting, it is plain, still manages to repress racial hostility beneath such issues as economics and peace, understating the degree of tension that actually exists. These figures suggest that the Wallace percentages in the northern cities would be multiplied three, four, or five times in a straight black-white confrontation.

The ominous turn that the racial struggle has taken emerges even more sharply when one plots the Wallace vote on maps. In city after city, the conflict takes on a territorial, almost "border war" form. Never is the Wallace vote sprinkled evenly or randomly through a city; always it is packed into compact white worker neighborhoods which confront heavily black districts, almost like two hostile nations. The low-Wallace white precincts are nearly always in parts of the city far from the black areas.

In Columbus, Ohio, for example, 48 per cent of the known white precincts in the whole city recorded a Wallace vote of at least 15 per cent. In South Columbus, though, as much as 85 per cent of the white precincts ran that high for Wallace.

Similarly, in Baltimore, 55 per cent of the known white precincts in the whole city voted at least 15 per cent for Wallace. But in East Baltimore all but 3 per cent of the precincts were that high. The middle-ground white precincts—where Wallace got under 5 per cent—lie at the opposite end of the city, to the Northwest.

In Gary, Cleveland, and Newark, this territorial splitting of the city into two belligerent halves is virtually complete. All but a handful of precincts were either heavily for Wallace or predominantly black. But even in cities such as Chicago or Philadelphia, where Wallace's pull was more limited, one finds the same pattern. The heavy Wallace areas—the six

Chicago wards which voted at least 15 per cent Wallace or the fifth of Philadelphia's known white precincts which did—all border on the heaviest Negro residential expansion. The wards which seem free of racial polarization are in parts of the city which are not affected by the spreading Negro areas.

One gets the feeling that in these and other cities, polarization is at an early stage and has not yet spread as widely as in Gary, Cleveland, or Newark.

Ironically, not poverty but prosperity has been intensifying this racial polarization in our northern cities. The unprecedented boom of recent years has quickened the residential mobility of much of the urban population. Appreciable numbers of black families have been able to push up out of slums into quite good housing. At the same time, though, the movement of whites to the suburbs has been speeded up.

Although Negro numbers in the suburbs have been rising, the net effect of all this residential reshuffling has been to leave segregation of blacks and whites as strong as ever.

The black ghettos, in short, have been transformed into Black Cities on the move, pushing ever deeper through the larger city. By 1968 the Black City in Detroit had spread over nearly 40 per cent of the voting precincts; in Baltimore to over a third of the city; in Philadelphia to almost a third, including the precinct where Girard College, endowed to educate only white Protestants, is located.

As new expanses of "turf" have been—and continue to be—transferred to black control the whole integration issue has been transformed. Officially the goal remains intact, and school busing and other efforts still are pushed, but effective integration appears to have collapsed. Streets on which whites and blacks have lived together for any length of time are rare. Where black and white neighborhoods adjoin each other the trend is for the races to be pulled apart.

Inside the spreading Black Cities few whites are left to integrate with, while black militancy seems directed toward driving out what white presence remains, such as white shopkeepers and teachers.

Simultaneously, in the white neighborhoods bordering on these Black Cities resistance has been mounting to any action that may weaken neighborhood control. This explains why my interviewing in the 1968 campaign showed almost as strong a desire to repeal the open housing law and end school busing in the North as in the South.

It also helps explain the strategy of the Deep South in demanding equal enforcement of school desegregation in the North, hoping that it would stir northern voters to revolt against integration.

In that connection one should note that these feelings were not created by the agitations of either Wallace or Senator Stennis, but are the result of uncontrolled population movements, quickened by prosperity.

As late as 1958 the streets in South Philadelphia welcomed home Pete, John, and Paul and were not a DMZ of racial tension. A Jewish community lay between them and the nearest Negro residences, but as the Jews moved out the blacks pushed down until they met with the resistance of these Italo-American families.

The racial views of these Italo-Americans could not be labeled extremist. While 12 per cent of them voted for Wallace, the preponderant majority felt that "he would swing the hammer the wrong way" or "he hates the colored" or "he'd set this country back a hundred years."

But these families stood as one in their determination not to be "forced out" of their homes by blacks moving into their streets.

Despite the requirements of the open housing law, one never sees a For Sale or For Rent sign. If someone is in the market for a house, the word gets passed around through friends and relatives. On Emily Street a young married couple talked happily of how "We'll move across the street into our own home next month." Meanwhile, they were living with the wife's parents; a few doors away was the house owned by his parents.

Many families have lived on these same blocks for three generations. From the outside, their row houses look like the drab, unpretentious structures one would find in any worker neighborhood. But inside, many residents have employed their own construction, carpentry, or stonemason skills to make ornate banisters, marble fireplaces, and bathrooms set in tile of varied colors and design, and to erect statuary in their backyards.

Everyone interviewed wanted school busing ended. Since nearly all the children in these families attend Catholic schools, they are not troubled directly by school integration.

But to these Italo-American families the presence of almost any black person in the neighborhood seems like a hostile invasion. A cab driver's wife was particularly incensed that the few Negro children attending the Catholic school "don't show any respect for the nuns." She went on to explain: "They use curse words to them, but the nuns are afraid of them. If my kids did that, I'd want the nun to smack 'em good, show 'em respect."

The chief annoyance appeared to be the daily trek through the neighborhood of young blacks to and from South Philadelphia High School and the Bok Vocational School, both predominantly Negro.

Some residents protested, "It's dangerous how the colored flock around the Catholic schools" or "They come through here after school and frighten us." A construction worker pointed down the street and grumbled, "They pull down that doctor's sign every week." A storekeeper told how "they steal pies and cakes."

A few weeks before the election, a neighborhood boy

was cut in a quarrel with a young Negro near the Bok School. In the days that followed, black students walking through South Philadelphia were stoned. The blacks retaliated by overturning garbage cans, the Italo-Americans by marching on the Bok School. As incidents and protests spread through the city, schools were shut down, then reopened under police guard.

That students walking through a neighborhood can almost close down a school system may seem incredible, but incidents like these also point to how quickly the dynamics of racial conflict have changed. In 1964 Barry Goldwater tried to link the racial angers of the white South with anti-Negro resentments in the northern cities but failed disastrously. In the twelve largest nonsouthern cities, Goldwater's vote dropped to a new Republican low of 26 per cent.

After 1968 an alliance between the white South and northern urban dwellers had to be put down as politically possible.

Here again one should note how deceiving the voting returns can be if one looks at only the citywide totals. If one adds together the vote for the twelve largest nonsouthern cities, the Democratic share of the two-party vote in 1968 was 66 per cent, which was 2 per cent higher than in 1960. But this "gain" is misleading. Wallace drew 534,253 votes in these twelve cities, 6.5 per cent of the total. Thus the Democratic boost came about through the balancing off of two conflicting voting trends.

In every city a greater Democratic solidarity was shown by Jewish and, even more so, Negro voters. Blacks cast not only a heavier proportion of the total vote in each city than in 1960 but a higher percentage, by 10 to 15 per cent, for the Democrats.

Against this, the Democrats suffered sizable losses in white areas. In 1960, when John F. Kennedy swept South

Philadelphia with three-fourths of the vote, Nixon carried just one of its 131 precincts. Four years later, Barry Goldwater won twelve South Philadelphia precincts; Nixon in 1968 lifted that to forty-five precincts. He drew 40 per cent of South Philadelphia's vote, which, with Wallace's 12 per cent, left Humphrey the first Democratic candidate since the 1920's to fall short of a clear majority in South Philadelphia.

Similar Democratic defections of twenty or more percentage points since 1960 have taken place in white neighborhoods in other northern cities. In Chicago's four westside wards, across which Martin Luther King, Jr., staged his open-housing march in 1966, the Democratic share of the total vote dropped from 66 per cent in 1960 to 42 per cent in 1968. Nixon edged Humphrey with 43 per cent, while Wallace drew 15 per cent.

In Gary, Nixon actually won a majority of the white vote that lies south of the Calumet River; Humphrey dropped to only 31 per cent, compared with 67 per cent for the Democrats in 1960, while Wallace drew 26 per cent.

In the five white wards of East Baltimore the Democrats fell from 72 per cent in 1960 to 46 per cent in 1968, with Wallace drawing 21 per cent.

The Baltimore vote also reveals how thin was Humphrey's edge of victory in some states. His plurality in all of Maryland was only 20,000 votes, as against a 98,000 plurality in the city of Baltimore. Wallace drew 179,000 votes in the state.

These are sizable presidential defections, but still nowhere as heavy as the swings of white Democrats against black candidates for mayor. In fact, at the local level in many cities the New Deal coalition no longer exists. Yet one difference from the South should be noted. The racial angers of white southerners get directed against the national government and erupt in presidential voting; in the northern cities the white protests which are targeted against racial changes at the local level have spread only in part to national voting.

If there is to be a reconciliation among the New Deal voting elements in the North, it would have to be a street-scene affair carried through not in Washington but in hundreds of neighborhoods across the country. This would require a keener understanding of the forces cracking our cities apart than has been shown in the past.

## 2. Unraveling a Coalition

Virtually every big-city election in years to come is likely to be dominated by racial conflict. If past practice continues, each of these contests will be televised and headlined as a fresh round in the ceaseless struggle between those "bad guy" bigots and those "good guy" champions of racial enlightenment.

But in all of these elections the most important single force will not be the "backlash" politicking of the candidates but the moving vans that have been shuttling between the cities and suburbs. The 1968 voting reveals that these suburban migrations, piling up over the years, have passed the tipping point, upsetting long-established political balances and plunging our cities into the grotesque new world of polarized politics.

In 1968, for the first time, the total vote cast by our twelve largest nonsouthern cities dropped below the vote cast by the suburbs around these cities.

Some of the figures in Table 2, reflect the lower voter turnout in 1968. But the shift in the political balance in unmistakable. Between 1952 and 1968 the suburban vote jumped 37 per cent, while the city vote was dropping 21 per cent.

In the North, at least, the Supreme Court's "one man,

one vote" ruling has been reducing the political strength of the cities in relation to the suburbs, which is not too hopeful an omen when the cities are bidding so desperately for financial aid from Congress and state legislatures.

TABLE 2

*Total Vote Cast in the Twelve Largest Nonsouthern Cities and Suburbs, Presidential Elections 1952–1968*

|      | CITIES | SUBURBS |
|------|--------|---------|
| 1952 | 10,324,000 | 6,284,000 |
| 1956 | 9,643,000 | 7,080,000 |
| 1960 | 9,636,000 | 8,264,000 |
| 1964 | 9,274,000 | 8,519,000 |
| 1968 | 8,112,000 | 8,591,000 |

Nearly half the big-city drop came between 1964 and 1968, indicating that the decline is quickening. Perhaps more significant than the size of the population loss is the harsh Darwinian process of selection which brought it about.

It would be difficult to organize a process more surely calculated to aggravate racial strife. Within the cities lopsided black concentrations account for an increasing share of a declining population; the whites left tend generally to be older and poorer families who can't afford to move. In most northern cities they usually are factory workers, either from southern and border states or Catholics, descended from Italian, Polish, Hungarian, Czech, Slovenian, and other Eastern European immigrants, who tend also to have strong community ties.

As long as they remained in the cities, the better-off groups constituted a "middle ground" between the blacks and the immobile "ethnics." But as the exodus to the suburbs continued the "middle ground" has narrowed steadily, and our cities have moved from coalition politics toward the politics of polarized confrontation.

In Detroit, for example, "liberal" control of the school

board had been insured through a voting coalition of blacks, organized labor, and Jews. When the Jewish families left for Southfield and other suburbs, this coalition collapsed. The two new school board members who were elected in 1967 came from the two racial extremes—one was a black militant, the other the candidate of the civic groups who wanted to kill school busing.

At this point no stabilization of the spreading Black Cities is yet in sight. The Census Bureau has reported a slowing of Negro migration from the South, although the movement could pick up again if one of the tobacco harvesters now being tested proves really successful or if most people quit smoking. But even if the Negro inflow halts, a further spread of the Black Cities is certain. In no city do blacks have adequate housing. The high births of previous years will also be projecting a much more rapid rate of increase for young blacks of marrying and voting age than for whites.

A special census tabulation estimates that by 1975 Negroes will comprise 25 per cent of all youth between twenty and twenty-nine living in the twelve largest nonsouthern cities. In 1965 the black proportion in that age group was only 20 per cent.

It is people who make government what it is, and as the population makeup of a city is changed, its politics change.

Through the 1968 campaign, as pointed out earlier, my interviews showed that the voters in the nation generally favored a middle-course racial policy. But the white flight to the suburbs has made it virtually impossible to carry out an effective middle-course program. We have deceived ourselves—as we may have wanted to deceive ourselves—into thinking that words or intentions make a policy. Our talk has been of moderation, but our feet have carried us toward polarized conflict.

In this polarization equation, the diversity of white population equals time. Some of our larger cities have more time for racial adjustments; but as the suburban drain continues even these cities will move toward a further tightening of black-white relations.

Of all our cities, Cleveland offers perhaps the best locale for examining this uprushing future.

The speed of racial change has been quicker there than in most cities. In 1958 Cleveland's four Negro wards cast roughly 36,000 votes. By 1969 the black voter registration had more than tripled, spreading through fifteen wards stretching over nearly twenty square miles, an area as large as the whole city of Newark.

The suburban migration, in turn, has left Cleveland with a white population that is overwhelmingly of worker background, including expanding numbers of hillbillies and Puerto Ricans.

As the first major city in the nation to elect and re-elect a black mayor, Cleveland has also had more experience with the actual operation of polarized politics than any other American city.

Does electing a black mayor yield a formula for white-black reconciliation? What can a black mayor do? What is beyond even the most successful black mayor?

No Berlin Wall or iron curtain limits movement between the white neighborhoods on Cleveland's West Side and the black areas that lie on the East Side of the Cuyahoga River, but, to most whites and blacks the two parts of the city are like separate countries eyeing each other across a frontier of fear.

Two illustrations may give a sense of how intimately these fears cut into the lives of ordinary Clevelanders.

A retired engineer had talked of how he "was forced to move to the West Side" and then added, "my wife is buried on the East Side. Whenever I go to put flowers on her grave I carry a gun in my car. If any nigger tries to stop me, he'll get a bullet for his trouble".

Not far from the Cleveland airport a young mother fondled her baby boy as she explained, "He's three months old but his grandparents haven't seen him yet. They live over on the East Side, in Sowinski, and are surrounded by colored. They want to see the baby so bad, but they don't drive and they're scared to go out of the house and wait for the bus. Nobody here will take me over to see them, we're so afraid to go over there."

"My husband will be getting out of the Air Force next month," she continued. "Then we'll take the baby over for his parents to see. We're just counting the days until he gets back".

The deep cleavage that separates whites and blacks is also etched into the voting returns of the two Stokes victories. At first glance the election results in Table 3, seem a picture of unyielding hostility and embattled prejudice. In 1969 Stokes bettered his 1967 citywide plurality by just 1,772 votes, raising his percentage of the total vote by only four-tenths of 1 per cent.

### TABLE 3
#### Two Close Ones: Cleveland
#### Mayor's Vote 1967 and 1969

|  | FOR STOKES * | |
|---|---|---|
|  | 1967 | 1969 |
| Negro Wards | 95% | 96% |
| White West Side Wards | 19 | 20 |
| Citywide | 50.3 | 50.7 |
| Plurality | 1,679 | 3,451 |

* Percentage of two-party vote.

However, a less rigid picture emerges from five weeks of interviewing in the city and by comparing the two elections precinct by precinct. It then develops that the two years of Stokes's first administration brought significant shifts in racial feelings among both whites and blacks.

For Negroes Stokes's first administration meant a remarkable lift in morale and in actual benefits.

A twenty-eight-year-old domestic remarked, "I never saw a snow plow on our street before Stokes became mayor." Other Negroes talked buoyantly of "all the different kinds of jobs that have been opened up to us" or of how "the police aren't as nasty as they used to be" or of how "we feel part of Cleveland now."

The economic boom has also brought many of Cleveland's Negroes out of the slums into middle-class neighborhoods. On one street a forty-five-year-old widow who worked in a plastics factory remembered that she was working the night shift when she first heard that Stokes had been elected. "I had no radio," she recalled. "Then the white workers came over and told me what had happened. They were so happy for me. It was wonderful."

She also talked of trying to get a job during the day so "I can go to high school for night classes and get my diploma."

"Some say violence is the way to get the things we need that we don't have," she said. "But I don't go along with that. Militancy means take. I want to get things on my own."

Among whites, however, having a Negro mayor had differing impacts.

An air-freight driver recalled, "It doesn't sound nice to admit it, but I couldn't vote for Stokes last time on account of his color. We'll vote for him this year because without a Negro mayor we would have had more racial trouble."

This sense that "there would be a lot of trouble without Stokes in" was sufficiently strong so that in half of the white precincts on the West Side Stokes gained, percentagewise, over his 1967 vote.

But in the other half of these precincts his vote dropped, reflecting intensified racial angers.

A pipefitter's wife remarked, "My husband is more against the colored than before. He won't even let our kids watch TV programs with colored on them."

Why should white voters in the same city react so differently to the Stokes record? One key force turned out to be the nature of the spreading Black City itself. As it expands territorially, the Black City becomes a city of nomadic conflicts. Bitter emotional tensions shoot off between blacks and whites—over jobs, over crime and ineffective policing, over the uneven burden of taxes, and, above all, over living space.

The new votes that Stokes picked up between 1967 and 1969 came mainly from people who were largely untouched by these conflicts—young lawyers, teachers, junior executives, better-educated white-collar people. In both campaigns Stokes was backed by the two Cleveland newspapers and had the financial support of the banks and leading industrialists. Many of his white supporters leaned toward the Republicans.

Some who had been raised in the suburbs had decided to start their married life in the city. A twenty-four-year-old lawyer, a Nixon supporter born in Cleveland Heights, said, "Stokes has given Cleveland the image of a city on the go, a city that's concerned about housing, pollution."

Others welcomed the Negro economic advance. The branch manager of a bank reported, "A lot more Negroes have white-collar jobs at the bank since Stokes got in. The more they get into white-collar fields, the more they'll be accepted when they move into white neighborhoods."

In the whole city Stokes carried one white precinct by a majority. This was the one containing the Chesterfield Apartments, a new high-rise downtown high-income development.

Another white precinct where Stokes did quite well, drawing 33 per cent of the vote, lies close to the western city limits and includes St. Joseph's Academy.

A St. Joseph instructor who voted against Stokes in 1967 shifted to him in 1969. She talked of how the student nuns look to Stokes "to set a good example for Negroes generally" and to bring to the fore "Negroes whom people can admire."

But where people felt themselves caught up in conflict with Negroes, Stokes lost ground in 1969. These losses were heaviest among worker families, usually Democratic, with lower levels of education. Some of the angriest protests were voiced by young whites just entering the labor market who felt that the "coloreds get preference on all the jobs."

One twenty-one-year-old youth talked wistfully of how, "I really wanted to be a policeman. I was going to take the test but figured there was no use. They'd hire more colored than white."

He had picked up a job as a sheet-metal worker, explaining, "I'm trying to learn a trade. In a couple of years I'll try for my rating as journeyman."

Then his anger flared: "These colored want these journeyman jobs without waiting. Why are they better than I am?"

The twenty-one-year-old daughter of a construction foreman remarked, "I was lucky. Right after I started at the supermarket the manager said they could only hire colored from then on."

But the most intense conflicts were generated by the physical spread of black residential areas. This point should be underscored in double strokes.

Widened visibility is needed to understand how the racial crisis in our cities is changing. For some years TV cameras, newspaper headlines and government reports have been trained on the ghettos with their seemingly unchanging slums. Any number of government reports have emphasized that the "solution" to racial conflict is to eliminate poverty.

But alongside of the pictures of ghetto conditions should

be placed pictures of what happens when blacks move out of the slums into better housing areas. The racial conflict is then seen not simply as a matter of poverty, but also as the impact of Negro progress and, in part, as a population struggle of the sheer numbers of Negroes on the move.

For one round of interviewing I decided to check the Cleveland precincts with the heaviest Wallace showing. In East Side wards where sizable numbers of whites still lived, thirteen precincts voted at least 30 per cent for Wallace; another thirty-seven precincts gave him at least 25 per cent.

Visiting these precincts was like inspecting a stretched-out war front. Each Wallace precinct was like another outpost marking the borders to which Negro residential movement had pushed. On some streets the families who had voted for Wallace in 1968 were already gone, the area having turned entirely black by 1969. Other streets simmered with the strains of neighborhood transition. At still other points the whites had drawn an unyielding line that permitted no blacks to pass.

Interviewing in "Little Italy" was literally like visiting a besieged fortress. "I have five rifles in my closet," a thirty-four-year-old truck driver remarked casually. Other "defenders," as these Italo-American men called themselves, talked of the "ingenious" alarm system they had set up to alert "every house" that "the colored are coming" as soon as any crossed the nearby New York Central Railroad bridge. Vowed a garbage collector, "Not one of them will get out of here alive."

A housewife recalled, "Once a sniper got to the top of a corner building and started firing down into our streets. My girlfriend and I were out in the car. We were so scared we squeezed down on the floor. One defender got in and backed the car out for us. None of ours got killed, but the defenders killed the sniper."

In many cities like Newark, Chicago, and Philadelphia

the white group in most bitter conflict with the blacks is the Italo-American. Competition over city patronage is one factor. Generally, Italo-American mayors came into office after World War II. Now, after only a few years in power, they find themselves being challenged by the blacks.

But the heart of the conflict seems to be the special attachment that Italo-Americans have for their homes and for living together. In Cleveland's Little Italy, as in South Philadelphia, residents pointed across the street to "the house where I was born" or a few doors away to "where my mother was born." Often the feeling was expressed, "You don't have closeness like this anyplace else."

"All over the East Side, the colored move in and the whites leave," said one city worker. "We decided if you stand your ground you get further."

Little Italy's "defenders" like to boast, "This is the only place in Cleveland where a woman is safe walking by herself at three in the morning."

Still, living in fortified fear has its drawbacks. The twenty-three-year-old wife of a truck driver complained, "My parents live three streets away, I'd stay here the rest of my life, except I want something better for my children. I don't want them to have to worry about trouble and killings. I don't want them to have to hate the colored like we learned to. We're moving to the suburbs next month."

Vigilante resistance takes not only clannish solidarity, but physical vigor to fight back. In most neighborhoods penetrated by Negroes, the whites are generally quite old. Often they suffer the peculiar helplessness of being trapped by their own lifetime savings.

On Korman Avenue, an eighty-year-old man was wearing khaki trousers and a shirt that seemed to have been bought at an army surplus store. When I spotted him, my memory flashed back to news pictures of the Great Depression that I had never forgotten, of how ragged were the "bonus army" marchers who were chased out of the Anacostia Flats in Washington.

"All I have to live on is my Social Security," he explained. "Last week these hoodlums knocked me down and took twenty dollars out of my pocket. I want to move away. But how can I? My house is all paid for. If I moved I'd have to get a big mortgage that I couldn't pay. I have to stay here."

As he turned to walk away he remarked bitterly, "America was a wonderful country when I came here as a young man. There's nothing here for a white man any more."

That remark stung, perhaps because of my own immigrant background. I had read any number of articles analyzing the "bigotry" and "prejudice" among so-called "ethnics," usually written as if these people were a subhuman species. Still here were men and women who had lived according to the values extolled by this country. They had worked in sweaty factories and mills, disciplining their desires to be able to save regularly so they could pay off the mortgages on their modest frame homes. When they got too old to work, they would be secure; they would have a place to live on which no rent had to be paid, with no need to seek charity, welfare, or the uncertain mercies of grown children and in-laws.

But the changing city had converted these values into virtual prison walls. What part of the "backlash" feelings in the northern cities is stirred by prejudice, what part by the impact of change?

Another cluster of high Wallace precincts brought me into Cleveland's "Little Hungary" area. Along Buckeye Road were Hungarian restaurants, bakeries with trays of strudel in the windows, a dancing master who still gave ballet lessons, and such quaint drinking places as "The Old Hog Saloon."

In no other Cleveland area I visited was the anguished

complaint of "we need more police" voiced more widely. It was not the increase in homicides that bothered the residents but the petty thefts, muggings, and purse-snatchings.

Why this was the special agony of these people became clear as I went from house to house. At one home on Honeydale Avenue, a thin, frail woman answered the door. It was an effort for her to speak. She explained, "I don't vote any more. I'm eighty-eight. When I go to bed at night I never know whether I will wake up in the morning."

As I started to leave she added, "I hope the white people win."

That aged lady and her dream of a white mayor was typical of the neighborhood. Almost all the homeowners were gray-haired. Virtually everyone I talked with felt the neighborhood was doomed. When the old people died, there would be no young people to buy their homes, which would then be sold to Negroes.

Still, the white families left wanted to stay in the neighborhood as long as possible. If crime were not checked they feared more whites would be driven out faster.

"If we only had enough police to stop these purse-snatchings," said one teacher and her husband, "we might be able to stay here for years."

A druggist on Buckeye Road explained, "We no longer make any deliveries after six because my customers are afraid to open their doors after dark."

As we talked a tall man came in and asked, "Can I have this prescription filled? My mother just got knocked down on Forest Avenue and her purse was snatched. This will quiet her nerves."

When I left the area I felt both sad and angry. Why couldn't a housing policy be devised that would provide Negroes with the housing they needed without uprooting a piece of Europe that could never be reassembled again? Then I thought of the many cities I had been in where urban renewal or freeway construction had displaced blacks and other poor people with little regard for their feelings. Strange, how much attention is paid to employment and how little to how or where people live.

In several changing neighborhoods Negro families were interviewed as well. For them the move into their own homes was a heartening event.

Some volunteered "how much better police protection is in a neighborhood where whites still live" than in the older black areas; also how much better the schools were, at first—until more and more Negro families moved into the area.

A forty-two-year-old brickmaker and his wife had moved into the Sandusky area, when it was still predominantly white, from the slum area of Hough, where four days of rioting took place in 1966.

"When we first got here the schools were wonderful," the wife recalled. "This year all of a sudden the schools are overcrowded. The school wrote us a letter asking us to sign up our children to go to classes in the church."

Part of the problem is that the whites left are usually old and have few children, while the Negroes moving in are in the prime of life with many more children than nearby schools can accommodate. It is a perverse process of selection that the test of integration so often hinges on age groups who have so little in common.

Questions on how the two races got along brought mixed replies like "the kids play together but no one visits" or "many of these white people can't even speak English."

A retired printer said, "I've noticed Negroes are accepted better when there are just a few moving in."

A forty-four-year-old rail inspector remarked bitterly, "It makes me feel good to know we can chase them. Whites don't understand we don't care about being around them either."

The ring in his voice was one of pride.

Signs of whites and blacks learning to live together were rare. But the evidence of Negro economic improvement was impressive. The political effect was also visible.

Each white person who moved to the suburbs or died off was one less anti-Stokes vote, while each additional black of voting age was a new vote for Stokes. The pace of neighborhood change was important in solidifying Negro political power in the city.

On the East Side, at least thirty-six precincts which were white in 1967 had turned black by 1969. In these precincts the Stokes vote jumped sixteen percentage points over 1967, bettering his 1967 plurality by 3,200 votes, which was close to his total plurality of 3,451 through the whole city.

Stokes's re-election, in short, was made possible only in part by the new strength he had gained among some whites, which offset his losses among other whites. Most of his 1969 plurality came from the loss of white population. In both elections Stokes needed about a fifth of the white vote to win. If the prevailing trends of population change continue, a black mayor would need fewer and fewer white votes to be elected.

This clear Negro dominance seems already established in the Democratic primary. In 1969 Stokes would have won the Democratic nomination even if almost the entire white vote had gone to his opponent.

Similar population shifts are taking place in other cities. When the 1960 census was taken, the city of Newark was still two-thirds white. By 1967, when the July rioting left twenty-three persons dead, the white population had dropped to 38 per cent. Replacing the whites who left the city were Negro migrants from the South, Puerto Ricans, and Cubans.

The same selection process which thinned out the white

population also eroded the city's economy. Per capita costs
for health and welfare increased to where they were twenty
times as great in Newark as for some surrounding communities; taxes on a $10,000 house rose to $661.70—double
the rate in the suburbs.

By 1968 the Black City had spread over roughly half of
Newark's precincts. In comparable Negro areas, Humphrey
did 11 per cent better than John Kennedy had in 1960,
but the predominantly white North and East wards, which
had voted 68 per cent for Kennedy, gave Humphrey only
48 per cent, with 16 per cent for Wallace.

The 1968 city council election seemed like a test run
for the 1970 mayoralty election. There were thirteen candidates for the two at-large council seats at stake. Three-
fourths of the votes, though, were cast for four candidates:
two blacks who lost, and two Italo-Americans who won. The
precincts where Wallace drew 15 per cent or better voted
95 per cent against the two black candidates.

One top black candidate lost by only 79 votes; the other
by 3,295. Could the Negroes elect a mayor in 1970?

Of the whites remaining in Newark, a fourth were fifty-
five years of age or older. Of Newark's blacks, 40 per cent
were youngsters under fifteen.

Or would they have to wait until more black youngsters
reached voting age?

Similarly, in Detroit, had the mayor's election come a
year or two later rather than in 1969, County Auditor
Richard Austin would probably have been elected instead
of being defeated by only 1 per cent of the vote.

This black push up the housing ladder is not unlike
the great trek out of the slums of the white immigrant
groups during the first third of this century. But thus far,
it is producing quite different political results.

For the immigrants the city served as the equivalent of

the western frontier, an old tenement trail, along which they moved, neighborhood by neighborhood to middle-class country.

Although rocked by gang fights, racketeering, and other friction, their climb was, on the whole, a unifying force through which "wops," "micks," "kikes," "hunkies," and other minority groups learned to live with one another and through which the New Deal coalition was formed and consolidated.

Today the city is serving as the urban frontier for blacks, Puerto Ricans, and other minorities, who are also reaching out into "nicer neighborhoods" to register their gains. And these gains have been considerable.

But in its political effects, the outward and upward push of the blacks through the same ladder of neighborhoods that the immigrants climbed has seemed more like a coming-apart process, as if it were unraveling the New Deal coalition with each neighborhood that the blacks penetrated.

If the New Deal coalition, born of the city, should die of it, two factors will be mainly responsible. First, in all the years it held political power, too great an emphasis was placed on high employment, and not enough on housing and dwelling policies.

Perhaps that was unavoidable considering that the Roosevelt coalition was brought together in a despairing recoil against the Great Depression, which gave white and black workers a common interest against the employers who had thrown them out of work.

But the New Deal never did acquire the sensitivity to block-busting that it had to union-busting. It never did develop a common interest in living together that could be shared by whites and blacks; nor did its housing and dwelling policies reconcile the interests of the central cities and suburbs.

President Johnson's "Great Society" failed politically on

this same dwelling front. Pushing the Gross National Product ever higher strengthened the politics of working together, black unemployment being cut by a third. But this same GNP aggravated the lack of a politics for living together.

If it ever was possible to develop a pattern by which whites and blacks could live alongside each other, that possibility was ploughed under by the mechanization of cotton in the 1950's—the second factor destroying the New Deal.

The displacement of sharecroppers coincided with the big movement to the suburbs that followed World War II. In just ten years, between 1950 and 1960, our twelve largest nonsouthern cities lost more than 2 million white residents while gaining nearly 2 million Negro residents.

For all the other New Deal elements immigration had been cut off in the 1920's, which helped them stabilize themselves socially. But not the Negroes. They found themselves exposed to the leveling forces of southern Negroes drifting northward in numbers too large for any city to manage.

Squeezed between the inward flow of blacks, and in some cities other minority elements, and the white movement to the suburbs, our larger cities lost those wonderful powers of social unification which they once had and which came to political fruition with the New Deal.

Nor has any new urban entity appeared to fill the need for unification.

The great separation between blacks and whites will not be undone quickly. But before one decides that the New Deal coalition is dead and can be shipped off to the funeral parlors, at least one further question should be explored.

Can it be that whites and blacks would get along more easily if they stayed separate? What is happening inside the Black Cities?

## 3. The Gun on the Hill

Shortly after Martin Luther King's assassination I was asked to design an interviewing survey to determine whom Negroes would choose as their new leader.

My response was: "The survey would be wasted. No one would be picked. The time is past when any one man can speak for Negroes generally."

That judgment was based on my interviewing of Negroes, which had shown that King had been losing popular support for six to eight months *before* his fatal mission on behalf of the Memphis garbage collectors. Particularly among younger, more impatient blacks the comments ran:

"King has outlived his time" or "He had a purpose and accomplished it; now he's passé" or "King was our savior in the beginning but he's outmoded now."

Significantly, all the blacks interviewed, both King's critics and admirers, had agreed that he symbolized the hope of further integration and of negotiating with the white man.

The riotings in the summer of 1967 marked, I believe, the turning point away from King's philosophy. After those "rebellions," as the riots were often described, many Negro college students began referring to themselves as "blacks" and wearing natural hairdos.

After that summer the more articulate Negro opinion tended to push "blackness" as an ideology, to denounce integration and school busing, and to proclaim a separate black society as their goal.

This concept of "two Americas," one black, the other white, has been applauded by some whites; by two groups, in fact, who ordinarily would never be found in agreement. Southern segregationists praised black separatism even as the KKK in the 1920's supported Marcus Garvey's dream of "back to Africa" nationalism. At the opposite end of the political spectrum, some white liberals seized upon the idea of black self-rule and "black action" as if it were the solution to racial problems.

But neither the segregationists nor the white liberals have fully appreciated how deeply torn most blacks are by the concept of black power. To many its main appeal is the sense of identity and pride they draw from the concept, along with the hope that blacks will be able to pool their energies to advance themselves economically and perhaps be able to push for integration at some future time, "when the black is better organized."

But for others who are militant, black power has another meaning. Its special strength is the firepower of oversimplification. It is the gun on the hill, strategically placed so that it commands all the approaches to the Black City and so that its rapid "black, black, black" can mow down any competing ideology.

To whites the gun on the hill is trying to say, "You can deal with us only on our terms"; to blacks it is saying, "You must join us so whitey will have no other choice."

Black power, in short, represents less a form of withdrawal than a struggle for community control and establishment of a new pattern of white-black bargaining on the basis of greater black pride, even at the point of a gun.

Can a constructive sense of pride be separated from the gun on the hill? That is one of the more agonizing riddles posed by black nationalism in its varied forms.

Black studies can be welcomed in colleges as a means of strengthening the sense of black identity, but often these programs are also designed to organize political eruptions and even to test techniques for revolution.

The shootouts between Black Panthers and the police in an increasing number of cities have raised the same vexing questions. Can armed bands of nationalists be tolerated in our cities? Must the guns be taken away by force?

Would doing so inflame the Negro community and worsen racial relations?

Here again the experience of Mayor Stokes in Cleveland is revealing.

Before going to Cleveland I had puzzled how seriously one should take the black nationalist ideology. The idea of setting up a separate black nation seemed such a fantasy. Where in this country could blacks acquire the territory on which to establish a "separate black society?"

After several weeks in Cleveland, I began to wonder how much of the "fantasy" lay on the white side, whether the emergence of Black Cities, stretching for ten, twenty, or more miles, did not provide in street reality, the "territory" for at least a beginning pass at setting up a "nation."

Were the racial fastnesses of Hough and the nearby parts of Glenville, which most whites and many blacks feared to enter, really so unlike the Sierra Maestra mountain where Fidel Castro hid until he was ready to make his bid for power in Cuba?

I was also struck by how easily the black nationalist ideology could serve as a cover for crime and lawlessness.

One issue that threatened Stokes's re-election chances was a controversy kicked up by demands of black militants that they be given franchises for two McDonald hamburger restaurants on the East Side. The McDonald people protested that the terms amounted to extortion under threat of being driven out of business. Both the Cleveland *Press* and *Plain Dealer* sided with McDonald; many whites were provoked to anger.

One afternoon I met with several black nationalists in Glenville who explained the reasoning behind the McDonald demands. One declared, "Any white-owned establishment operating in the black community owes something to that community. Part of its profits should be given back to the community."

"What if a man decides he doesn't want to make such a contribution?" I asked.

"He shouldn't stay in the community."

"Who decides that he has to get out?" I asked.

"We do."

Were such demands tantamount to buying "protection"? Ideologically the nationalists could contend, as they have, that they recognized no laws made by the whites, but only the laws they themselves laid down.

As we talked I thought of a luncheon session that I had had with five black students at a small college in Ohio. To them "the ghetto" was like a colonial country in Africa that was trying to shake off the rule of an imperialist foreign power.

The students seemed to regard all property in the Black City as "ours." They talked of "taking over the banks" and other white-owned enterprises and of starting new ghetto businesses "with the help of government financing."

In the course of an angry attack on "the profits that white people take out of the ghetto," one student interjected: "We should run all our own businesses. Why do these Jew merchants keep coming back? In Washington we burned them out once. They got their insurance. They ought to let the blacks take over their stores."

A few weeks later in Washington, D.C., a clothing store owner found that the skylight of his store had been broken open and some eight thousand dollars' worth of clothing had been stolen. As reported in the *Washington Post*, this was the fifth time the store had been burglarized. The thieves had left a note: "Get the hell out of here or we'll come back and get you."

Stalin had been a bank robber before the Russian Revolution, but Al Capone had never been a revolutionist. Where "ideology" ended and crime began in the Black City was an almost invisible line.

How did the mass of Negroes in Cleveland feel about black nationalism? In interviewing Negro voters in seven different wards I probed for their reaction. Some of the findings were illuminating.

First, Stokes's being mayor had given Cleveland's Negroes a far greater sense of pride than could come from any act of black nationalism.

One question put to Negroes was "What does Stokes being mayor mean to you?"

Two responses were repeated most frequently: "He's an inspiration to my sons, something to look up to and work toward" and "He has shown white people what an intelligent Negro is capable of doing."

Most Negroes, in short, felt that they shared a personal stake in Stokes's own success as mayor. When they said, as many did, "he's done a wonderful" or "beautiful" job as mayor, they were flexing their own muscles of pride.

This feeling that Stokes's success was their success brought to the surface sharp and even angry criticisms by many Negroes of black nationalist actions that might contribute to his defeat. Nearly two-thirds of the Negroes interviewed criticized the McDonald demands as "unreasonable"; many said, "Stokes should have stepped in and settled the situation earlier."

One thought was expressed quite frequently, "We should build our own restaurants" and "not try to take away McDonald's hard-earned business."

A short-order cook who had worked for McDonald's felt, "Stokes should condemn the black nationalists. They're not helping uplift the blacks. They're thieves, crooks, murderers, and dope artists."

A widow who sold real estate said, "The problem of the nationalists is that they have nothing to work at and to keep busy so they create a lot of disturbances."

The black nationalists were also criticized for trying to

indoctrinate young Negroes.

One mother complained, "The nationalists are grown men and dropouts hanging around schools harassing kids, trying to force them into wearing Afro hair styles."

A woman on welfare protested, "Last week my two daughters held a party at home and some black nationalist youths tried to break it up because they weren't invited."

Many of these same Negroes, though, also defended the black nationalists because "they bring out problems that whites refuse to believe" and "most whites never cared about us before they had the nationalists breathing down their backs."

Stokes had also come under attack for marching with armed bands of black nationalists in commemoration of the 1966 Hough riots.

The less militant Negroes thought "he should be friendly to the nationalists to keep them quiet." But others thought, "Stokes should march to show pride in his color."

A cigarette stamper declared, "No one gets heated up when the army or other military groups parade with arms and weapons. The idea of that march was to show the whites that blacks are prepared to fight for freedom all the way down the line."

A thirty-four-year-old plumber defended Stokes by saying "The Nationalists marched with weapons to show the symbol of what they were preparing for: an end to former oppression. They were revolutionary but the weapons weren't loaded."

This same phrase "the weapons weren't loaded" was volunteered by other Negroes. It seemed to emphasize the one thing they wanted to hold on to—the threat of being able to make trouble if they had to. They wanted to keep some sort of gun on the hill, even if it wasn't loaded.

At this point one comes to a basic source of white-black tensions: the extent to which the "bargaining" between the races has been based on a precarious balance of mutual fears. Earlier I quoted the Negro who observed that white people feel that racial problems are well in hand if things are peaceful and quiet, while the Negro is concerned with getting his rights. If whites understood their own feelings they would realize that some recognized mechanism is needed to enable blacks to voice their grievances. Or how else are they to make their discontents visible?

Having white-black relations hinge on mutual fears is a precarious and fickle business. The thought that Stokes might prevent racial violence was the main reason he drew a significant white vote in 1967, the peak year of rioting through the country.

In his re-election bid he gained some new support because of the general feeling that Cleveland had suffered less racial unrest than other cities. Ironically, these lessened racial fears also cost Stokes votes, since some of his 1967 supporters felt that a black mayor was no longer worth the same weight in taxes.

A forty-eight-year-old engineer recalled how "frightened people were of race riots two years ago. We voted for Stokes because we thought he'd be able to calm the colored down.

"Today," he continued, "the immediate need for a colored mayor isn't as strong. I'm inclined to switch to Ralph Perk. He has a better fiscal background than Stokes."

What conclusions can be drawn from Cleveland's experience?

A new realistic definition of integration is needed, one which recognizes that residential segregation in itself does not cut off steady gains toward ever-fuller integration. This becomes all the more important in view of all the talk of the collapse of school integration.

Nearly all of Cleveland's Negroes live in segregated neighborhoods. Since Stokes's election, though, the blacks have made dramatic progress in being integrated into the life of Cleveland, through a wider array of jobs, residential mobility, political power, patronage, and, what sums it all up, a growing sense of constructive pride.

A thirty-one-year-old cabinetmaker remarked, "Whites look at you as a person quicker now than a few years ago."

How is that pride built? My stay in Cleveland left me feeling that what is done politically may be more important than what is done economically, though the two should march together.

If the right man can be found, a city would be wise to elect a black mayor, preferably while whites still represent a majority of the city's population. The comments of some Negroes made clear how much more Stokes's victory meant to them because some white people had voted for him.

"You can see racial relations are improving," remarked a forty-two-year-old truck driver. "Ten years ago no whites in Cleveland would have voted for a Negro mayor."

A black mayor also becomes at least one stake that whites and blacks share. This in turn, gives whites a leverage inside the black community that can probably be gained in no other way. To protect and hold that stake, we have seen, blacks opposed nationalist actions inside the black community that might hurt Stokes; they have also felt some restraints on their own behavior.

"Negroes listen better since Stokes has been in," explained a forty-eight-year-old cook.

Another Negro said, "He can tell people not to tear things apart but to wait for improvements."

In a polarized city, white voters also need *visible* evidence of racial progress; perhaps even more so than in a city that is not divided. A thirty-seven-year-old mechanic who services business machines on Cleveland's East Side confessed, "I used to be afraid to look at a colored man because he might think I was prejudiced. The fact that we've both got a colored mayor is something we now have in common and can talk about."

A Negro winning an election has a totally different kind of impact than appointing a Negro to the same post. Freedom has a different walk than dependence. I decided to test the difference in the District of Columbia, which also has a Negro mayor, Walter Washington, who is appointed by the President. I did a little interviewing of Negroes, asking the same question I had asked in Cleveland—"What does Walter Washington being mayor mean to you?"

Few blacks had any warm, positive reaction. In Cleveland, a majority of the Negroes interviewed in 1969 remembered exactly what they were doing when they heard that Stokes had been elected.

A cleaning woman who was working alone in a bank at night recalled, "I was playing the radio real loud. When I heard Stokes won I went around the bank whooping and hollering."

In the District of Columbia, no black person interviewed could remember what he was doing when he heard that Washington had been appointed.

The democratic power of the election process should not be underestimated. It is a means by which people identify with their leaders; the more impersonal our society becomes, the more important becomes the use of that identifying process.

The very fact that Stokes has had so much going for him with the mass of Negroes gives special significance to the problem areas where he has had no visible affect—most noticeably on crime, which has been rising as rapidly in Cleveland as in other cities.

We may as well lay aside all those eloquent government reports which have repeated the generalities that the only solution to crime—to quote the Violence Commission— is "reconstructing urban life," and which then follow with proposals that billions be spent on improving education, job opportunities, housing, recreational facilities, etc.

The harsh political reality is that these billions are not going to be made available. Also the fact that considerable economic improvement in Cleveland has changed so much of Negro living, but not crime, suggests that crime has some specifics of its own which need to be dealt with directly, with whatever funds are available, expanding the effort as more funds come in.

Not all of Cleveland's crime is racial. On the white West Side, which attracts a steady influx of hillbillies, the youth gangs who roam the deteriorating neighborhoods are white. One of their specialities is the speed with which they can strip cars of parts which "customers" have ordered in advance.

For some whites and blacks, crime has become a form of gainful employment, yielding higher financial rewards and prestige than other employment. Often it is argued that since the unemployment rate does not include part-time workers, joblessness among Negroes is understated. If the ever-ingenious Bureau of Labor Statistics worked out a measure of the extent of gainful employment in crime, the unemployment rate would drop appreciably.*

Another key factor is the territorial struggle that has come to structure the whole urban crisis. The Black City itself is experiencing its own territorial conflict, between neighborhoods into which Negroes who make economic progress are moving and the poorer areas, including Hough and nearby parts of Glenville, which are controlled by black nationalists and where crime is heaviest.

The Hough-Glenville area, which most whites and many blacks fear to enter, seems deliberately walled off from the

* This is likely to be of rising future importance. To evade the Justice Department, the Mafia in New York City have subcontracted some operations to Negroes, giving them a larger stake in what is probably Harlem's biggest single industry.

rest of the city.

Market surveys conducted by the newspapers have blank spaces for parts of these neighborhoods. "We've stopped sending interviewers in there," explained one surveyor, "because they're always robbed." Visiting these streets is like visiting a bandit or revolutionist stronghold.

One sees little evidence of the prosperity so evident in middle-class Negro neighborhoods, unless it is in how well-dressed are the men in their twenties and thirties standing on street corners in midday. Many stores remain empty since the white merchants have left.

A nurse's aide complained, "The nationalists run out the white businesses and the stores the colored own now, you can't get what you want from them."

Another reason why the area doesn't respond to general economic improvement is that the same process of selection that moves whites to the suburbs operates inside the Black City. The Negroes who better their lot move out of Hough and Glenville to homeowning areas. Their leaving tightens the hold of the militants on these neighborhoods. Many of the families left in these nationalist strongholds are headed by women on welfare with no male wage-earner—and can't move.

Andrew Brimmer, the one-time Negro banker who is a member of the Federal Reserve Board, has warned of the "dangerous widening" of accomplishment between the expanding Negro middle class and the less educated militants in poorer black neighborhoods.

The conditions in poorer neighborhoods—welfare problems, the drug traffic, poor schools, crime parading as an ideology—have to be dealt with directly. They do not respond to a general improvement in the economy.

This expansion of Cleveland's sizable middle class has strengthened the conservatism of many Negro families; too much so, contend some blacks.

In the Lee-Seville area, the better-income homeowners voiced strong opposition to a Stokes proposal to erect a low-cost housing project in their neighborhood.

One middle-aged auto worker tried to explain: "We're not against these people coming in, but someone ought to teach them how to live before they are brought out here. We have worked hard to keep eyesores out of this neighborhood."

The fact that Stokes has drawn full support from the whole of the Black City holds out an "iffy" chance that a black mayor may prove the instrument of pacifying the black nationalists. In varied ways Stokes has tried to make the more militant leaders part of his administration—by giving a job to one, a project to another.

When Martin Luther King, Jr., was assassinated in 1968 this gamble paid off. Although racial disorders broke out in more than a hundred cities across the country, Cleveland remained quiet. The day of the assassination Stokes walked the ghetto streets, into the bars and pool halls, talking to everyone about the importance of keeping quiet. He also made the rounds of the militant leaders. Among the places he visited was a bookstore and Afro culture shop called "Ahmed's Shop."

Shortly afterward, Fred Ahmed Evans, a black nationalist leader and decorated Korean War veteran who dabbled in astrology, was given a $10,000 grant for an African crafts project. Evans spent the money on guns for his followers.

The guns were used in a shootout with the police—no one ever determined who fired the first shot—on the night of July 23, 1968, in which ten persons were killed—three black nationalists, three policemen, and four black civilians.

The next day Stokes made a critical decision—to move all white policeman from the tense Glenville area, leaving only Negro policeman and black leaders to restore law and order. No further killing took place after "black control" was established, although looting continued.

More than a year later, during his re-election campaign, Stokes's decision to pull out the white police was still one of the most emotionally divisive issues throughout the city.

Several factors explain why the memory of the Glenville shootout churned up such turbulent emotions.

Stokes's action made clear that he was not going to act as "the white man's nigger." Substantial numbers of Democrats had voted for Stokes in 1967 "because he was a Democrat and I thought maybe he could calm the colored down." They swung against him when, they felt, "Stokes showed he would favor his own people against the whites."

The Glenville decision also touched off a bitter, seemingly unending, feud between the police and Mayor Stokes.

The police felt humiliated and ashamed by Stokes action.

The mother of a policeman who had been in Glenville during the shootout related how her son felt after the bodies of the slain policemen were pulled out. "Mom," the son told her, "when the order came that we couldn't go back in there we just stood there and cried like jerks."

Another policeman said, "Glenville drew the line. You knew exactly how Stokes would go from that time on. It was the clue for permissiveness."

Some Clevelanders interviewed during the re-election campaign felt that after Glenville the police resorted to a deliberate slowdown in answering calls for police protection. Every policeman I interviewed during the campaign talked openly of wanting to see Stokes beaten, often saying, "We have to have a showdown whether the Negroes will obey the law."

This "racial showdown" feeling was echoed by many white voters. Among the whites interviewed half of them felt "there will be more racial trouble if Stokes is defeated." And yet most of them said they would support Stokes's opponent, Ralph J. Perk, the county auditor.

Asked what should be done "if trouble develops" many replied, "meet it head-on" or "let the police have a free hand."

On election day, several hundred policemen took off their uniforms and went into Negro polling places to challenge the voters.

After the election, in hopes of resolving the feud, Stokes named General Benjamin Davis as his new safety director in charge of the police and firemen, and also brought in a new police chief.

The balance of mutual fears in Cleveland remains a precarious affair, held together by a Stokes victory margin of less than 1 per cent and a rebellious police force.

For those who want an instant solution, the Cleveland story may seem frustrating—as is our racial experience in every part of this country. When one considers the enormous difficulties to be overcome in bringing whites and blacks together, what has been done in Cleveland seems a good beginning.

At best, though, it will take some years to learn what really works. In the meantime, white-black relations could explode in any of several cities. It is during this period that uncertain racial tensions could have their greatest political impact, particularly if the Republicans press the racial issue in hopes of winning a party majority.

Still, such a strategy could produce results as surprising as Mayor John Lindsay's off-Broadway rehearsal in reshuffling our parties.


## 4. Cops and Mayors

An imaginative playwright setting out to dramatize how our racial conflict might build up into a political showdown that would throw American politics into upheaval might come up with a three-act drama along these lines.

Act One would open at a Republican presidential convention with the more conservative Republicans demanding a strict law-and-order platform plus a quick and open offer of coalition with the white South, in the process defeating the liberal Republican wing and driving out such senators as Charles Percy, Jacob Javits, Hugh Scott, Clifford Case, and Mark Hatfield.

In Act Two the Democrats, assembled at their convention, would try to counter the GOP by putting together a poor man's version of law and order in an attempt to hold the white workers in both the North and South.

This strategy would so enrage the more liberal Democrats who feel strongly about civil rights that they would bolt the Democratic convention, taking with them all the black delegates. Those liberals and blacks would then form a new all-liberal coalition, joining with the liberal Republicans who had been ousted from the new all-conservative GOP.

The final curtain would then come down with a resounding election victory for whom ever the playwright thought would save the nation.

Such a script would bear a pretty close resemblance to New York City's mayoralty election in 1969. At stake in that vote was not simply who would be elected to try to govern the nation's largest city, but what might happen if racial conflict became the issue that forced a realignment of both the Democratic and Republican Parties.

In defeating Mayor John Lindsay in the mid-June Republican primary, the more conservative Republicans were trying to purge the GOP of "liberals" who, in conservative eyes, "have never been real Republicans." They were also striving to give a big forward push to the "southern strategy" of alliance with the South by demonstrating how badly the Democrats could be split by the law-and-order issue.

The fact that State Senator John Marchi ran a poor third,

drawing only 23 per cent of the total vote, flagged red signals of caution to President Nixon. Further, the $3 million in campaign funds that were reportedly raised for Lindsay, and the impressive list of Republicans and business leaders who supported him, made clear that any move that stamped the GOP as anti-Negro would split wide the northern Republicans.

Temporarily at least, the bargaining power of the liberal Republicans may even have been strengthened by the demonstration that Negroes and Puerto Ricans would forsake the Democratic Party en masse for a man who was fighting their battle.

But the southern strategy was only slowed, not killed, by Lindsay's impressive personal triumph. Nor could his victory be accurately described as any indication that the "law and order" issue had been laid to rest, even in New York City.

On the contrary, the voting reveals that the polarization of racial feeling has become probably the strongest political force agitating New York City's voters.

How deeply embedded these tensions are becomes evident if one turns back three years to the vote in 1966 that killed the Civilian Review Board, which Lindsay had set up to hear cases of alleged police brutality.

Lindsay won re-election with 42 per cent of the city's vote, which was 5 per cent higher than the losing vote in favor of the Review Board; but borough by borough, assembly district by assembly district, his 1969 showing scales quite closely to the Review Board vote.

Of New York City's sixty-eight assembly districts, only twenty-one cast a majority vote to retain the Review Board. All twenty-one were won by Lindsay with a clear majority. In addition, he carried three other assembly districts by a majority; these had voted 44 to 49 per cent to keep the Review Board.

At the other extreme, seventeen assembly districts went from 75 to 85 per cent to abolish the Review Board. Only one of these districts gave Lindsay as much as 31 per cent of the vote. Also included in these seventeen districts are twelve of the thirteen districts that Nixon carried in 1968, as well as twelve of the thirteen where Wallace drew between 8 and 10 per cent of the vote, his best showing in the entire city.

The close scaling between the vote for Lindsay and the Review Board also holds for the assembly districts at the city average. Eleven districts voted no more than 3 per cent above or below the 1966 city average of 37 per cent to keep the Review Board. All but two fell within 3 per cent of Lindsay's citywide average of 42 per cent.

That a Police Review Board vote three years old should structure the 1969 balloting for mayor may seem astonishing when one looks back upon Lindsay's exciting re-election campaign and the many things that happened in his first term as mayor.

After the election his victory was credited to a remarkable variety of influences: (a) the famed independence with which New Yorkers toss aside party loyalties; (b) his strong denunciation of the Vietnam war; (c) the split in the conservative vote; (d) the surprising World Series triumph of the Mets; (e) the *Daily News* poll; (f) the low voter turnout; (g) his skilled television performance; (h) Mario Procaccino's anything-but-skilled TV performance.

On top of all this were Lindsay's racial ups and downs as mayor. New Yorkers split in 1967 over whether Lindsay had been too lenient in tolerating looting that stopped short of violence. The next spring he seemed unbeatable politically when the city was spared the riotings that followed Martin Luther King's murder; by October of 1968 he looked like a sure loser as he was booed in the synagogues because of the bitterness that came with the ten-week teachers' strike over school decentralization.

Lindsay's campaigning undoubtedly shifted his vote upward from what it would have been right after the summer primary. But the really remarkable fact is that in the face of all that happened, the 1969 voting for mayor across the whole city flowed into the grooves of emotion that had been dug and channeled in the 1966 battle of cops and mayors over the Review Board.

That fact cautions against leaping to the conclusion that voting on racial issues means a swing for either "liberalism" or "conservatism." That was how the Review Board referendum in 1966 was pictured by the more liberal New York newspapers—as a test of liberalism and support for civil rights.

But my own interviewing at the time showed that for most New Yorkers voting to end the Review Board was a vote against rising crime and quickened Negro residential movement.

A fourth of the Negroes and Puerto Ricans interviewed voted to abolish the Review Board. With few exceptions, their reasoning was "I don't want to cripple the police" or "there are too many thugs who try to take advantage of the police" or "sometimes the police must be hard and even use force."

Among the whites interviewed, of those who wanted to kill the Board, one in five said that either they themselves had been robbed or mugged or that a member of their family had been.

Among those who voted to keep the Board, only one in ten said they had been the victim of some crime.

Of those who wanted to keep the Review Board, one in twelve had had a run-in with the police; of those who voted to abolish it, only one in thirty complained of having been mistreated by the police.

Many of those who favored abolishing the Review Board

had pro-civil rights feelings.

A Bronx photographer who favored passage of an open housing law but opposed the Review Board had been held up twice in his studio.

He explained his opposition to the Board by saying, "I don't believe police attack people who are nice characters. If criminals think they're in danger of police then maybe they won't molest other people. Police brutality charges are false. To deal with Negroes, you must be tough, you must use a firm hand. If Negroes want to get ahead it's wrong to loot."

The assembly districts which voted near the city average—63 per cent—to abolish the Board were the heavily Jewish areas. These districts went overwhelmingly against Goldwater in 1964, and just as heavily for Hubert Humphrey in 1968, indicating that their 1966 vote on the Review Board did not mark "any swing to the right" politically. They were troubled about crime and police protection.

Still, the three years between 1966 and 1969 brought some significant changes in the voting.

New York City is generally pictured as the home of "the eastern liberal establishment," and to Spiro Agnew, as it was to William Jennings Bryan, it remains "enemy country."

The net political reading from New York reveals much the same trends of racial voting that we have noted in other cities, the same spreading of territorial conflict, that is being intensified by population shifts.

This can be seen when one checks the assembly districts that show the biggest departures from the 1966 Review Board vote.

In nine assembly districts, Lindsay's tally jumped between 10 and 15 per cent over the vote to keep the Review Board. Five of these districts have had heavy increases in Negro and Puerto Rican population. One, the Grand Concourse section in the Bronx, was once symbolic of Jewish middle class progress; the other four radiate from Bedford-Stuyvesant in Brooklyn.

Two of these—Bushwick and East New York—still rank low in their Lindsay support, and in both the influx of Negroes and Puerto Ricans is fairly recent. In 1966 only one-seventh of the precincts in these districts voted to keep the Board; in 1969 Lindsay carried more than four in every ten precincts.

As one moves out of these Negro or Puerto Rican areas into the heavily white precincts, the Wallace vote jumps as high as 16 per cent. But even in these precincts the new births foreshadow a further rise in the Negro and Puerto Rican vote. In the Bushwick precincts where Wallace drew 16 per cent, white families accounted for 82 per cent of the births in 1966; just one year later the white proportion of births dropped to 70 per cent.

The other four assembly districts where Lindsay scored gains of 10 per cent or better over the Review Board referendum were in Manhattan, where Lindsay really won the election. He drew 66 per cent of Manhattan's vote, for a 218,000 plurality. In the rest of the city he ran 60,000 votes behind Procaccino. None of the four boroughs outside Manhattan gave Lindsay more than 39 per cent.

The Manhattan showing reflects in good part the mayor's success in stabilizing the borough racially. During his first administration, Lindsay gave every possible priority to expanding Manhattan's impressive office-building complex, which constitutes the city's largest source of payrolls.

As part of this program, the erection of new high-rise apartments, many of them cooperatives, was encouraged, as was the remodeling of older buildings to provide quarters for single girls and younger couples who worked in downtown Manhattan.

Manhattan is the only borough in the city whose white

population has increased. In stabilizing Manhattan, however, Negro and Puerto Rican residential pressures were shifted to the other boroughs, particularly to the Bronx and Brooklyn. Lindsay's vote through the whole of the city, in short, reflects both his success and failure in racial stabilization.

Nixon's 1968 vote reveals the same gap between Manhattan and the other boroughs. The President carried a mere 3 per cent of Manhattan's precincts against Humphrey, compared to 13 per cent of Manhattan's precincts in 1960. In the other four boroughs Nixon won a third of the precincts against a quarter of them in 1960.

As Table 4, shows, Nixon's heaviest gains came in the Bronx and Brooklyn. Since these are the boroughs in which Negro and Puerto Rican numbers have increased most rapidly, the table understates Nixon's 1968 gains among white voters over his 1960 vote.

TABLE 4
*Nixon's Gains in New York City*

| BOROUGH | PROPORTION OF PRECINCTS NIXON CARRIED | |
| --- | --- | --- |
| | *1960* | *1968* |
| Bronx | 12% | 22% |
| Brooklyn | 16 | 23 |
| Queens | 39 | 46 |
| Staten Island | 74 | 86 |
| Manhattan | 13 | 3 |
| WHOLE CITY | 21 | 27 |
| CITY, OUTSIDE MANHATTAN | 24 | 33 |

One final set of voting statistics may complete the picture. Table 5 lists the twenty-six assembly districts where Lindsay drew less than a third of the vote. One notes, first, how close is the correlation between the low Lindsay showing and the low vote to retain the Police Review Board.

But when these assembly districts are divided into two groups—the thirteen districts carried by Nixon and the thirteen Humphrey won—it then becomes clear that these racial angers have not ended voter loyalty to the two parties.

TABLE 5

*Race and Party Loyalty in*
*New York City: 1966–1969*

| ASSEMBLY DISTRICTS FOR NIXON | | 1968 PRESIDENT | | 1966 PRO- | 1969 MAYOR |
|---|---|---|---|---|---|
| | | NIXON | WALLACE | REVIEW BOARD | LINDSAY |
| Brooklyn | 49th | 62% | 7% | 15% | 18% |
| Brooklyn | 50th | 60 | 7 | 15 | 22 |
| Staten Island | 58th | 57 | 10 | 16 | 16 |
| Queens | 20th | 56 | 8 | 19 | 27 |
| Queens | 30th | 55 | 10 | 15 | 22 |
| Queens | 28th | 55 | 8 | 19 | 27 |
| Staten Island | 59th | 53 | 9 | 19 | 20 |
| Queens | 22nd | 51 | 6 | 29 | 32 |
| Queens | 34th | 50 | 9 | 19 | 26 |
| Queens | 29th | 49 | 9 | 19 | 24 |
| Bronx | 80th | 49 | 9 | 19 | 24 |
| Queens | 32nd | 48 | 7 | 23 | 29 |
| Queens | 33rd | 47 | 8 | 20 | 28 |
| ASSEMBLY DISTRICTS FOR HUMPHREY | | | | | |
| Brooklyn | 46th | 22 | 3 | 32 | 29 |
| Brooklyn | 39th | 24 | 3 | 31 | 29 |
| Bronx | 82nd | 30 | 5 | 29 | 31 |
| Brooklyn | 48th | 32 | 4 | 28 | 25 |
| Brooklyn | 41st | 32 | 4 | 26 | 31 |
| Brooklyn | 47th | 33 | 4 | 27 | 26 |
| Bronx | 83rd | 38 | 5 | 27 | 31 |
| Brooklyn | 42nd | 38 | 5 | 25 | 24 |
| Brooklyn | 35th | 40 | 10 | 21 | 26 |
| Brooklyn | 51st | 41 | 6 | 26 | 30 |
| Brooklyn | 53rd | 43 | 9 | 20 | 28 |
| Brooklyn | 38th | 44 | 8 | 21 | 31 |
| Bronx | 85th | 46 | 7 | 22 | 24 |
| CITY AVERAGE | | 34 | 5 | 37 | 42 |

All thirteen Humphrey districts were won by Procaccino, while Marchi carried only eight of the thirteen Nixon districts. A precinct analysis of the vote points to some shifting of Marchi supporters to Procaccino as the candidate most likely to beat Lindsay. But the returns indicate that the anti-Lindsay Democrats are not ready to swing Republican for president.

A quick note might be added about Governor Nelson Rockefeller's vote in 1966, which was not structured by racial tensions. His highest percentages came in seven Manhattan assembly districts, but he also carried eight of the thirteen AD's that Nixon won in the other boroughs. Rockefeller, in short, carried districts both high and low for Lindsay; some which favored keeping the Review Board and some which voted overwhelmingly against the Board.

In planning his 1970 re-election run, Rockefeller had to decide in what direction he was to move politically. The announcement that Nixon will campaign for him in New York state suggests that Rockefeller would be looking for more conservative support than in the past.

For the Democrats the meaning of what has been happening in our northern cities, not New York alone, seems clear. The New Deal coalition in these cities cannot be held together unless effective means are developed for coping with the effects of the suburban drain of white population and the spreading movement of blacks and other minority elements through the cities.

Prejudice, bigotry, racism—whatever the term employed —is part of the difficulty, but the critical problems are those of a great population movement—and struggle—which began in the rural South and has been pressing inexorably through the cities and out into the suburbs.

One is tempted to write that the "liberal" Democrats misjudged the law-and-order issue; but more likely they tried to talk it down because they could think of nothing effective to do about it. They have hoped that "massive funds" could become available to "restructure urban life," but there seems only a remote chance politically that the billions being sought will become available. Despite those handicaps, the real issue of law and order—to find the means through which whites and blacks can live together in racial peace—has to be met if the Roosevelt coalition is to be revitalized.

For the Republicans the significance is mixed. In both Cleveland and New York anti-Negro feelings among white workers have brought some shifts in party loyalty to the Republicans, while many more Democrats say, "There is no difference between the parties any more," which could presage even larger shifts in the future. But the clean break in party loyalty on a major scale which would crack the Roosevelt coalition for good has not taken place.

Simultaneously, some efforts are being made to forge a business-Negro political alliance whose implications could be far-reaching.

The pattern may not be as evident in New York City as elsewhere, since New York has always had business leaders and persons of wealth with liberal inclinations. But in Cleveland, Stokes won Republican votes and drew his main financial support from industrialists and bankers; similarly in Detroit, Richard Austin, in his bid to become the city's first black mayor, had the backing of Chrysler and other auto executives.

A business-Negro combination would be facilitated by the fact that there are no conflicts over "living space" between better-income whites and the blacks. A number of cities—New York, Chicago, Philadelphia, Cleveland, Atlanta, Detroit—have been building high-rise apartment houses to help stabilize their "downtown" areas and to lure back white families from the suburbs. In all these developments, residents cast low votes for Wallace.

Over the last decade as well, better-off whites have tended to vote on the same side as Negroes in a succession of racially sensitive elections in both the North and South— in Boston against Louise Day Hicks for mayor, in Little Rock against the segregationists who wanted to keep Central High School closed, in Atlanta against Lester Maddox's two efforts to be elected mayor.

More significant than any open political commitments, which are few, are the decisions of so many business leaders to remain in the central cities with their plants and investments. On the night of July 23, 1967, when much of Detroit was afire, one can visualize GM, Chrysler, and Ford executives mounting to the top of their office headquarters for a better view of the flames. Inevitably the question must have come to their minds—do we get out of the turbulent, riot-torn inner cities or do we stay and work for order?

In Detroit the decision made was to stay. The auto companies have not moved work from the inner-city plants to other sites; the General Motors headquarters building has been redecorated at quite an expense.

Such decisions of business leaders across the country are obviously not part of any politics to save the New Deal coalition. These acts of selection must be looked upon as part of the political struggles of the future, which will be fought inside both the Republican and Democratic coalitions.

With their present population makeup, the big cities are no longer viable governing units. Their dominant need is for additional financial resources to meet their problems. Their politics in the future is likely to become a claimant-city politics that will seek to pressure state and federal governments for funds and grants.

Inside the cities varied political alignments will be tested—to determine which best fits the needs of claimant politics—blacks allying with business, white workers turning

Republican, New Deal elements trying to revive their coalition.

John Lindsay, the handsome, personable WASP campaigning so naturally on ghetto streets and in synagogues, may gain his place in history as the first of our big-city mayors who recognized, as so many university presidents have, that their essential function has become that of fund raisers. He may also become the spokesman for a new urban sectionalism which is ready to be born.

But before we get into the implications of claimant-society politics, let us take a look at developments in the South and how Nixon is doing with the special political temptations of southern cooking.

*FIVE*

# THE POLITICS OF UPBRINGING

## 1. A Two-Party South?

FAIRLY OFTEN in my interviewing throughout the South I thought about how much of the 1968 vote had actually been settled twenty-five years earlier. Repeatedly it would develop that why one voter supported Nixon, another Wallace, and still another Humphrey was determined by the kind of upbringing they had had, by how their parents had talked about Negroes, or by the fact that "my father once belonged to a labor union" or by a longing that "everything should be like it was back in Mississippi."

On one southwest Miami street two neighbors, living side by side, picked "racial violence" as the biggest problem before the country, but in revealingly different terms.

The wife of a roofer recalled, "When the Republican convention was here I prayed for rain to keep the Negroes off the streets so there wouldn't be any trouble."

Her next-door neighbor, a construction supervisor, declared angrily, "Shoot a few. That will stop them!"

A Wallace supporter, he wanted to scrap every civil rights law enacted over the past decade, declaring, "Just put the son of a bitch back into his place and keep him there."

The roofer's wife, who favored Nixon, when asked whether schools should remain desegregated, replied quickly: "Oh, you must do that! Without education we'll never learn to live together."

Why did these two Miami homeowners, on a par economically, differ so strongly in racial feeling?

The Wallace man, it turned out, had been born and reared in the harsh rural poverty of Georgia, with its strict segregation taboos. The roofer's wife had come from Philadelphia, where, she remembered, "there were always colored children in my school."

In an age of moon-landing technology it may seem ironic that the past should still exert so powerful a hold on people's political thinking. Still, this clash of upbringings, not only among different southerners but between northerners and southerners, seems likely to shape the party realignment now taking place in the South.

At stake in Nixon's southern strategy is who is to be changed by the process of realignment. Will the South become more like the rest of the nation or will the rest of the country be southernized?

How Nixon presses his southern strategy will also determine whether liberal Republicans in the North may be driven out of the GOP as Mayor Lindsay has virtually been, as well as the nature of the Nixon coalition after he has left the White House—will it be a broadly based center party or one pulling the nation ever more strongly conservative?

Will the South and its problems come to dominate the Republican Party as the Negro and his conflicts have the Democratic Party?

Varied party patterns will be developed by Republicans in different southern states. Virginia's Governor Holton highlighted his inaugural message with the pledge to end racial discrimination in the state government, perhaps reflecting the fact that 16 per cent of the Old Dominion's vote is cast in the suburbs across the Potomac. At the same time Florida's Governor Claude Kirk was searching publicly for new ways of stalling desegregation, perhaps reflecting his sensitivity to the fact that half of Florida is a suburban expansion of the North and the other half a population spillover from Georgia and Alabama.

But the eleven southern states have also persisted as a sectional force which differs markedly from the rest of the country. The South remains *the* section in the country where business enjoys the widest permissiveness, where labor unions are weakest, where the economic dependence on military installations is unusually high, where Negroes still struggle for political visibility, where welfare payments are lowest.

In one of its parting projects the Johnson Administration selected some 256 counties in the country for an emergency $10 million program of food and medical aid; of the counties 206 were in the eleven southern states. Ten of the eleven secession states—Louisiana the exception—have right-to-work laws; only three have laws setting miminum wages, none higher than $1.25 an hour.

Given this wide disparity, realigning with the South becomes something of a problem in political genetics: which genes and chromosomes, interests and prejudices, of one mate are to be dominant and which are to be recessive?

Southerners also play the "game of politics" differently than do northerners. The term "two-party politics" doesn't mean the same thing in Dixie as in the rest of the nation. In some southern states the dominant elements will try to control both major parties even as they shift Republican nationally. We may still have one-party states. In Congress the southerners can be expected to try to maintain their control of strategic committees by re-electing key Democrats.

Strom Thurmond, John Tower, and other southern Republicans will be bringing Nixon, as has already happened, all kinds of "suggestions" calculated to strengthen "our Republican friends" in their states—quotas on textile imports, softening compliance with desegregation, naming southerners to the Supreme Court, weakening the voting rights laws, lesser changes in oil depletion taxes, how military contracts should be shared, larger appropriations for the Charleston naval facilities, and so on. As is always the case in such situations, more will be asked of Nixon than any have a right to ask. What will he be wise enough to turn down?

Before he is through with his southern strategy, President Nixon will have undergone a harsher testing of both his character and political shrewdness than has befallen any previous president.

In terms of the voters, the opportunity—and problem—that Nixon faces can be seen in Table 6, which traces the presidential voting of the two streams of anti-New Deal insurgency that developed in the South.

The economic insurgents centered in the southern cities, who sought to counter the influence of organized labor, have followed the same pattern of Republican voting as has the whole nation, going for Eisenhower twice, splitting almost evenly between Nixon and Kennedy, and dropping against Goldwater.

The urban economic appeal of the Republicans, in short, has been firmly structured since 1952 along the same income lines as in the nation generally.

But not so the racial insurgents who rebelled against the rising Negro political influence in the North. The southern racial vote, as reflected in the 157 black-belt counties—where Negroes outnumber the whites but were unable to vote until recently—has never moved with the rest of the country.

While the Democratic Party served as a one-party monopoly that kept Negroes from voting, these black-belt counties were the most loyal of Democrats, holding firm even when other parts of the South were breaking against Al Smith in 1928. In recent elections these racial insurgents have fluctuated wildly in their Republican support. After giving Eisenhower 41 per cent of their vote in 1952, they dropped to 29 per cent in 1956. Goldwater's support jumped to 62 per cent. But virtually the whole of this vote was swept away when Wallace ran.

TABLE 6

*Race vs. Economics: Presidential Voting of
Southern Cities and Black-Belt Counties*

| | CITIES | | BLACK BELT | |
| | REPUBLICAN | THIRD PARTY | REPUBLICAN | THIRD PARTY |
|---|---|---|---|---|
| 1928 | 49% | — | 17% | — |
| 1948 | 33 | 21% | 7 | 53% |
| 1952 | 54 | — | 41 | — |
| 1956 | 55 | 4 | 29 | 16 |
| 1960 | 50 | 3 | 31 | 14 |
| 1964 | 48 | — | 62 | — |
| 1968 | 39 | 26 | 18 | 44 |

The 1968 voting broke with all past patterns. The collapse of Democratic loyalties among white southerners could hardly have been more complete. With 31 per cent of the vote in the eleven secession states, Humphrey carried only 237 of the South's 1,105 counties, and 154 of these were in Texas—the only southern state he won.

But Nixon picked up few of the pieces. He drew only 34.6 per cent of the South's vote, to 34.4 per cent for Wallace, winning twenty-four fewer counties than in 1960. His vote, moreover, was swelled by appreciable numbers of Wallace supporters who, as the campaign closed, switched to Nixon rather than see Humphrey elected.

After the 1968 election returns were in, some observers pinned the "conservative" label on both the Nixon Republicans and the Wallaceites, as if the full 5,073,409 Wallace votes in the South were Nixon's for the taking. Actually, though, the Wallaceites and Nixon Republicans represent two clashing streams of southern life, culturally, economically and historically.

Until now the main thrust of the Republican upsurge in the South has been borne by the expanding, business-minded middle class in the cities, the well-educated and generally respected management types.

The Wallaceites, on the other hand, have long been among the bossed, often ridiculed as "rednecks" and "crackers." Their family roots are largely rural and they tend to cling to much of the old Bible Belt morality. In Memphis, Houston, and Richmond the Wallace precincts have voted most heavily "no" to liquor by the drink, while the strongest Nixon precincts have voted most heavily "yes." Both Wallace and Georgia's Governor Lester Maddox are teetotalers, as is Senator Strom Thurmond.

When Howard Calloway, heir to the Calloway fortune, ran as a Republican for governor of Georgia against Maddox in 1966, a popular political anecdote was: "When Calloway was born and the doctor slapped him on the butt that made him a millionaire." Calloway's father had been a director of several banks, U.S. Steel, and Shell Oil. Many leading Wall Street financiers went hunting on the Calloway estate.

Maddox's father was an Atlanta steelworker who lost his job in the Depression. Then only twelve, Maddox had to drop out of school to work full time as a delivery boy and soda jerk.

These economic differences run generations deep, at least on the Wallace side. Many Wallace supporters are lineal descendants of the millworkers and poorer farmers in Georgia whom Tom Watson rallied in the 1890's in his Populist assault on the wealthier landowners, and later in his anti-Negro race for the U.S. Senate. In Augusta, Wallace carried one ward, the fifth—then and now the millworker ward—which Watson won regularly.

To merge the Wallaceites and Nixon Republicans into a unified political force would be a considerable political achievement. What mixture of racial and economic policies can Nixon offer that would accomplish this merger? Can he appeal to the Wallace voters on anything but race? If so, how? If not, how far can he go and remain acceptable to the rest of the country?

## 2. "Rednecks" on the Move

For more than a century the city of Richmond has been regarded as a political weathervane for the state of Virginia. In every presidential election since 1864 the city voted for the same candidate as the state as a whole, and the percentages were usually quite close. In 1968, though, while Nixon was carrying Virginia, Richmond went for Humphrey with 49 per cent of the vote and Wallace tallied 11 per cent.

This shattering of a century-old precedent was not the result of changed political thinking in Richmond; rather, it reflected a striking transformation in the makeup of the city's population. The Kerner Commission had predicted that Richmond would be over 50 per cent Negro by 1971. But the Commission had not reckoned on the quickened residential push of the blacks, which sent nearly all of Richmond's white workers scurrying into suburban Henrico and Chesterfield counties. By 1968 Richmond's Negro population, by local estimates, had passed the 50 per cent mark, doubling the number of heavily black precincts where Humphrey drew his vote.

For the Democrats, taking Robert E. Lee's favorite city —along with Atlanta, New Orleans, Norfolk, Little Rock, Memphis, and other southern cities—was not really good political news. Mainly, these victories indicated that blacks, as in the North, are being concentrated inside the cities while whites are moving out to the rapidly growing suburbs. Around Richmond the suburbs have nearly quadrupled their vote since 1952.

When one maps this growth and analyzes the voting of the urban south, four striking facts emerge:

1. Unlike those in the North, the southern cities have been expanding their voting power. Between 1952 and 1968 the number of voters in the twelve largest southern urban counties rose 80 per cent, from 1,605,000 to 2,882,000.

2. Despite this expansion, the class structure of the South does not appear to have changed. In every southern city and suburb, the high-income Republicans remain apparently secure from Negro residential encroachment and more than token school desegregation. Always the competition for housing and the possibility of school integration on a major scale bring black and white workers into conflict.

This distribution of conflict, as we will see, is one key to Nixon's neighborhood school concept. In every southern city checked, home construction for the well-to-do has been pointed in one direction—southward in Charlotte; northward in Atlanta, Dallas and Raleigh; westward in Richmond and Houston—while housing for black and white workers has been built in another direction.

3. Most Wallace supporters share a common sense of identity and self-awareness which suggests that they have the makings of a new political force. When they come to the "big city" from the countryside they seek out people like themselves. When they move to new homes and better neighborhoods they follow one another, retaining their own group consciousness.

4. In talking with Wallaceites,—particularly those under thirty-five—one is struck by how few fit the old stereotypes of the southern poor white or "redneck."

The Wallace people do share a sense of poverty, but it is of the deprivations with which they and their parents grew up, not a current condition.

The prosperity of the last few years has given many of them their first lip-licking taste of the good things in life. They want more and are prepared to work hard for it, with both wives and husbands holding down jobs.

How this upward drive shapes their racial and economic thinking will probably determine whether they turn Republican, go back to the Democrats, or remain ready to support a third party.

The worker suburb of Glen Lea northeast of Richmond is fairly typical of these "rednecks" on the move. Two months before the election a majority of those interviewed talked of going for Wallace. In the last week of the campaign so many switched to Nixon that the final count gave him 53 per cent to 36 per cent for Wallace and only 11 per cent for Humphrey.

The frame or brick houses in Glen Lea cost around $12,000. There are few sidewalks, and interviewing after a rain means sloshing through the mud. Still, on one street of twenty homes, ten had boats in their backyards. The homes are kept scrupulously neat inside; couples under thirty tend to have modern furniture that is laminated and inexpensive. Bookcases are rare but most of the homes have large stereo consoles, wide-screen color television sets with remote control, and air-conditioning units.

Of those interviewed, two-thirds had come to Richmond from rural areas, and almost none had ever been out of the South. With only rare exceptions, they shared an ingrained, almost religious prejudice that the races ought to be kept separate. More than half of those interviewed were Baptist. One remark was repeated, as from a Sunday school lesson, "God didn't intend for whites and blacks to mix."

The thought of even token integration was resisted. A

bricklayer's wife who had planned to vote for Wallace but shifted to Nixon on election day was troubled by the fact that there were "one or two colored" in the school her children attended.

"I think ahead, you know," she explained. "I'm afraid for the day when my little girl comes home from school and asks me if Mary can stay overnight at our house. Then when Mary comes it turns out she's colored. What do I do then?"

Many of those interviewed had fled to Glen Lea from neighborhoods in Richmond where Negroes had begun moving in, and they were ready to flee again. They talked fearfully of how the city might annex the county and extend the bus lines to Glen Lea, which would bring out the blacks. Most of them had already picked out places they would move to. A forty-seven-year-old construction worker figured: "As soon as they run the bus lines here, the niggers will take over. We got about five years at the most. We're gonna buy ourselves a house and a nice piece of land in Hanover County."

This readiness to take residential flight seemed to be almost an instinctive reaction. None felt they were in economic competition with the Negro. This point was checked out carefully. At least three-fourths of those interviewed had or still worked with Negroes; almost no one was troubled by the experience.

Their determination not to live near Negroes seems to have been structured inside of their minds in childhood and has been strengthened by their economic climb. When they register their gains by moving to a nicer house, a nicer house means, of course, one in a white neighborhood.

The importance of keeping separate from Negroes was revealed in their replies to the question, "What do you tell your children about the colored?"

The few who had said they would remain in Glen Lea

even with Negro neighbors replied, "I've told my children to respect the colored" or "I've told them the colored have the same rights we have," often adding, "I want my children to get along, things aren't separate any more."

But among those who had already mentally packed to run from Glen Lea, typical comments were:

"I told my kids just what my daddy told me—the colored got their place and you gotta keep 'em there. And he told me never to call 'em Mister or Miss—you call 'em Uncle and Aunt."

"I don't teach Denise to hate the colored but I teach her there's a line. You have to instill that in a child."

"Bonnie has been told not to be rude, but I don't want her mixing with them."

"Stay away from them—that's what I tell my children."

One wondered whether this meant that the next generation would carry on the same resistance to integration as their parents.

On the economic side, their strongest resentments were against paying taxes, particularly for programs designed to help Negroes.

Some pro-Wallace families, in fact, seemed angrier over "welfare handouts" than over racial desegregation efforts.

A service manager, not long from Danville, said, "My mother-in-law got us to register to vote because she's so excited about Wallace. She says Wallace will cut out this welfare stuff for women who have illegitimate children. Mom doesn't think they should be paid for any illegitimates. I don't go that far. I can understand letting them make one mistake, just one baby."

A candy vendor's wife who was employed as an insurance clerk had pinned onto her coat a button that read, "I work for a living."

"I don't mind a sales tax," she explained, "because everybody pays it, but I don't like my taxes going to people who don't work."

These anti-tax sentiments are not confined to welfare but extend to all sorts of issues. In the 1968 voting three referenda were on the ballot—bond issues for new college buildings and mental hospitals, and legalization of the sale of liquor by the drink. The suburbs where Wallace drew his heaviest vote were strongest in opposition to all three issues, as Table 7 shows. The suburbs where Wallace did worst—all were over 75 per cent for Nixon—strongly supported all three issues.

TABLE 7

*Wallace Vote in Relation to Bond Issues,*
*Richmond Suburbs, 1968*

| HIGHEST WALLACE | FOR WALLACE | AGAINST COLLEGE BUILDINGS | AGAINST MENTAL HOSPITALS | AGAINST LIQUOR BY THE DRINK |
|---|---|---|---|---|
| Eanes | 51% | 70% | 57% | 45% |
| Highland Springs | 40 | 59 | 45 | 39 |
| Montrose | 39 | 53 | 42 | 36 |
| Glen Lea | 36 | 55 | 41 | 42 |
| Ratcliffe | 35 | 49 | 38 | 30 |
| Glen Echo | 32 | 44 | 39 | 30 |
| LOWEST WALLACE | | | | |
| Ridge | 9 | 29 | 26 | 22 |
| Maybeury | 7 | 29 | 20 | 19 |
| Spottswood | 6 | 28 | 21 | 20 |
| Rollingwood | 6 | 30 | 21 | 18 |
| Derbyshire | 5 | 24 | 18 | 17 |
| Tuckahoe | 4 | 27 | 18 | 17 |

Glen Lea's residents were somewhat more sympathetic to mental hospitals than to additional college facilities. Roughly six in ten voted in favor of the hospital bond issue, but only 45 per cent for new college buildings. Those who opposed financing new colleges usually felt "it would be all right if everybody's kids could go but mine won't." A traffic signalman who voted for the bond issue said: "I'd like for my children to go to college. But the first demonstration they get mixed up in, out they go and off to work."

This tendency to vote against bond issues characterizes pro-Wallace precincts throughout the South. Their expectations of what government should do for the people run low. Southside Atlanta, where Maddox drew most of his support, invariably registered sizable opposition to improvements favored by the Northside Republicans. In both Miami and Nashville, the Wallace areas opposed consolidation of the city and county. In New Orleans in 1968 the strongest Wallace wards went heavily against giving the city the power to assess property owners for the cost of sewers, sidewalks, and water improvements.

These low desires for government services seem part of a strong sense of economic individualism that is shared by many in the South. Theirs is not the thinking of people brought up in an affluent society. Theirs is the acquisitive drive that characterizes a society in an earlier stage of economic development, with little surplus to be shared.

With what political party are these anti-tax and anti-government feelings identified? As of 1969, the answer was none.

In this respect the pro-Wallace voters differ sharply from the white-collar, middle-class southerners who identify their aspirations for the future with the expansion of business enterprise and the Republican Party.

But the Wallace people do not identify readily with business, possibly because of their own worker ties; also, they do not like rich people. In discussing school desegregation, complaints like these were often voiced:

"The Republicans and Democrats both have money—enough money so's they don't have to send their children to mixed schools. Wallace doesn't have that kind of money."

"Wallace is the workin' man's man. These rich politicians can send their kids to any school they want."

Near Richmond an electrician's wife who voted for Wallace remarked, "I'm glad he didn't get in. He's so head-strong. I regret not voting for Nixon. I'm beginning to lean Republican. I think they'll get us out of Vietnam."

Still, in talking about where she and her husband might want to live, she pointedly excluded the solidly Republican sections of Henrico County, explaining, "I wouldn't want to live on the West Side. They're a different kind of people over there; they're not friendly like here. They act like they have so much; they're so conceited."

The strength of these split-party feelings was evident in the 1969 voting. In the Richmond area, the strong Nixon precincts went Republican for both governor and lieutenant governor. The heavy Wallace areas, though, voted Republican for governor but Democratic for lieutenant governor. The younger Wallace backers often have little sense of party identity; their shift to Nixon on the election eve was marked.

"We intended to vote for Wallace right up till the last day almost," recalled the twenty-nine-year-old wife of a Richmond fireman. "He was stern with people. I liked the way he talked when he said if any of 'em lay down in front of my car I'll run 'em over. That's what I'd do, I'd run 'em right over. But I knew that all the colored would vote for Humphrey. So my husband and I decided that voting for Nixon was the best thing."

Asked what was the big difference between the Democratic and Republican Parties, she replied, "It's just the way each man talks. If they make sense to people who don't have a lot of education, then I'll vote for him."

A twenty-seven-year-old sprinkler-system installer switched from Wallace to Nixon because "there was no use throwin' away my vote."

Before the election, he had described the difference between the parties this way: "One side has plenty of money and the other side doesn't." He then added, "I'd have to say the Democrats are better for us cause they're supposed to be more for the working people."

After the election, his wife explained, "We're glad Nixon's in and not Humphrey. The Democrats are better for us, but we needed a change this time. I can see me and my husband voting Republican again."

Asked what she thought the role of government should be, she replied, "First thing I have to say is that taxes are outrageous. As far as school systems go, that should be a state-controlled thing, not government-controlled. I hope Nixon leaves the schools more to the states."

For the immediate future, school desegregation dominates the thinking of these families, particularly those with children, and is likely to trigger their voting. Over the long run, though, a Republican appeal to their individualistic economic drive would probably provide a more lasting basis of political identification than the racial issue.

If these anti-tax and anti-government Wallaceites were to be absorbed into the Republican Party, their influence would operate to sharpen the clash in economic thinking between southern and northern Republicans, particularly over welfare-state issues. The pro-Wallace injection would stimulate the acquisitive hormones in Republicanism, even perhaps to rejuvenating McKinleyism, and weakening the restraining sense of social responsibility.

On the conflicts looming for the 1970's over whether higher tax revenues should be devoted to expanding public service or to reducing taxes, the Wallaceites could be expected to line up on the side of cutting taxes.

The economic drive of the pro-Wallace people also seems likely to move them in a different direction from the Negroes. The blacks' dependence on government appears to be increasing, and they will remain a powerful pressure for greater public spending. The Wallaceites, their votes on bond issues would indicate, will tend to align against public spending and perhaps even for a crude equivalent of *laissez faire* individualism.

If that is what happens—that the Black Cities on the move and the rednecks on the move should diverge into conflicting economic directions—it would be one of the great ironies of history.

Both whites and blacks are seeking to avenge themselves on the poverty of the past. Economic change and progress are supposed to level local prejudice and unify people nationally. But memories of the poverty suffered twenty to thirty years ago have sharpened a militant hunger for a larger share of the better things. The prosperity of recent years has also given the once-poor of both races a rising confidence and economic strength with which to fight one another politically. Or can the trajectories of their clashing upbringings still be altered?

### 3. *"Nixon Likes the South"*

While Eisenhower was in the White House, the unannounced racial strategy of the Republicans was to keep the heat on the Democrats. This was accomplished by advancing some integration, never going too far, but with sufficient impact to make civil rights Democrats feel they had to outbid the Republicans by doing still more for the Negro.

If the northern Democrats responded they would widen their split with the white South. If they did not, the way would be open for Republican gains among the Negroes.

The key elements of those policies have been the underpinnings for Nixon's southern strategy. The central aim has remained to divide the Democratic Party, this time with finality by developing racial policies acceptable to at least the majority of white southerners. While doing this, Nixon has been careful to keep open the possibility of future Republican gains among Negroes.

Nixon's zigzagging toward his goals has often given the appearance of confused policy. But by early 1970, he seemed close to locking up nearly all of the South, thanks in part to the Supreme Court's "terminate dual systems at once" decision of October 29.

Before the Court's decision was made, Nixon had managed to establish in the minds of southerners that "he likes the South more than Johnson did" and "he's slowed desegregation down some."

This took a bit of effort since the Nixon Administration could not come out openly in opposition to desegregation. The first attempt to get a message of sympathy through to the South, in the summer of 1969, was blurred somewhat by conflicting stands taken by Mitchell and HEW Secretary Robert Finch, who in those days often referred to himself wryly as "the house liberal" in the Nixon Administration.

The Mitchell-Finch differences were criticized as evidence of "administrative bungling." More likely, they were intended to encourage southerners to read what they wanted to in the new HEW guidelines.

But doubts as to where Nixon's political heart lay were swept away that August when Finch asked the Supreme Court to delay ordering desegregation in thirty-three Mississippi school districts.

Some interviewing in Memphis shortly after the opening of the 1969 school year yielded comments like these from Wallace supporters:

"The Republicans do more for the South."

"They've given in to Mississippi, giving them time to adjust, not pushing them."

"I'm not sure I'd vote for Wallace again. I don't think we could do much better than Nixon."

In Ripley, Tennessee, an electric company supervisor said, "Nixon is more interested in how southerners feel. It's because of Wallace, though."

Some southerners, in fact, took the Administration's request to postpone school action in Mississippi as meaning, "Nixon will go along with freedom of choice." So encouraged were several school boards that they reneged on desegregation plans they had already approved.

Much of this pro-Nixon feeling in the South has to be credited to the attacks by northern liberals and Negro leaders on Nixon's policies and by the Senate's rejection of the nominations of Judges Clement Haynsworth and G. Harold Carswell to the Supreme Court.

A construction company owner reflected a generally held sentiment when he remarked, "I didn't think much about Haynsworth's nomination until the niggers and liberals started hollering about it. Then I figured Nixon was okay naming him."

The nomination of Judge Carswell re-emphasized Nixon's apparent determination to remake the Supreme Court so it would be more to the South's liking.

This prospect of a changed Court is Nixon's strongest political asset in the South. The one battle most white southerners feel they are fighting is with the Court, and Nixon has effectively identified himself with that cause. When Judge Haynsworth was certain to be rejected, Nixon refused to withdraw the nomination, preferring to go down in public defeat with the South Carolinian and the South. Again the President rejected overtures that he agree to the Senate's sending Judge Carswell's name back to the judiciary committee. Part of the art of politics is knowing how to pick one's enemies; Nixon seems happy while humming "in Dixieland I'll take my stand."

This change in the Court might take time, but that could prove a political advantage during at least the next two presidential elections. After the confirmation of Chief Justice Warren Burger, two, perhaps three, more appointments would be needed to establish a pro-Nixon majority among the nine justices. The resignation of Abe Fortas had left one opening. The other vacancies could be expected with the retirement of Justice Hugo Black, born in 1886, and William O. Douglas, born in 1898, and who uses a pacemaker for his heart.*

While these changes were taking place, tensions over the Court would heighten; at some point the balance determining the Court's majority might even hinge on the appointment of the next justice. Even after the balance had changed, Republican orators in later elections could stump the South warning that a Democratic victory would bring back "that old Warren Court" and the use of federal troops to enforce desegregation.

Nor has Nixon been fuzzy in his own thinking about the changes he wants to see in the Supreme Court's interpretation of the Constitution. In public utterances he has stressed consistently the importance of the "neighborhood school," with "a minimum" of school busing. In private talks with intimates he has also been inclined to favor "freedom of choice," which, in theory, permits white and black students to pick the school they want to attend.

In actual practice, Negroes have often been intimidated from choosing white schools. In 1968 the Supreme Court declared that freedom-of-choice plans were not producing desegregation and ordered that new approaches be tried. At that time—fourteen years after the 1954 school decision— only 20 per cent of all black students in the South were attending mixed schools.

These two labels, the "neighborhood school" and "freedom of choice" should be pinned to all civil rights war maps, since each corresponds to the political needs of the two main divisions of the White South. In the pro-Wallace rural areas, where there are no sharp patterns of residential segregation, "freedom of choice" is the favored means of evad-

---

* The retirement of Justice M. Harlan, born in 1899, would make a third vacancy.

ing integration. In the cities, where Nixon's political strength lies, the "neighborhood school" can be easily managed to limit integration to little more than a token basis.

We have seen how the spreading Black Cities and suburban migration have pushed school integration out of physical reach in the North. A similar development is taking shape in the urban South. Real-estate planning in many southern cities, as noted earlier, has guided new residential construction to produce clear neighborhood patterns, separating the well-to-do from white workers and blacks.

In addition a second defense in depth against desegregation has been prepared in the nearby suburbs. Following the 1954 school desegregation decision, there has been a steady movement of white workers out of the cities into school districts which are overwhelmingly white. Even if the blacks follow, little more than token desegregation is likely in these suburbs for some years.

In New Orleans public schools, for example, black children outnumbered whites two to one by 1969. But in nearby Jefferson Parish, which more than doubled its vote after the Court's 1954 decision, only 2 per cent of the precincts are Negro.

In New Orleans and Memphis, before the school decision, whites and blacks often lived on adjacent streets. Now in Memphis, more than half of the children in the public schools are Negro. Suburban Whitehaven, south of Memphis, has leaped from 3,000 voters in 1952, to 16,500 by 1968; only 3 per cent of the voters are black.

More than twenty-five Atlanta schools were desegregated, only to be resegregated as whites moved away to nearby Cobb and DeKalb counties. By 1968 black children accounted for more than 60 per cent of Atlanta's school enrollment.

Only a small part of the flight to the suburbs has been from areas where schools had been integrated. Most of this movement, as in Glen Lea outside of Richmond, has been of white families whose children have never gone to an integrated school. In the South one cannot say that school integration has failed. There hasn't been much of it for long. The prosperity of the Great Society years accelerated the outward rush, nullifying part of the step-up in enforcement of desegregation that was pressed since 1968.

Both in southern and northern cities, in short, population movements since 1954 have brought into existence a widening territorial separation of the races. School desegregation is still attainable, but not without busing; also the physical distances involved are generally much shorter in southern cities.

For several years a new approach to integration has been needed—one that would be reasonable but firm in enforcement and go beyond mere desegregation to equalize access to technical training and to lift the quality of all schools including those still segregated.*

In his desegregation statement of March 24, 1970, Nixon demonstrated a lawyer's skill in picking up all the available arguments for a changed approach to integration. But his use of these arguments to idealize the "neighborhood school" simply ratifies and perpetuates the evasions that have taken place since 1954. That is how his statement will be interpreted in the South.

Repeatedly in my interviewing, when southerners were asked why they were fighting desegregation, common replies would run, "I want to see my children graduate first" or "We don't want any mixing until we can move out to the suburbs."

The President seems to be searching for some short-cut legal formula which can be cited as evidence of compliance so as to lift enforcement pressure from the South. But given the prevailing patterns of mobility, to freeze around the

* See my *White and Black*, written in 1964, for a more detailed exposition of why integration policy needed to be changed.

neighborhood school will divide our society geographically into segregated and racially polarized areas. It would restructure the whole urban South in the image of racial conflict. His approach also clashes with Supreme Court decisions since 1968, which have tended to demand "affirmative" action and "a plan that promises to work realistically now."

Nixon's desegregation statement is a remarkable political document. It marks perhaps the first time that a president of the United States has undertaken to advise the Supreme Court publicly on how it should alter its judicial opinions. The statement seems also to be an effort to solidify public opinion behind Nixon's views and, if need be, against the present Court. The statement is also likely to serve as Republican campaign material in the 1970 and 1972 elections. Certainly in the South the guidelines Nixon has enunciated will be interpreted as a promise of how the new "Nixon Court," if it comes into existence, will change the law.

What prompted so abrupt a departure from the original strategy of disengagement that Nixon and Mitchell started with? Their clear aim, at the outset, was to get out from under the task of direct enforcement. This was to be accomplished in slow-moving stages:

1. Desegregation would continue, but on a basis more friendly to the South, until a new "Nixon majority" came into being on the High Court.

2. Gradually enforcement would be turned over to each southern state. This would be brought about by filing statewide suits, as with Georgia, and having the Courts issue desegregation orders directly to state officials.

3. For a time bitter clashes might be provoked between state officials and the Courts but each year one, two, three new, sympathetic judges would be appointed by the President to the lower federal courts, *if the Senate confirmed them.*

4. In time, the white South could look forward to a pace

of desegregation determined by a "strict constructionist" Supreme Court, a growing proportion of friendly judges in the lower federal courts and state governments which had fought integration in the past. Whatever this combination decided the constitution meant, the Man in the White House would disclaim direct responsibility.

For the Negroes, their alternatives would be to accept this dispensation of justice, revolt violently, or move North.

I realize it oversimplifies a complicated problem, still one point should be stressed. The basic, crumbling weakness in the present situation is Nixon's desire to avoid developing and administering a reasonably-paced program of desegregation in the South. The courts cannot administer such a program. Most of the Southern states are not likely to do so. No *de jure-de facto* formula can overcome that gap.

While the Administration was nursing this strategy along, the Supreme Court was becoming more impatient. In December of 1968, Justice Hugo Black, in an interview with Eric Severeid and Martin Agronsky, revealed that he thought using the phrase "with all deliberate speed" had been a mistake. It would have been better, Black felt, to "force the judgment on the counties affected that minute." This thinking was reflected in the October 29 decision to desegregate "at once" that was written by Justice Black.

The Administration was caught off-balance by the Court's ultimatum, but the southern political leaders were not. As a group they probably have been the shrewdest, toughest political operators in the nation. While northerners, both Republicans and Democrats, fretted a great deal about saving the world, the southerners concentrated on holding control of the key committees in Congress. Country-bred, their approach to politics was more that of the hunter than of the political lawyer doing business while playing golf at the country club.

Skill in hunting meant that one knew when to wait,

when to lie low in the grass, how to deploy decoys and yield ground that couldn't be held; how to stalk in relation to shifting winds so the scent of the hunter would not reach the prey; also when to close in for the kill.

The Court's "at once" decision brought the whole integration effort within southern gunsight.

The first action was to blur the issue to divide and perhaps test the "northern liberals." This was done in the amendment to the HEW appropriations introduced by Senator John C. Stennis and which called for desegregation guidelines being "applied uniformly to all regions of the United States" and "without regard to origin or cause of such segregation." Surprisingly weak resistance was shown by northern liberals, many of whom, like Senator Abraham Ribicoff of Connecticut, seemed tired of fighting the issue.

While the Stennis amendment was coming up for a vote, Nixon indicated publicly that he favored "the concept," although later shifting his position. Charges were made that he was beholden to Stennis, who is chairman of the Senate Armed Services Committee, for supporting the ABM missile program. But Nixon's commitment to easing desegregation in the South is certainly several years old. It undoubtedly was strengthened by the fact that in 1969 all but four of the South's twenty-two senators voted in favor of ABM deployment.

But more revealing were the effects of the telegrams and letters of protest that poured in from Charlotte. A Fourth Circuit Court order had suggested as a guideline that each of Charlotte's 102 schools reflect the racial composition of Mecklenburg County, which was 71 per cent white and 29 per cent black.

Charlotte was definitely not "Wallace country," to be shrugged off by the White House. It was North Carolina's great stronghold of Republicanism, having given Nixon his biggest 1968 plurality in the state. Charlotte was also a

classic example of how most southern cities are laid out socially and revealed why the Court order that had been
issued would be opposed as a social disaster.

On my first visit to Charlotte, in 1950, I was shown
rather nice homes that were being built and sold to negroes
in the North end of the city. I was also shown the fine
homes for well-to-do white families which were being
erected in the suburbs *South* of the city. The new court
order meant not only that some children would be bused
the physical distance from one end of the city to the other,
but over the social distance between blacks and Charlotte's
wealthiest and most prestigious families.

Some of the white children scheduled for transfer to
all-black schools were to come from Myers Park, long the
social center of Charlotte's oldest and wealthiest families,
with the city's largest churches, an art museum, and little
theater. The earthquake quality of the social shock the
Court order had upon Charlotte's ruling class can be sensed
from the local quip that "Charlotte believes in the Brother-
hood of Man, the Fatherhood of God and the Neighborhood
of Myers Park."

The White House hastily improvised a "plan" to try to
modify the Charlotte order on appeal. It seemed unlikely
that other circuit court orders would be as severe as Charlotte's. One February order in Orlando, Florida, sanctioned
neighborhood schools even if all black. Still, a critical political threat to Nixon had been raised.

If the Court's "at once" decision were extended to the
South's cities, the spine of Republican strength in the South
would come under the rack. To hold to a "disengagement"
strategy that left things to the Court could threaten to cost
Nixon the whole South. The administration had to intervene
and try to work out more reasonable plans of integration
for its own political supporters.

Within the White House, it was also feared that events

might push the President into confrontation with the Supreme Court. Hoping perhaps to influence the Courts and
head off harsher rulings, the President decided to make public the guidelines he was prepared to follow.

But how would the Supreme Court respond? Would
it bend to his statement? Accept parts of it? Reject it
completely?

When the appropriate cases reach the Court, one can
assume that Justice Burger will argue the President's side.
If overruled, Justice Burger could be expected to move into
public dissent. The lines of conflict would be drawn openly,
between the President and the Court, between the present
majority and what a new "Nixon Court" would do.

Were that to happen, Nixon against the Court could
become the decisive issue of the 1972 campaign.

### 4. Nixon to Wallace to the Court

At least one intriguing omission is contained in the President's lengthy desegregation statement. Virtually nothing
was said about the problems of the nonurban South where
the "neighborhood school" is not a common concept and
where Wallace drew his heaviest vote.

Like all acts of selection, the fact that Nixon avoided
this aspect of the racial tangle is revealing. To have met
the needs of the rural South Nixon would have had to argue
for something like "freedom of choice," specifically rejected
by the Supreme Court. Forced to make his own choice,
Nixon went for urban rather than rural interests in the South.

Did that mean he was conceding a sizable share of the
southern vote to a third party? The urban South gave Nixon
a 631,000 plurality over Wallace; but this was balanced off
by a Wallace plurality of 597,000 in the rest of the South.
Nixon's net plurality for all eleven states was only 34,000.

Those figures would not spread cheer inside the White

House. Still, my own political judgment is that in any re-peat performance of the 1968 Nixon-Wallace contest, nearly all of the high cards would be in the President's hand.

His first ace—and for most of the South this could be de-cisive—only Nixon can change the makeup of the Supreme Court to satisfy southern aspirations.

Nixon's second ace would be his total performance as president, which extends, of course, beyond the aggrava-tions of race to the war and the economy. If by 1972 Nixon has handled these problems well, he would be strengthened everywhere in the nation. Only if he failed as President would he be in deep trouble, in so much trouble that the electoral votes Wallace might be able to control could be important.

The joker in the pack—the card that would cause Nixon trouble—is that the urban South is so much more adept at evading integration than is the rural South, where Wallace drew his heaviest following.

The logistics of racial conflict become transformed when one drives out of the cities into "Wallace country"—those parts of the rural South with large concentrations of black children.

In these rural areas the whites cannot escape desegrega-tion by moving away from the blacks. Children are bused to school normally, which often means driving white chil-dren past black schools each morning and black children past white schools. With only one or the other of two schools to choose from, compliance with the Court often means busing white children to a school which has been all black or in which whites are outnumbered by Negro children.

In these areas white parents have tended to defy the government openly or turn to private white schools, and if parents knuckle under they do so while keeping a revenge-ful vigil for the first political opportunity to break free.

Stantonsburg and Saratoga, eight miles apart in the tobacco belt of eastern North Carolina, are two towns where just such a shuffling of white and black children took place in the fall of 1968. Almost every parent interviewed broke into outraged protest which wound up with the declaration, "A vote for Wallace is the only way to stop this."

In 1960 Kennedy drew 85 per cent of the vote in these two towns; Johnson slipped to 68 per cent and Humphrey to 17 per cent, with Wallace drawing 65 per cent of the vote.

In all rural areas with heavy numbers of black children the desegregation battle is likely to be prolonged and bitter. Where public schools have become virtually all-black, financing them will become a new, embittering struggle. Even where the races are mixed, the conflict will persist. Black children in the South as in the North lag in reading and writing, largely because of poor schooling. For integration to be successful these educational disparities must be overcome. Many white parents fear, as a Stantonsburg merchant protested, that "integration puts slow children in with smart children. This slows my child down, so it's not right. Negroes have rights, but they have to earn them just like anyone else."

Other white parents are chilled by the thought of their sons or daughters being outnumbered by blacks or being taught by black teachers, who usually, although not always, have less training than white teachers.

An elderly farmwife in Saratoga told of how "my daughter-in-law got killed in an accident and left three little children. My son works in Wilson, at Burlington Mills, so we take care of them. The oldest is in the second grade. They've just moved the whole second grade from the colored into the white school. There are more colored than whites in his class. He has a colored teacher. What kind of education will he get?

"Why can't they leave us alone?" she demanded. "All my life we've lived separate. That's how it should be again."

Even in a favorable political climate integration would be difficult. If, in these integrated classes, teachers pay more attention to white children, what happens to the black students, who need remedial help? Will frustrations lead black parents to echo demands of militants in the North to "let us have our own schools"?

While parents and teachers struggle with these anxieties, court decisions would be tossed around among Nixon, Wallace, and the Supreme Court. The Justice Department, instead of taking on individual school districts, decided to go the slower way of statewide suits against the high resisting areas. The threat of a racial third party will not be felt until after the 1970 elections. In any event the Republicans would be reassuring their Deep South constituents that once "the Nixon Court" comes into being some ingenuity would be found to interpret away the more difficult problems.

Unexpected developments or miscalculations of the contending forces are always possible, and Wallace might be able to extend his appeal to carry North Carolina and Tennessee. I doubt that this will happen. A more realistic assessment would note that the areas of heaviest racial sensitivity have been strongly Democratic in the past and that Wallace's agitations would hurt the Democrats more than the Republicans.

Of the 571 southern counties that Wallace won, 294 gave Nixon less than 20 per cent of the vote, and another 106 between 20 and 24 per cent.

When the whole struggle is over, Wallace may find that—against his own desires, perhaps—he has served the GOP as a "secret weapon" to keep the Democrats divided in areas where the Republicans have little appeal.

In North Carolina Wallace cut deeply enough into the Democratic vote in 1968 for Nixon to carry the state. Wallace's best showing came in the tobacco counties of eastern

North Carolina, long the most racially sensitive part of the state—and the most loyally Democratic. These counties paid little heed to Strom Thurmond's Dixiecrat run in 1948 and held out against Eisenhower in 1952 and Goldwater in 1964, though he received more support than Eisenhower did. Wallace swept the area.

Often it is contended that if the South were left alone, the rapid pace of social change and economic prosperity would liberalize race relations without government intervention.

These tobacco counties of eastern North Carolina furnish an interesting test of that theory. Few areas in the country have undergone more extensive change over the last generation. Between 1950 and 1968 the number of farms was reduced at least by half. As farms became fewer, a fourth to a third of the Negroes, often the better workers, migrated from the area, many moving on to Washington, Baltimore, Philadelphia, and New York.

At the same time, in the towns, employment in factories and service occupations, as clerks, salespeople, and typists, nearly doubled. Car pools have also been taking farmers' sons to factory jobs as far North as Norfolk and Richmond in Virginia.

Even smaller towns have been brightened by modern ranch homes or new industries. Highways have been widened to accommodate monster trailer trucks that rumble by. New hospitals have been built and old courthouses renovated.

The net effect of all this prosperity and change has been to improve the economic lot of the Negroes, but also to stiffen white opposition to desegregation and to weaken loyalty to the Democratic Party.

For the tobacco farmers—and tobacco remains the largest single source of revenue in the area—prosperity has meant a tightening labor supply which leads many farmers to grumble, "If things keep up like this I'll have to quit farming."

Near Sims, a youngish farmer, always a Democrat before, was shifting to Nixon. He complained, "Our prices stay fixed, but our costs keep rising. "I'm paying twice as much for my labor and they don't do anything like the work they used to. Next year I'm going to rent out my tobacco allotment. It takes too much labor. I'll just raise corn and soybeans that I can manage myself."

The tight labor supply pleased the Negroes interviewed. Jobs were easier to get and pay was higher. But among the whites the short labor supply seemed to tighten political and racial nerves generally. In Zebulon a filling-station owner complained: "We need a change in Washington. No one you hire these days wants to work the way we used to."

Near Wendell a farmwife grumbled: "It's become so much harder to get along with colored people—the woman who used to work for me won't ever come out anymore." She then added, "These riots are terrible. The colored are out of hand."

But it was the welfare program that these farmers fastened on as the main target for their economic frustrations. Much of the labor required during the intensive harvest period has traditionally been performed by Negro women and youths. "Welfare pays these women," the angry complaint ran. "They won't work any more."

No one interviewed seemed to have a clear cause-and-effect picture of what part of the labor shortage could be attributed to welfare and how much of it reflected other trends of change, such as the exodus of Negroes from the area and the steady rise in town employment.

The minds of most hard-pressed tobacco farmers were riveted to the thought that their labor difficulties could be eased if people on welfare "are made to work instead of being handed things for nothing."

Nor have good jobs and high earnings made nonfarm workers more amenable to desegregation.

In the thriving city of Wilson, a waitress announced she would cast her first vote for Wallace because "he'll give us back our schools." Her husband worked in the Thermatics plant near Elm City, and with two incomes the couple was "better off than we have ever been." This new sense of economic independence made her more assertive of what she regarded as her rights.

"I have the right to send my child to the school I pick," she declared. "Next year I hear they're going to send her to the colored school."

That waitress reflects a new strain of racial resistance in the South. In a prospering democracy, how far can compulsion be pushed without stirring resistance, without people using their growing economic strength to fight back?

The prosperity of recent years has been stimulating voter independence through the whole country. In the rural South the ties of agricultural interest that bound the farmers to the Democratic Party and helped repress white racial resentments in the past are falling slack as farm practices change. The expansion of nonfarm employment has been giving people greater economic mobility and made them more free-footed politically.

Rapid economic change widens the range of choices open to people. Auto dealers in these rural areas now sell more cars to factory workers than to farmers. Tight labor demands remind people that their bargaining power is pretty hefty, a feeling that is reinforced when family income is fattened by wives and husbands both working. Their aspirations for their own children rise.

Can desegregation continue to be imposed on people, against their will, when their political and economic sensitivities are quickening? If not, what then happens to racial change in the South?

## 5. Our Racial Dilemma

Like all dilemmas, our racial dilemma is more easily stated than resolved.

One horn of our troubles is that residential mobility in both the South and North limits the school integration that is possible, although this may change as more black families move into the suburbs. We have also seen that prosperity stiffens the determination of southern parents to educate their children as they please. Southerners generally have caught the political scent of vote-hungry Republicans.

The other horn of the dilemma is the fact that the changes in southern racial practices during the last generation have taken place under compulsion.

Nearly always, white southerners have continued protesting: "We don't want things crammed down our throats," even while resisting every change unless forced by court orders and even the use of troops.

If government enforcement were lifted, the record to date indicates that desegregation in some parts of the South would slip backward, while in the Deep South it would be hailed as a mighty political victory and a vindication of racism.

That isn't a development to be shrugged off lightly as if it were just another lawsuit or just another election. The really critical question of enduring importance is whether a nation, like an individual, can change the effects of social character and upbringing. We are agreed that what is left of the legacy of slavery in this country should be gotten rid of.

For the first time in our history we stand close to being able to end racial discrimination by law and beyond that to keep open the possibility of whites and blacks learning how to live together as equals under the law.

To lose this now, to let our efforts lapse when this great advance is so close at hand, would be not an American tragedy but the tragedy of America.

The choices we face as a nation should not be confused. Differences between the North and South remain critically important. In the North school and residential segregation is kept high largely because of the great population movement of blacks from the rural South, which has created veritable Black Cities in our urban areas. With this has come a social disorganization that has plunged many public schools into disorder, leading black as well as white parents to shift their children into private schools.

In the South, though, the issue has been primarily political and psychological. Many southerners will argue "God intended the races to stay apart," which no northerner believes. Also in most of the South the degree of actual integration was small until 1968.

Court orders which demand that each and every school be integrated may be extreme, but that does not mean that the choice before us is either to follow such a statistical formula or to abandon integration. We still have time to work with reasonable formulas of integration.

Earlier I reported that after Senator Goldwater's defeat I found southerners ready to accept a greater degree of integration than ever before, but that the march from Selma to Montgomery kept alive and strengthened their desire for political revenge. The abandonment of desegregation would repeat the political mistake of 1965, only this time it would be the black people who would nourish their hatred and wait for political revenge.

A suggestion I proposed in 1964 while writing *White and Black* may still have some value. My thought was to create a Racial Peace Commission in each state where it was needed, and to charge it with setting forth in precise detail what further desegregation steps would be taken *voluntarily* in that state over the next three or four years.

Some variant on that proposal might prove workable today—that is, in as many disputed school districts as possible to have some agency work out a detailed program of desegregation for the next few years that would be generally satisfactory to both whites and blacks in the area and that would be carried through on an agreed-upon timetable.

Placing each state or school district on record as to what it would do voluntarily would help redefine the issue— whether there were genuine difficulties in complying with the Court's decision or simply willful determination not to obey the law. One cannot expect agreement to be reached everywhere, but to the extent that there is agreement on action to be taken voluntarily, a new atmosphere might develop in the South.

To reinforce such understandings, special federal funds should be made available to improve the quality of education for youngsters of both races. President Nixon has talked of $1.5 billion for aid in desegregation and lifting the educational level in "impacted" schools. That is fine as a starter. Continued funds for these purposes will be needed.* One main reason why black families sought integration was to gain for their children the same quality schooling that white children received. They felt that only by moving blacks into the same schools as whites would as much effort be made to educate them.

What would happen if integration efforts do collapse and the white South is left alone? Some judgment on that score can be drawn from the responses of typical white southerners when asked: Which of the civil rights laws enacted over the last fifteen years would you keep? Which would you want ended?

---

* Under Nixon's "New Federalism" funds would go to state governments which have shortchanged all-black schools in the past.

The responses indicate fairly dramatic progress in gaining acceptance of the public accommodations law enacted in 1964. Of the southerners interviewed during the 1968 campaign, six in every ten agreed that Negroes should be able to eat in the same restaurants and use the same hotels as whites.

In 1961, when I questioned a cross-section of white southerners on these same practices, only 39 per cent of those interviewed were ready to accept whites and blacks eating in the same restaurants.

As can be seen from Table 8, similar advances were recorded in southern approval of Negroes being able to attend the same churches as whites and sit anywhere on local buses.

TABLE 8
*Attitudes of White Southerners Toward
Civil Rights Practices*

|  | APPROVE | |
| --- | --- | --- |
| THAT NEGROES SHOULD: | 1961 | 1968 |
| Be able to vote | 95% | 99% |
| Work with whites | 80 | 87 |
| Attend same schools * | 70 | 65 |
| Sit anywhere on local buses | 51 | 72 |
| Attend same churches | 40 | 63 |
| Eat in same restaurants | 39 | 61 |

* The 1968 question on school desegregation was not comparable with the 1961 question, when southerners were asked "Which would you rather have: the admission of colored children, or a shutdown of public schools?"

In Siler City, North Carolina, a forty-year-old pharmacist explained why he had changed his views on the public-accommodations law. "People were afraid the colored would take over, but that hasn't happened," he said. "As long as they have the money it's okay."

Once the new laws took effect none of the fears and bugaboos that had been predicted in advance materialized.

It was the touch of reality, of living with the changed situation, that reconciled southerners to the new laws. Had they not been put into effect, the protests might have dragged on endlessly.

One of the saddest aspects of Nixon's effort to freeze around "the neighborhood school" is that it can cut so drastically the opportunities for such unifying experiences, for whites and blacks to learn through the touch of reality that the races can get along together.

Actually, though, the extent of progress in the South is not as high as Table 8 would indicate. A more revealing political picture emerges when one separates the responses of the Wallace and Nixon supporters. We then see that opening hotels and restaurants to blacks and whites and even riding on the same buses are still fighting issues to many Wallaceites, but are shrugged off as meaningless by the pro-Nixon voters.

Table 9 should be looked on not as two columns of percentages but as a quick profile of the racial attitudes of two social classes, bearing in mind that the Nixon supporters generally are the business elements and the key leadership in most communities.

TABLE 9

*Attitudes of Nixon and Wallace Voters in the South Toward Civil Rights Practices*

| | APPROVE | |
| | NIXON | WALLACE |
| THAT NEGROES SHOULD: | VOTERS | VOTERS |
| --- | --- | --- |
| Get equal pay for same job | 94% | 72% |
| Work with whites | 91 | 73 |
| Attend same schools | 87 | 34 |
| Sit anywhere on local buses | 85 | 56 |
| Attend same churches | 83 | 46 |
| Eat in same restaurants | 75 | 44 |
| Stay at same hotels | 74 | 38 |
| OPEN HOUSING LAW | 18 | 12 |
| SCHOOL BUSING | 13 | 10 |

The essential question is: will the Nixon supporters use their leadership to have their own views prevail? Or will they adjust their views to get the political support of the Wallaceites?

That the attitudes of the Wallaceites can be changed is indicated by the survey results.

Roughly a third of the pro-Wallace southerners did want to repeal every civil rights law that has been enacted and "put the nigger back into his place the way it was before that Supreme Court started telling us what to do."

But two-thirds of the Wallaceites conceded grudgingly, "I don't like this integration, but it's gone too far now to be reversed." A relaxation of federal enforcement would increase the proportion of those who would turn back the racial clock.

The strong opposition to school busing shown in Table 9 among both the Nixon and Wallace supporters confirms the fact that white southerners generally are still not reconciled to much more than token desegregation.

The Nixon supporters, being better educated and free from the fear of Negro residential encroachment, are relaxed rather than uptight in their racial thinking. What structures their racial views is their intense business-mindedness. They speak up most forcefully in favor of Negroes being able to work on the same job as whites.

As a General Electric sales engineer near Richmond explained: "When it's a matter of hiring them, the businessman has to hire a Negro if he's qualified. Business has to be integrated, and the colored deserve equal pay if they can do the job."

In opening new job opportunities to the blacks, many southern businessmen prove surprisingly "liberal."

Pursuit of their own self-interest would probably lead southern businessmen to other "concessions" to Negroes. Some southern Republicans may also prefer racial policies which would leave open at least the possibility of a Republican-Negro political alliance. In the North the exodus to the suburbs tends to leave blacks and low- to moderate-income whites in the central cities. But in the South the population elements left as white workers abandon the central city are Negroes and well-to-do whites. They have a common interest in developing a workable way of governing the city; they could also share mutual political interests, particularly against the rural-dominated state legislatures.

In every southern city the Republican residential areas are positioned, as we have noted, to be free of the residential conflicts that divide white and black workers. Whether the business elements ally with the black or white workers, or play off one against the other, will probably vary from city to city, perhaps from election to election.

Urban Republican leaders in the South are not likely to be in any political hurry to cut off all Negro support through an all-out bid for the Wallace vote. After all, between 1960 and 1968 alone the number of Negroes registered to vote in the South jumped from 1.5 million to more than 3 million.

Atlanta's rapid and profitable growth was built on a political alliance between Northside business leaders and Negroes, but the rising proportion of blacks in Atlanta may have upset this alliance. At least in the 1969 mayoral contest, the business leaders decided to run their own man, Rodney Cook, without Negro support. The Southside Maddox-Wallace supporters, after their own candidate lost in the primary, also backed Cook, but he was defeated by former vice mayor Sam Massell, Jr., who is Jewish and who drew 92 per cent of the black vote plus slightly more than a fourth of the white vote. In the contest for vice mayor, Maynard Jackson, a Negro attorney, won handily, with nearly a third of the white vote.

The testing of southern businessmen, though, is whether they can look beyond immediate profits. On the racial issue, there is no other leadership in the South. It is also Nixon's opportunity and testing. What kind of leadership will he give to the South?

School desegregation does not seem to touch the sense of business interest. The typical comment runs, "I'm not against integration, but I'm against the government forcing it."

Many southerners are sincerely troubled with uncertainty over what school desegregation may bring. The thirty-nine-year-old wife of a Richmond restaurant owner remarked: "My children have been going to school with colored. They get along real well."

She then called in her fourteen-year-old daughter and asked how she felt about the one Negro girl in her class.

Her daughter laughed and said, "Mom, you know she's one of my five best friends."

"All the ones I know are real nice kids," she continued. "I don't know what you're worrying about, Mom."

As her daughter left, the mother shook her head and said, "I just don't know. I should be happy she gets along with them, but in a way it scares me. I'd hate to see her get to like them so much she'd get involved."

This sort of mixed-up feeling is not unusual. Some parents are troubled by talk that "school desegregation will lead to intermarriage." Others puzzle over how to instruct their children in view of the continued resistance to desegregation.

When a Raleigh salesman's wife was asked, "What do you tell your children about the colored?" she replied, "I'd know better how to bring her up if I knew what kind of society she will be living in. Will it be integrated or segregated?"

At stake in the integration battle is not simply what may be expedient for tomorrow, but how the racial thinking of the South is to be structured for generations to come. President Nixon, Attorney General Mitchell, and Mr. Agnew will have no trouble finding legal language that can be interpreted in different ways. The real test is how parents will explain to their children what the President has said and done. We can be sure the explanation will be in plain English, without legal loopholes; also that it will help shape future racial attitudes in the South.

Some of the voters interviewed still are repeating to their children "exactly what my daddy told me."

In a comfortable brick home on Kennington Road, in Southeast Raleigh, a four-and-a-half-year-old was playing in front of the television while I interviewed his parents. The mother favored Nixon because "my father was a Republican." Her husband, a printer who was strongly for Wallace, had been born in eastern North Carolina.

"My father hated niggers," the printer recalled. "He used to say put them all on a boat and ship them back to Africa."

What would he tell his children? "Pretty much the same thing," he replied.

"Oh no!" exclaimed his wife. "You can't fight it. He has to learn to accept some change."

Other southerners are trying to break with the past. Next door to the printer a young man in his early thirties who ran his own car-wash business, remarked, "I hire colored people all the time. The ones who come in from the country are good workers. The ones who have lived in the city never stay long on the job."

When I asked what he told his children about colored people, he replied, "I've told my eleven-year-old, you're going to school to get all the learning you're able to take and after that it will be up to you. No one is going to cut you off from something you want to do. You don't have to hate or fear anyone."

Still others are projecting the more liberal attitudes of

their own parents.

A twenty-four-year-old graduate student in chemistry talked of casting his first vote for Nixon. His father, a factory foreman, had voted Republican in King William County, Virginia. One of the son's earliest childhood recollections was how "the house of a Negro neighbor burned down and how he had his meals with us for six months."

What would he tell his children about Negroes? "My wife and I have thought about it," he replied. "We wouldn't want our children to marry coloreds but we're going to tell them we'd like you to look at a person and not see what color he or she is. When they grow older we hope they'll understand the problems people have with mixed marriages. But we can understand that people can fall in love with each other. We'll leave that to them. They'll have to make the decisions themselves."

The Nixon years will prove particularly critical. Racial progress in the South has reached a point where, if school desegregation could be enforced firmly and doubts as to its permanence removed, mixed schools might be given sufficient time to gain acceptance and one troublesome era could be packed away in the attic of history. If that happened, it would be one of the greatest possible contributions to a new American unity. The more likely prospect, though, is that southern and Republican impatience will try to push the pieces of conflict back into the old mold.

If the South's uncertainties and resistances are strengthened, the gap of time between the polarizing northern cities and the evading southern cities will widen. Can a new generation bring more change?

# SIX

# THE YOUTH CRISIS

### *1. Oh, Those Birth Statistics!*

WHEN THE STORY OF the Johnson Administration comes to be written, at least the more kindly disposed historians may marvel at his incredibly bad luck in deciding in 1965, of all years, to plunge the nation into a deeper Vietnam conflict.

No worse year could have been selected for such an action.

For 1965 was destined to mark the emergence of a new political force, one which in the three years that followed was to disrupt hundreds of college and university campuses, undercut support for the war, split the Democratic Party, and contribute to Johnson's decision not to seek re-election.

Homer would have blamed the behavior of his Greek gods for this preordained rigging of history. Actually, what was responsible was the intimate behavior of earthlings—specifically, of those millions of G.I.'s who returned home from World War II in 1946 and promptly married, and whose wives almost as promptly—in 1947—begat babies in record numbers.

Exactly eighteen years later, the number of males reaching draft age leaped spectacularly. The 1964 count of eighteen-year-old males stood at roughly 1,401,000. Just one year later the figure had jumped 35 per cent, to 1,897,000, continuing at roughly that level in the years after. For 1972 the annual figure was projected to pass 2 million.

More than any single factor, it is this spectacular increase in sheer numbers that has given this generation its distinctive stamp, making it the human carrier of so many diverse unrests and giving it an almost instinctive predisposition—if in doubt, change.

Because of their numbers, almost everything that happened to them was to have a chain-reaction effect. The Vietnam war was to agitate them into a unifying grievance against society; their numbers were to render tragically obsolete the form of draft that was in operation; with 34 per cent of all eighteen- to twenty-one-year-olds attending college, our institutions of higher education had to expand and change. These youths were also to constitute a sufficiently large commercial market so that it was profitable to sensationalize them as a self-conscious subculture.

For some years to come these numbers will continue to generate pressures for entry into society, for new types of careers, new standards—or lack of standards—of personal behavior, new concepts of politics.

With the draft, if ever a crisis could have been averted this was it. The births after World War II warned unmistakably of the approach of a profusion of males far beyond any foreseeable military needs. In 1962, in fact, Secretary of Defense Robert McNamara ordered a study of how the draft should be changed.

But the Pentagon manpower planners, reasoning that the situation was "not expected to become acute for two to three years," contented themselves with requesting mere renewal of the Selective Service Act, unchanged. Also recommended was continued study of the problems that would come with "an emerging surplus of manpower . . . in the fiscal years 1965–1968."

The minimum draft reform needed—but which was not to be carried through until 1969—was a relatively simple one. As Selective Service operated, a potential draftee remained subject to call at any time between his eighteenth and twenty-sixth birthdays, a seven-year itch of uncertainty which would become unnecessary with so large a manpower pool. The sensible change would have been to reduce each youth's draft exposure to a year or two.

The old policy of selective uncertainty did stimulate "enlistments" to avoid being drafted, a psychological feat in which General Lewis B. Hershey took great pride. Beyond that, no vital military purpose was served. In fact, prolonging the anxieties for so many millions of families was probably the worst possible form of draft for a limited war, since, as will be seen in a later chapter, it undermined morale at home and unavoidably divided the nation.

This failure to adjust the draft in 1963 can be said to mark the beginning of our youth crisis. The absence of draft reform would mean that when our involvement in Vietnam deepened, for every young man taken into the service, three to four times as many would feel they had to find ways of evading the draft, postponing career decisions, and building up resentments against society.

These grievances would enable tiny minorities of student agitators, often fewer than a hundred on a campus, to radicalize a sizable part of all college students across the country. Anti-draft sit-ins and other "peace" demonstrations were to bare the critical weaknesses of our universities— from the lack of authority of college presidents to faculty desires to be considered as "the university" but not to bear the responsibility of running it—inviting further student onslaughts and even armed upheaval at Cornell and San Francisco State. By 1968 the "youth crisis" had been transformed into a larger, more ominous crisis of the university.

In whatever fashion this crisis is resolved, it will leave

doubts about our ability to see through any future foreign policy, which conceivably could shake the peace in the entire world.

Curiously, through all these happenings the same unchanging label of "generation gap" was usually employed to caption what was going on. From the beginning it has been a misleading concept that blocked understanding of the nature of the youth crisis. For one thing, the term implied that the basic trouble was a clash between two generations, of young people differing so much from their elders that they could not communicate with one another—a thought that was picked up by Nixon's speechwriters and led him to pledge an "open dialogue" in his administration.

But the crisis has never been one of communication, or of "alienation." The real gap has been a "fitting into society" gap; of how a particularly populous generation, while resisting an unpopular war, was to mature and find entry into society. Where would they fit readily? How would they—or society—have to be changed for each to come to terms with each other?

How has this conflict moved up to now? Where is it heading in the years ahead?

## 2. How to Make Radicals

By 1968 most of the public saw the campus disorders as a defiance of reason. Some persons said sympathetically, "I can understand why students protest against the war" or "They seem to want better teachers." But generally the tactics of disruptive dissent had shouted down whatever sympathy people might have felt or any merit they might have seen in these demonstrations. Fair numbers of voters concluded, "They must be communist-led"; many more decided, "We need to crack a few heads together" or "Those kids should be given some lessons in respect and discipline."

An elderly machinist in Rock Island, Illinois, carried this feeling to amusing lengths during the 1968 campaign when he volunteered that although he was a Humphrey admirer he intended to vote for Nixon.

"I want to teach these young protesters a lesson," he declared angrily. "They don't know how bad it is to live under a Republican president. When Nixon gets elected, he'll show them what they will be losing."

Why should a politics of physical violence—seemingly the very antithesis of rational behavior—take hold at, of all places, our leading intellectual centers?

Much of the mystery evaporates if one examines in patient detail who these campus rebels were and how they were brought together.

From interviews spread over four years with more than eleven hundred students at thirty-seven college campuses, one can identify at least three distinct streams of protest among the students who described themselves as part of the "New Left."

1. Easily the most important single stream was the sons and daughters of one-time socialists, communists, and other leftists. These students comprised the organizing core for the Students for a Democratic Society; they also supplied the "revolutionary" ideology and tactics.

2. Sizable number of "draft insurgents" arose, concerned primarily with protesting against the war. Their interviews reveal no evidence of political radicalism until our involvement in Vietnam.

3. Lastly, there were the "career rebels" who rejected money-making pursuits in favor of "working with people and ideas"; quite often they had businessmen fathers.

The hippies, overpublicized because their long hair and masquerade clothing make such good TV copy, have not been especially important politically.

The real drama of campus rebellion has revolved around the fusing of the old Marxist addiction for playing at revolution with the current grievances of the draft insurgents and career rebels.

The offspring of the old-time leftists—Staughton Lynd and Bettina Aptheker come to mind as two much-publicized examples—can hardly be pointed to as evidence of a "generation gap." Far from being in family revolt, these students were projecting the radicalism of their parents.

Some of these rebels reported troublemaking childhoods, but others, even if they wanted to rip society apart, seem to have been almost model children who got along quite well with their parents. Asked how they would bring up their children, they replied, "Much the same way," often adding, "but I wouldn't be as protective as my parents were."

The sense of grievance that animated these radicals did not originate in any current performance of our society, nor was it caused by the war, nor by how the colleges they attended were being run.

Few of their families were religious. Particularly along the eastern seaboard and in California, many were Jewish and had always thought of politics in abstract, utopian terms.

From their leftist parents most of them had inherited an anti-business, anti-capitalistic bias. These biases were not acquired through the disciplined study of Karl Marx or other socialist writers. The Marxist slogans and phrases such as "make a revolution" or "it's the system" were picked up in casual family talk and flowed as spontaneously in their conversation as "come seven" from a crap-shooter snapping his fingers.

Virtually all recalled having been exposed to intense political activity while young and having been members of high school radical groups.

"My father brought me up to be a radical," remarked an SDS leader, a history major, at the University of Pittsburgh.

At Cornell, an education major recalled, "I was only five when my parents—they were communists—took me to my first demonstration."

A senior at Yale who was going on to graduate school "because there's nothing else to do to avoid the draft" had accompanied his parents on a peace march in 1962. He considered himself "more radical" than his father, explaining, "I have a taste for anarchism; my father doesn't."

Nor could any possible restructuring of the universities satisfy them. For them the specific issue of agitation was less vital than to be "agin" something.

At the University of North Carolina, the son of a National Farm Organization organizer remembered the satisfaction he derived from his first demonstration: "I felt the way I did when I gave up religion," he said. "I felt I had kicked something. I was free."

This "agin' everything" and "kick something" desire would probably have remained a minor nuisance if the war and draft had not developed as "the cause" to agitate the students generally.

I recall how gloomy the head of the SDS chapter at the University of Texas was during the winter of 1965. He talked sadly of the small SDS membership and said, "We protest against anything that comes up, hoping to find some issue that will arouse the students." He was particularly depressed because an SDS effort to organize draft-card burnings and a "strike" against the draft had fizzled that October not only in Texas but across the nation.

At that time, in the fall of 1965, our Vietnam policy was supported by two of every three students interviewed, which was no different from the sentiment of the public generally. Some students grumbled, "I'm as much for peace as anyone" but still felt "we can't back out now" or "we have to stick it out."

The first anti-draft demonstrations were regarded by most students as more of an emotional outburst than a political revolt. They reacted to two youthful pacificists who had burned themselves alive with "They needed therapy" or "They were either very religious or very sick."

In response to the question "What kind of students take part in these demonstrations?" nearly everyone distinguished three types of participants:

Some demonstrators were pictured as "sincere" or even "rampant idealists." Others were dismissed because "they're trying to avoid the draft, that's all."

Still others were termed "just hangers-on out for kicks."

At New York University a twenty-year-old coed had been invited by a classmate to a demonstration. She recalled: "I asked him, 'What are you demonstrating against?'

"He said: 'You name it. We'll march for a couple of hours, then get a six-pack and go over to so-and-so's and talk about truth.'

" 'Oh,' I replied. 'You mean you want a cheap date.' "

Another NYU student went back to the Greek philosophers to explain why he approved of the draft.

"I read in Plato that a man is unable to do everything for himself," he said. "That's why he forms a government. The group protects him. Since he can't live without government, he has to accept its obligations and rules."

The first of the draft-card burnings were denounced by college presidents and prominent public officials, including President Eisenhower. Some students were fearful that the demonstrations might bring a draft crackdown on students generally, and others were so angered that they donated blood or marched in parades in support of President Johnson's policy.

"Usually I don't go for that kind of thing," explained one senior at Columbia, "but I had to show that not all students agree with these demonstrations."

Still, even though there was little open opposition to the war in 1965, as I went from campus to campus, I was struck by how demoralizing an impact the draft was having.

At every college, students talked openly of how "I'm here to avoid the draft." To hang on in school, many were taking courses they disliked or in which they had little interest.

A Stanford senior enrolled in the School of Education confessed, "I hate teaching."

A doctor's son at Michigan was ready to graduate from law school, but said, "Taking a Ph.D. will keep me free of the draft for three more years."

Others were troubled that so many of their friends seemed concerned only with staying out of the war. A graduate student at Columbia volunteered: "A third of the fellows causing space problems in colleges would not even be there if the draft were fair. In my class, twenty out of fifty are there to stay out of the Army."

At Manhattan Junior College, a Negro, when asked about the draft, said: "I just came from the library. Two fellows are in there pitching pennies. They ought not to be deferred for that."

Since only a small proportion of the available males could be taken, the Selective Service had been extremely liberal in granting deferments to anyone going to college. One effect, though, was that many of the students felt themselves draft evaders.

This often stirred a sense of guilt or exaggerated attacks on society beyond the campus, as if the students were seeking to justify their own withdrawal.

"You think the real world is out there," I would be lectured, "but the real world is here; we understand reality."

When asked about his ambition, a student at CCNY replied, "Right now it's to stay out of the Army and get through school in one piece."

He then added: "I often think that leaving school and getting a job is like jumping off a ledge. Rather than be dangling out there you just stay in school."

At Berkeley one group of activists were expounding on how "cold, cruel, and impersonal" business was. They blamed it for every known fault they could think of. One Iowan said, "I worked for business for two years. All I found was that it was boring."

Another Berkeley student talked of "the ordeal I went through" in answering an advertisement for someone who could help paint a houseboat.

"I was afraid to answer the ad," he recalled. "You know, society is so strange. I had to go down to see the houseboat owner but I wasn't sure what to do. I thought about it all day. Finally I took off my boots and put on shoes; I combed my hair; I even put on a tie."

He got the job with hardly any questions asked.

Other student reactions seemed truly tragic, such as declarations of "I'm going to Canada" or boasts of having faked or experimented with homosexuality to avoid being drafted.

After listening to such tales, I would think how senseless it all was. If all these young men who considered themselves draft evaders had been inspired to stage one grand demonstration to end all demonstrations and had gone to Selective Service headquarters to volunteer en masse, most of them would have been turned down. They would have been told the services simply had no need for them.

The anti-society phobias stirred by the draft were also being fed by widespread political restiveness and a groping search for new careers. At every campus two conflicting trends of political change were going on.

One in every eleven students from Democratic families was becoming more conservative and switching to the Republicans. Generally these converts came from poorer families—they were sons or daughters of an Akron rubber worker, of a bookbinder in New York, a policeman in Providence, a shoemaker in Chicago, a tenant farmer near Memphis, a steelworker in Pittsburgh, a union organizer in Richmond.

All were targeted toward professional or business careers and believed that "a man ought to make his own way without government help."

These Republican converts were particularly numerous in the South, where backgrounds of family hardship generated a philosophy of competitive individualism, the same trend we have observed with the younger supporters of Wallace in the South.

In their racial feelings, though, young southern conservatives are far more liberal than their parents. The same college students who opposed repeal of right-to-work laws and who objected to raising the minimum wage supported most of the civil rights laws.

Among students with Republican parents, in contrast, one in seven had turned Democrat, socialist, or anarchist. This leftist trend centered almost entirely around the offspring of middle-class and well-to-do families.

Among these career rebels were the son of a real estate developer in Los Angeles, a geological consultant in Oklahoma, a wholesale druggist in Baltimore, and a purchasing agent in Battle Creek, Michigan.

Generally they talked of wanting careers in public employment, college teaching, or university research, or of "working with people."

Often these students resented bitterly their fathers' business occupations, protesting, "I don't want to just make money like my father" or "I couldn't stand dog-eat-dog competition."

At Northwestern, the son of a lumber dealer had refused to go into the family business. "Business and the

Republicans aren't human," he explained. "I'm a people person, so I want a people job."

At Columbia, an eighteen-year-old junior talked disparagingly of how his father had worked up to become the manager of a bank in Ohio and concluded, "If you're part of a big corporation you have to defer to stupid people—I'm a utopian. I'm for anarchism."

There they were, three outpourings of protest waiting to be brought together—those rebelling against the careers of their fathers, the draft protesters, and the SDS radicals looking for some cause to agitate. The catalyst that united them was the intensified opposition to the war in the whole country.

By the winter of 1966, in my second round of interviewing, faculty members and college administrators were protesting publicly against the war and were often encouraging the SDS in its demonstrations. Many campuses, in effect, had become staging areas for assaults on our Vietnam policy.

Possibly because the Selective Service Act was coming up for renewal in 1967, the draft had become the main target of protest, with students and faculty pushing a well-organized campaign to kill the draft and replace it with a voluntary army.

Three of every four students opposed a voluntary army as "impractical." Many anti-war protesters agreed that it wasn't workable, but still pushed it. As one Philadelphia student, who described his mother as an "intense" pacifist, explained, "We don't want a foreign policy that requires more than a voluntary army."

Student comments were also more bitter and more ideological than a year earlier. The war and the draft were being attacked not simply as "immoral" but as evidence of "a sick society" and of "a system that has to be changed."

At Fordham a policeman's son who still attended

Catholic mass regularly had, when first interviewed, supported the draft, saying, "If you're living in a country you owe something to it; there's no reason to defer someone because he can go to college."

Early in 1967 he complained: "With this Vietnam war they indoctrinate you into kill, kill, kill. Using any means of getting out of the draft is good."

A Negro from Evanston, Illinois, had told me in 1965: "It's my duty to serve my country. I know the word duty has gone out of style but that's how I feel."

A year later he was saying, "I don't believe in a peace-time draft."

Reminded of how he had felt a year earlier, he nodded agreement, but said, "Everyone I know is more radical than I am."

This solidarity of resentment on the campuses was another force contributing to the radicalizing of the students. At most colleges no figure of prominence was defending this most unpopular of wars; no longer was anyone bringing up Plato's view on a man's obligation to his country. Fears that draft resistance might be punished were also gone.

Capitalizing on these anti-war sentiments, the SDS pressed demonstrations against Dow Chemical, Army and Navy recruiting, ROTC, defense research, and anything else that could be made to stink of "war." When students were asked if the demonstrations were communist-led, the common response was, "Maybe some communists are involved," but that didn't trouble the students, since fighting the draft was their own personal battle.

Each succeeding year, as war resistance intensified, the radicalizing process cut deeper. Each year also brought some students closer to the end of their education—and closer, perhaps, to the war they hated.

Early in 1966 a Columbia College freshman had urged

escalating the Vietnam bombing because "it's to our national interest to stay in Southeast Asia." He talked of becoming a business economist and a Republican even though "my parents vote for any Democrat." At one point he volunteered, "The left wing is too vehement—even downright rude."

A year later he had changed sufficiently so that he thought, "We should get out of Vietnam." At that time it seemed that student deferments were to be ended and a lottery taking nineteen-years-olds put into effect instead.

"Being at the most draftable age," he said, "I'd rather the draft stay as it is." He also revealed he had begun smoking marijuana for the first time.

By April of 1968 he was one of the militants who seized the Columbia University buildings. He no longer wanted to become a business economist, saying, "I'm completely undecided about my career." He thought that "Senator Eugene McCarthy is the only one who favors the students."

At campus after campus the forests were dry and ready for burning and the hard-core radicals were playing with matches.

Throughout the 1967–68 school year my interviewing caught this tightening of emotional tensions at school after school. The draft law that had been passed on July 2, 1967, had aggravated the situation. Congress had changed the law so that on graduation seniors would be drafted first along with graduate students, whose deferments had been cut off.

By shifting the immediate burden of being drafted to seniors, the law solidified the anger of whole graduating classes. Moreover, these were the older students, including much of the nonradical leadership at the schools, who normally should have exerted a stabilizing influence on the younger collegians. Instead, they became among the more impatient and belligerent of the student leaders, ready to push their protest to a new pitch.

more impatient and belligerent of the student leaders, ready to push their protest to a new pitch.

The threat of being drafted also came at the point when their minds should have been occupied with thoughts of the careers they would follow in the outside world. Abruptly they found themselves questioning whether their whole education had any point.

That spring for the first time virtually every senior interviewed opposed the war. Many shrugged off all sense of purpose as far as their careers were concerned.

"We don't listen to the lectures any more," ran one typical comment. "All we talk about is whether the draft will get us when we graduate."

The sense of despair that gripped many of them was expressed by one graduate student of history at Columbia University who opposed the SDS seizure of the university buildings. Still, he confessed, "A few months ago I would have joined them. I was flirting with violence. I felt so hopeless about the draft I was ready to go to any limit.

"Then President Johnson announced he wouldn't run again. I decided the political system really works.

"Anti-war demonstrations are great," he added, "but I don't believe that violent overthrow of the American system is the answer."

The impact of the new law was not fully felt until the 1968–69 school year. Most of the graduating seniors went on to graduate school, gambling on the chance that they might not be pulled out, but their behavior differed markedly from previous classes. At Harvard Law School the faculty noticed that the incoming students spent less time studying and hadn't been at Harvard long before they were circulating petitions to have grades abolished.

The 1967–68 school year also brought an abrupt upsurge in Negro militancy, adding a new dimension of turmoil to the crisis in the universities. In the early war years Negro students had been much less opposed to the war than white students, stronger for the draft, and twice as many felt patriotism was important.

But the riotings in the summer of 1967 swung many of them to black militancy. Also the debate on draft reform had given considerable publicity to the fact that more Negroes—in proportion to their share of the population—were fighting in Vietnam than whites. But the new draft law, in granting all college students a four-year deferment, actually sharpened the discrimination against Negroes who couldn't get to college.

During the spring of 1967, two-thirds of the Negroes interviewed answered yes to the question, "Is it right for the government to draft young men?" That fall only half of them replied yes. When asked about Cassius Clay's claiming deferment as a conscientious objector, many Negro students who had been critical in the spring now replied belligerently, "You mean Muhammad Ali," using Clay's Black Muslim name.

Typifying this change in Negro feeling were remarks like these:

"The American black can't say 'Hell no—we won't go.' We have to wait for society to give us an even chance as the white to avoid the draft."

"The draft is right for whites, but wrong for Negroes. I don't think Negroes should fight."

At City College of New York a twenty-one-year-old student had criticized the anti-draft demonstrations when first interviewed, saying, "We ought to let the boys over there feel they're useful."

In the fall of 1967 he protested: "No draft law is fair for us. Negroes should all get together and protest. They can't throw us all in jail."

Asked why he had changed his views, he replied, "One of my friends came home from Vietnam. He saw a friend shot. He has no more mind."

He then talked of his own draft troubles. "I don't feel I owe the government three years of my life," he protested. "I've had a long struggle. At first I worked in the day and went to school at night. But I would have been drafted so I switched to day school. Now I'm having a difficult time financially. I've had to take two leaves of absence because of financial necessity.

"Last semester a friend got drafted in the middle of the semester. They may take me soon."

A welder's son, a twenty-year-old sophomore at CCNY, had urged a step-up in the Vietnam fighting when first interviewed. On the draft he had said, "Everyone should serve at one time or the other."

In September of 1967, though, he wanted to pull out of Vietnam and bitterly denounced the draft as "a system where the majority of white youths are deferred because they're in school, but blacks are excluded from the system and get drafted."

Earlier he had talked of becoming a teacher. When re-interviewed he said, "I want to go into law."

Asked the reason for the change, he replied: "As a lawyer I'll know what I can get away with. I want a gun. A lawyer will know how to get around it."

This militancy of the black college students marked an agonizing new turn in the crisis of the universities.

Many college administrators had struggled through the Vietnam years consoling themselves that the war would end sometime. With peace, they daydreamed, student radical-ism would die out. But after 1968 these administrators faced the more forbidding prospect of the universities being turned into a battleground for the nation's racial conflict whose end no one could foresee.

One night while the Columbia University buildings were still in SDS possession, a procession of perhaps seventy-five

Negro youngsters marched down Amsterdam Avenue onto the Columbia College walk. The two leaders were husky enough to be of college age, but the Negro youngsters seemed no older than ten or twelve. All were carrying candles, all were shouting rhythmically—whether in fun or anger was not entirely clear—"Burn Columbia down! Burn Columbia down!"

The universities had been unprepared to cope with the Vietnam agitations; they were even less prepared for this new black-studies crisis.

### 3. *The Chance That Was Missed*

One question naturally arises: Why did this steady process of student radicalization go unchecked for so long? What SDS was up to was always clear; so was the urgent need for draft reform. Yet every inaction and action of the university administrators only aggravated the difficulties, as did the changes made in the 1967 draft law.

Let us look at the draft first, and then at how the crisis at the universities changed.

On May 13, 1969, President Nixon requested Congress to revise the draft law to limit a youth's exposure to just one year. On reaching his nineteenth birthday a young man could let his name go into the lottery pool and, if not selected, would be clear of draft vulnerability unless a major war broke out. Or, at nineteen, he could take a college deferment for four years and then have his name dropped into the lottery pool for a year.

This plan to limit draft exposure to one year had attracted little attention when it was first advanced in 1967 as a minority-report recommendation of President Johnson's commission on draft reform. At that time, though, it was acclaimed enthusiastically by two-thirds of all the college students I interviewed, including pacifists and anti-draft militants.

The idea was picked up by Governor Nelson Rockefeller as his proposed draft reform in campaigning for the Republican presidential nomination. At every campus he spoke, the proposal drew cheers.

Had the proposal been enacted into law in 1967 much of the campus turmoil, including the seizure of the buildings at Columbia, might never had happened. By May of 1969, when Nixon revived the plan, any number of congressmen were agitating excitedly to 'do something" to quiet these campus rebels, but none of the members of Congress pressed for action on a new draft law. Not until mid-October, after much public prodding by President Nixon, did the House Military Affairs Committee report out a bill, which was then enacted into law on November 26, to adopt Nixon's request.

Why it was so difficult to obtain sensible draft reform? One could personalize the problem by pointing to the immense prestige of General Lewis B. Hershey, who performed so magnificently in directing the induction of 10 million men into the armed forces during World War II, but who never sensed how seriously the same draft methods could undermine morale in a limited war and with a manpower surplus.

Or one could blame the fiasco of 1967 on a breakdown of relations between the Johnson Administration and the House Military Affairs Committee, particularly two of its key members, Chairman Mendel Rivers of Charleston, South Carolina, and F. Edward Hebert of New Orleans.

My own belief, though, is that the critical influence was probably how the issue was debated in the country.

Neither apathy nor lack of attention was a problem with the 1967 debate on changing the Selective Service law. Far from being neglected, the debate was played out like a carefully constructed theatrical drama. The newspapers and TV looked to protesting students to provide the commotions that would point out what was wrong with the draft. The role of rational governmental authority was assigned to the twenty-member commission which President Johnson named, with Burke Marshall of civil rights fame as chairman, to recommend changes in the law.

As an added element of conflict the House Military Affairs Committee appointed its own commission, under General Mark Clark, to draft a competitive set of reform proposals.

Despite all this impassioned concern, when the final legislative curtain went down, a law making the draft worse had been passed; the public, moreover, still had no understanding of what the real draft-change issue was.

It was a mistake, first of all, to think that student protests were accurately defining the issue. In their marches and rallies and boycotts of classes the students complained bitterly of the inequities in the draft. But they were not really interested in obtaining a more effective draft law. Some student groups wanted to weaken the draft system to force us out of Vietnam. Others urged proposals, such as broadening the definition of a conscientious objector, which would have freed them from being called up. None of the campus proposals were really addressed to how best to draft those youths who would continue to be called up as long as the war went on.

Two distinctly different issues were being fought out—opposition to the war and reforming the draft—and these issues never got disentangled. In using the draft to attack the war, the student agitations and demonstrations probably prevented building up public support for a plan of draft reform that could be enacted.

In framing its report, the Marshall Commission had a choice of two main arguments for reform—that the draft was inequitable or that it kept millions of youths and their families in needless uncertainty in view of the swollen manpower pool. The majority of the Commission's members decided to make equity the issue and, with unpolitical thoroughness, proposed wiping out every vestige of unfairness. College deferments were to be ended so that those too poor to get to college—mainly blacks, of course—would not be discriminated against. Instead, everyone would take his equal chance through a lottery. The four thousand-plus draft boards were to be reorganized to end sectional and personal vagaries. The Commission also proposed that the order of calling up draftees be shifted to take nineteen-year-olds first, since this was what the Defense Department wanted.

The case against needless uncertainty was touched on but never really brought out. It never got into the public discussion.

The reaction in Congress was pretty cold, which was generally interpreted as reflecting General Hershey's known opposition to a lottery. But the Commission's recommendations also provoked strong opposition at every college and high school I visited.

For nineteen-year-olds any "equity" the lottery plan might have had was overshadowed by the angry thought of "why single out one age group to do the fighting?"

In peacetime this change would probably have been acceptable; in the midst of so unpopular a war it pushed draft discontent down into the high schools for the first time. Had the plan gone through, it probably would have spread anti-war and anti-draft demonstrations from the colleges into the high schools. Ten per cent of the high school seniors interviewed shifted from supporting to opposing the war. Some grumbled, "Here I've been working hard to get good grades and now they won't let me go to college."

How sensitive the students were to their own personal interests could be seen in how differently varied age groups reacted. Of the students who were nineteen or under only 8 per cent favored the Marshall Commission's plan, but nearly a third of the older undergraduates did. The older students offered such reasons as: "Younger kids make better soldiers" or "When they're younger they're dumber" or "You have more to lose with a twenty-two-year-old getting killed than a nineteen-year-old!" (Need one add that this last comment came from a twenty-two-year-old?)

The nineteen-year-olds saw things differently. They protested, "If they won't let us vote why should they draft us" or "They shouldn't interrupt your schooling." A Yale freshman contended, "A college graduate is more ready to face death than a freshman."

Actually, despite the many criticisms that had been voiced about how inequitable college deferments were, few students were willing to give up the 2-S deferment in their hand for the uncertain lottery in the bush. This proved true even with black students. The lottery had been pushed largely to end the criticism that a larger proportion of blacks than whites were being drafted. But most black students, even though they realized a lottery would help their race, still did not want to give up their deferments.

At Howard University, a twenty-year-old sophomore from Greensboro, North Carolina, remarked, "In the South, Negroes go first." Still, he felt ending deferments would be "too big a break out of your life."

Of the students interviewed in twenty-seven colleges and nine high schools spread through sixteen states, only 22 per cent favored drafting nineteen-year-olds through a lottery with deferments ended.

Among these same students, 41 per cent preferred the drafting of nineteen-year-olds, with student deferments kept as they were, which was the proposal advanced in General Clark's study for the House Military Affairs Committee.

But the plan the students really liked was the one which called for reducing the draft exposure of each student to a single year. Within the Marshall Commission, this proposal had been championed by George Reedy, Johnson's one-time press secretary, but had been voted down by a majority of Commission members. Although no headlines or TV publicity had been given the idea, as Table 10 shows, roughly two in every three students felt "it's the best idea yet."

TABLE 10

*Three Plans for Draft Reform:*
*Percentage of Students in Favor*

|  | ALL STUDENTS | 19 AND UNDER | BETWEEN 19 AND GRADUATE SCHOOL | IN GRADUATE SCHOOL |
|---|---|---|---|---|
| * Draft 19-year-olds through lottery ending college deferments | 22% | 8% | 32% | 25% |
| Draft 19-year-olds, no lottery, keeping college deferments | 41 | 37 | 44 | 50 |
| One-year exposure for all students | 65 | 72 | 60 | 69 |

* Note the low support for ending all college deferments which Senator Edward Kennedy has advocated.

Four reasons were volunteered most often in support of the plan:

"You know where you stand."

"You take your chance for one year and then you're off the hook."

"You can pick your own time to go."

"It doesn't interrupt your education."

Other students saw the plan as a means of reconciling a sense of guilt, expressed in the feeling that "I don't like to give up college deferments, but it's unfair to have the poor do the fighting."

The enthusiasm with which this one-year-exposure plan was greeted suggests that it would have quieted much cam-

pus unrest and might even have proved a constructive turning point in our whole youth crisis.

The results of my survey were made available to George
Reedy and to both the White House and the Defense Department. While the plan had its defects, it could readily
have served as the basis for compromise between the House
Military Affairs Committee and the majority recommendations of the Marshall Commission.

The law Congress passed in 1967 actually authorized the
President to go to a one-year-exposure plan. But two pro-
hibitions were laid down: there could be no lottery, and in
calling men in each age class the prevailing rule of "oldest
first" had to be followed.

The Defense Department felt it could not implement
the one-year-exposure plan without a lottery. The net effect
of the other provisions in the law was to place graduating
seniors and graduate students first in line for being drafted.

That the plan was aborted by technical difficulties and
not revived for two years makes one wonder whether what
was at issue was ever fully understood. Most of the com-
mentary on the new law dealt with it as a dispute over
the lottery method. In all the passionate debate on draft
change it was never made clear to the public or the Congress how needless was the uncertainty in which millions
of families were kept, how demoralizing the personal effects
were, and the disruption it caused in our universities.

### 4. On University Renewal

What has been happening to our universities provides
some insights into how dangerous leaving a crisis unresolved
can be to a democratic society.

During the early Vietnam years much was written about
how the student generation had become "alienated" by the
size to which universities had grown, by professors pre-
occupied with research leaving the teaching to youthful

assistants, and by students being treated as IBM cards instead of warm, loving bodies.

These and other practices probably needed reforming and later were to become active issues. But at first my interviewing revealed little evidence that they were particularly damaging to student psyches or that they were a significant cause of campus turmoil. What was rocking the campus lay beyond the university walls and out of reach, in the war and the draft.

Still, at some point in a crisis that remains unresolved frustrations apparently build up to a point where something has to give, and the crisis takes a new form.

This seems to have happened at Columbia in 1968 with the SDS seizure of the university buildings and the administration's decision to bring the issue to a showdown. When the use of the police to clear the buildings split the faculty, student unrest turned into a double crisis, going beyond resistance to the war and the draft to envelop the university as well.

The immediate issue in this new crisis which spread across the country centered around the university's ability to keep order on its campus, with or without the police, with a united or divided faculty. At Columbia, the commission headed by Archibald Cox, which investigated the campus disorders, picked up the thought of "restructuring the university" that had been advanced while the students were on strike. This became a common theme at other campuses as student pressures intensified.

Across the country, schools began yielding up some rule or ritual: a relaxation of curfew hours, wider student participation in faculty meetings, new courses, even the resignation of a university president.

These actions bought time for some schools but could hardly cool student impatience with the war and the draft. Nor have the "restructurings" been directed toward the deeper crisis that lies ahead of our colleges and universities.

At stake, of course, is what kind of intellectual legacy our universities will be able to pass on to future generations. On that score it is intriguing to note that the professional schools, such as those in medicine and engineering, have remained quiet through nearly all of the campus disorders, while the agitations and uproar have been most intense among students in the liberal arts and social sciences.

This contrast coincides precisely with what is certainly one of the gravest conflicts in our whole civilization, between the astonishing technological skills which enable us to land with split-second timing on the moon and our inability to perform in comparable fashion in governing ourselves.

What needs restructuring, at our universities and through the whole of our society is the fragmented manner in which the thinking, knowledge, and teaching of the arts of self-government are organized. Unfortunately the individual faculties—government, sociology, psychology, etc.— are the equivalent of craft unions and aren't structured to present a comprehensive, unified approach to governing ourselves. Yet this is what society needs.

We face little danger of being unable to transmit technological and vocational skills to future generations, but in the area of government and human problems what our universities can teach is being shaped by continued conflict.

The forces radicalizing our universities seem certain to run on for several years. Black-studies agitation will be bringing onto the campuses the pressures of another unresolved conflict that divides the nation. The black cause will probably prove a positive attraction for many white students. At Harvard Law School, nearly a third of the students do some kind of legal-assistance work in the slums of Cambridge and Boston. Similar involvements are found at most schools in or near a major city.

Often, in fact, such an act of involvement becomes part of the process of student political revolt. At Valparaiso University in northern Indiana, when I asked to meet with the leading student radicals, nearly half of the group were from Republican families. One senior had majored in business for his first three years, firm in his intention of joining his father's paper company. But in his senior year, he explained profanely, "I asked myself what the ——— am I doing? The Army will get me anyway." He switched his major to urban studies. "I'm a radical now," he added.

With him in breaking from parental Republicanism went a younger brother, also at the school.

Politically, we are likely to see some merging of black militancy and university radicalism. Any such alliance or coalition will also be markedly anti-war and anti-society, embracing faculty members as well as students.

We now have nearly half a million college teachers; the role of this professoriat has been made a major issue in California by Governor Ronald Reagan and seems likely to become an issue in other parts of the country. Many faculties are already ideologically split between those professors who believe a university should stick to education and research and the more "activist" professors who think the university has a positive mission to remake society.

The activists are unlikely to accept a quiet role for the university without a fight, a fight which could polarize much of academia as at some universities; where the Vietnam resistance has been pressed into efforts to halt university work related to defense.

The ranks of the activists have been swelled, in a perverse way, by the draft. It is from the graduate students and younger teaching fellows that future faculty members will be drawn, and almost to a man these graduate students have felt harassed by the draft. Some of them have been called up during the school year. Even if only one goes at any school, the others feel grimly reminded that their last academic supper may come soon.

The Congress that wrote the 1967 draft law certainly did not intend to radicalize university faculties, but that was its effect.

The anti-war feelings of many of the students have already been converted into a general hostility toward society. How long these antagonisms endure will hinge, I suspect, on two main influences: what kind of family upbringing they have had, and what happens to them when they leave school and go into "the world outside."

Why some students take to the barricades while others do not cannot be explained with any simple generalization. Once violence erupts and police clubs fly even quite conservative students may be swept up in the emotion that floods loose.

Still, my interviews reveal that resistance to radical action largely reflects the strength of the self-restraints that have been lodged within a student by his family upbringing. Often in discussions of the so-called "generation gap" parents have been pictured as being virtually obsolete. Actually, almost no restraint they planted in their children was without some continuing effect.

Among the "quiet majority" of students at every campus visited I found fewer nonreligious students, less of a tendency to smoke pot, and more of a feeling that self-discipline is a virtue on its own. The nonactivists were also more definite in their career choices than the radicals, many of whom had no idea of what vocations they want to follow.

But even among the nonactivists the generational trend is toward greater permissiveness.

Of the students interviewed, only a fifth said their parents were "not religious," but half of the same students described themselves as "not religious." This suggests that within one generation the proportion of "not religious" has almost doubled.

Nor is a strict childhood upbringing any longer the norm among college-going families. Only a fifth of the students interviewed reported having had a strict upbringing. Of these a third would raise their own children more freely, which suggests that further liberalization is likely.

More than half of the students would give their children much the same upbringing they themselves had.

While not the controlling influence, family environment does have a noticeable effect on how students feel about war issues.

Of those who described their upbringing as "pretty free," twice as many favored replacing the draft with a voluntary army as did those who had experienced a "pretty strict" upbringing.

Generally the influence of the college or university has been to weaken family restraints. Over the years many university professors have thought it was their function to debunk "small-town" morality and to downgrade religious beliefs, opening student minds to more "liberal" ideas. Thirty years ago that might have been an underdog viewpoint, but now greater permissiveness has become the prevailing conformity on the campus.

Student example also has a sweeping impact. In my 1965 college survey virtually every student who smoked marijuana was liberal politically. Less than two years later, a second survey revealed that substantial numbers of pot smokers described themselves as conservative politically; some were even supporters of Barry Goldwater and William Buckley. Nearly a third of the students from Democratic families who were turning Republican had smoked or still smoked marijuana.

One other characteristic of college youth should be noted—they are the first American generation to use psychology as an everyday tool. If you ask a student whether

he smokes or not, he is apt to reply, as did one Ohio State
sophomore, "I don't have a Freudian oral fixation."

Many of them have turned to psychology as a substitute
for morality; they also regard psychological manipulation
of human beings as a "norm" of American society; nor do
they hesitate to manipulate their parents or fellow students.
It is not that they are cynical. For them manipulation is
one of the facts of life.

Such changes underscore the importance of what will
happen when these students leave school. Will the outside
world stabilize them? Will they change society?

## 5. Doors to the Future

Perhaps the most revealing single question to ask any
young person is, "What career or occupation do you intend
to follow, and how does that compare with what your father
does?"

The responses to that query leave little doubt that the
choice of vocation operates as both the carrier of a young
person's sense of economic self-interest and as a major force
shaping the way he identifies with the future, both economically and politically.

This finding, in turn, provides some basis for looking into
the future in regard to both the special problems of entry
into society and the political impact that this generation is
likely to carry with it into the years ahead.

During the 1968 campaign a number of misleading
notions were circulated about the voting of young people.
Much was made of the question of whether Nixon would
be able to govern without the support of the young if he
were elected.

This question seemed to imply that "the young" shared
a single political viewpoint; this is not true. The question
also ignored the fact that Nixon actually fared a good deal

better with the younger members of Democratic families than with their parents, primarily because young people were less bound by Democratic Party loyalty and were more likely to be pursuing occupations with a business orientation.

To cite a typical shift: a marketing student at Villanova was voting for Nixon, while his father, a sheet-metal worker, was sticking with Humphrey. The student explained: "Dad still feels the Democrats are for the little man. I tried to talk him out of it and to explain that the Republicans need the small man, but he's too old to change."

Whether they vote at twenty-one or eighteen, young people start their political thinking by accepting the party their parents favor. Where breaks from parental loyalties occur, the most important reason is a changed sense of economic interest, usually reflected in the youth's career choice.

The predictable consistency with which career change links up with political change largely reflects the economic imagery attached to our political parties by students generally.

Whatever their political leanings—whether they are Democrats, Republicans, or shifters—the students agree in viewing the Republicans as "the party of business" and the "advantaged class," as cool to government spending and welfare, conservative, and slow to accept change.

The Democrats are seen primarily as the party of welfare and government spending, as "liberal" and eager to push for social change.

When a student breaks from his parents' party allegiance, it is almost always in terms of this accepted party symbolism.

To many older voters the main conflict between the major parties still is seen as that of labor against business. But with college students, the crucial political divider seems to have become whether one identifies with the public or the private sector of the economy, a division which was evident in interviewing I did as early as 1962.

At every college visited, the sons and daughters of Democrats turning Republican were motivated by an upward economic drive and a bend toward conservatism.

In contrast, the offspring of Republican fathers who were swinging Democratic were aiming for careers in government service, teaching at the university level, varied forms of research, social welfare, and psychology.

The importance of career selection in determining party choice is underscored by those students who say they are "undecided" politically.

Most of them turn out to be either undecided about the vocation they intend to follow or unclear about whether they will be working for private industry or in the public sector of the economy.

At Iowa State a twenty-three-year-old architectural student said, "My parents got only a high school education. I'll have totally different associations and a much higher standard of life."

Still, he explained, "I can't tell you which party I favor. I may make more money dealing with the government. Maybe government spending is good."

Similarly, a civil engineering major from Elgin, Illinois, predicted: "If my customers are private companies I'll stay Republican. If I work for the government I'll become a Democrat."

Again, it is not surprising to find so high a degree of career uncertainty among the student political activists. A career is the door through which a student walks out into the adult world, and many campus radicals have not wanted to open that door.

Of every ten "New Left" students interviewed, four wanted to stay on in college teaching, three talked of careers such as psychology, art, or journalism, while three more were undecided about what they wanted to do.

This intimate connection between career choice and political change can be used as something of a youth barometer to forecast the kind of storms likely to be kicked up in the future.

At least three pressure areas can be envisioned:

1. A good deal more political turbulence must be expected at a time of great occupational change, such as now, than we have been accustomed to in the past. By 1969 the number of young people—both men and women—between eighteen and twenty-four had risen to 23,600,000, which was 58 per cent higher than in 1955. It should not be surprising that the stormiest social convulsions have come in the universities and in the black ghettos, where the proportion of youngsters have increased at an even more rapid rate than among the whites.

The more successful these youths are in finding careers which absorb them satisfactorily into society, the less ferment there will be. This emphasizes anew why the needless uncertainty of the draft has been so disruptive socially and politically. Given the record numbers of young people, any action or policy that unnecessarily delays their entry into society should be ended, while any action that speeds their social adjustment should be favored.

The greatest unrest and instability is likely to be found among those who are undecided in their careers or who will have to fit into roles they don't like.

2. As this generation moves into the economy, it can be expected to remain a somewhat impatient element. Its members are likely to seek quicker promotion and not be content with simply waiting their turn to advance in any hierarchy. In fact, the clash between the generations might sharpen with time. One likely effect will be growing political pressures for earlier retirement, and earlier pensions, as this generation pushes against the adults standing in its way.

Its members are also more likely to favor innovation and

change, rather than preserving what exists, if only because they are inclined to think that the dice of change may roll more readily in their favor than the dice of stability.

In other words, not being part of the "in" group, some members of this generation are likely to be particularly sensitive to all of the entry problems of our society.

3. As important perhaps as the numbers of jobs that are available my be the kind of careers they will be seeking. This desire to go into new fields could have the greatest political impact and cause strong pressure for changes in how our society is organized.

It has become psychologically impossible for many young blacks to continue in the sort of work their fathers and uncles did. Beyond the need for higher-grade jobs, there is also the critical question of whether the careers open to them will take them out into the white world or keep them in the Black Cities.

On that score, some interviewing I did with black students on fifteen campuses is instructive. A special analysis was made of those students who were most belligerent and those who were most moderate. How and why did they differ?

A fairly sharp pattern emerged. The moderates were primarily youths with strong middle-class drives. Often their parents were white-collar people. Where the fathers were workers, the students had usually been disciplined, kept off the street, and given religious training. Also, the careers they intended to follow after graduating were ones which would bring them into contact with white people, such as architecture, sales, television, hotel technology, computer programming and engineering.

The militants, in contrast, talked of careers that would take them back into the ghetto "to work with blacks." Generally they were sons and daughters of workers, although some blacks of middle-class parentage have an idealistic urge to work in the ghetto.

Nearly all the militants thought "integration is a lost cause." An economics major at CCNY said, "This country will destroy itself before we get integration."

Asked about his career, he retorted, "What career? I'd sooner be on welfare than work. What kind of career could I have? A Negro can't get ahead at anything. Maybe there's one or two for show, that's all. You can't really do anything if you're black."

In contrast, students who saw themselves competing in a white world believed firmly that integration was bound to come, although they often added, "It has to come slowly."

At Howard University, one student who was the son of a refinery worker and was planning to be a doctor, explained, "We can't ask for all our rights immediately."

At Queens Community College, a nineteen-year-old sophomore who planned a career in electronic engineering thought: "Integration is not a lost cause, but you can't force it on people. I get along with everybody. My mother says we're making strides. We've got to push, but not too hard. I go along with her pretty much. We're pretty close."

What stood out, in short, was the extent to which the racial attitudes of both militants and moderates had been shaped by their own ambitions and experience with integration. Those who felt their families had gotten somewhere, or who thought the individual could get ahead on his own efforts, still had faith in integration as a goal; those who had not tasted the grapes were sure they were sour.

Here again it is the touch of experience that is needed to change racial feelings, even as it has been with southerners.

In the long run, integration will reflect the degree to which the career opportunities open to Negroes take them out of the ghetto.

It is remarkable how precisely the career conflicts among

our youth reflect the conflicts dividing society as a whole. The emphasis on black studies in our universities and high schools points to what could prove to be one of the sorest black vulnerabilities in the future.

In a rapidly changing society the need for blacks and whites is to acquire the skills that will give them the competitive mobility to keep up with rapid change. But the black militants fight for policies which would deprive them of these skills and which would perpetuate the lopsided Negro concentrations in our cities. In doing so, they risk repeating, with a reverse twist, the same kind of mistake that Booker T. Washington made in the 1880's and 1900's.

Those were the years in which the South was industrializing and textile mills, in particular, were being erected at a hectic pace. Still, at Tuskegee Institute, Washington continued to turn out graduates who would become teachers in rural schools, explaining, "We want to be careful not to educate our students out of sympathy with rural life."

He also urged each Negro to acquire a plot of land that he could cultivate and become self-sufficient, raising everything needed for his family, with the surplus to be marketed.

Today many of our central cities are being bypassed by the dominant trends of technological change. For black nationalists to demand black studies so as not to educate young blacks out of sympathy with ghetto life, and to preach independence and self-sufficiency inside a decaying city, could prove as irrelevant and behind the times as was Washington's dream of rural self-sufficiency for the Negro toward the turn of the century.

Washington's action can be defended on the ground that he had no other choice; whatever he did Negroes were going to be excluded from employment in the new factories being started in the South.

Today one justification that is made for black separatism is that Negroes need to organize so they can claim their proper share of the nation's economic resources. But tying black progress to the least efficient segments of the economy can defeat it.

In some cities blacks are buying homes in former white areas where the main sources of employment are old, nearly obsolete mills. Black economists would do more for their people if they directed black movement into the parts of the country with the most efficient industries.

With white students, many of those who are looking to the public purse for their economic future are sons of Democrats who appear to have inherited an anti-business bias. Others want to "work with people" because of their own personal psychological needs. Still others, including the offspring of affluent business executives, feel they are responding to the needs of the times, such as the problems of poverty, civil rights, and the urbanization of society. If careers in these fields do not expand as rapidly as these students would like them to, they are likely to become a pressuring force for greater government activity in these areas.

As one talks at length with these students it seems clear that for many of them idealism and self-interest intertwine. They urge large federal expenditures for fields in which they hope to work both because there are urgent problems in these fields and because they regard such spending as an investment in a vision of the future with which they have identified. In fact, they see government spending as a tool of capital investment in their own futures.

At Rutgers, a senior going into zoology research favored the Democrats "because they're more likely to support research." Asked how he felt about government spending, he replied, "Spending is what the government is for."

This conscious identification with the public sector is also reflected in the militancy with which some students and professors have tried to commit the universities to a more active role in dealing with social problems and, simultaneously, to reduce the role of universities in defense work.

The anti-war feelings that have sparked campus agitation over defense research have been reinforced by a desire for the government to favor the problems these students want to work on, the areas of enterprise they would like to see expanded.

The division of career choices among today's students will not revolutionize the American economy. A majority of this generation will be fitting themselves voluntarily into the established occupational structure. Still, this generation as a whole does place a higher value on the public sector than did their fathers. As they move off the campuses during the coming decade this influence will be felt in the conflict raging through the whole of our society over how our economic resources are to be allocated—for missile development or for the problems of the cities, for more luxurious private living or for higher levels of public expenditures?

This conflict, as we shall now see, is generating pressures to restructure our economy which are proving as frustrating as have been the efforts to restructure our universities.

# SEVEN

# A CLAIMANT
# SOCIETY

## 1. Captains of Public Enterprise

WHILE IN Los Angeles I stopped to interview a middle-aged man who was digging stake holes in his backyard. Asked how he was doing economically, he replied, "Lousy."

"What are you digging?" I inquired.

"A swimming pool," he answered.

That someone building a swimming pool for himself could complain of being badly off financially is a somewhat amusing example of the old American adage that the more people have the more they want.

The incident also points to a puzzling question that has arisen at varied points in this study—why has so much prosperity produced such unexpected and unsettling political effects?

In cutting federal taxes in 1964, President Johnson and the managers of the "new economics" operated on what seemed like a sensible theory. Stimulating economic growth would mean more resources to go around—a bigger pie to share—which would make it easier to resolve our domestic troubles and quiet the conflicts dividing the nation.

But that is not how matters have worked out. Between

1964 and 1968 the number of persons employed jumped by 10 per cent; unemployment was cut by one-third; and per capita income, even after taxes, rose 16 per cent.

Nor does the advent of an economy with a Gross National Product above a trillion dollars foreshadow greater contentment and an easing political strife.

The war and inflation can be debited for much of the discontent but our study suggests that the crisis runs deeper. Through much of our history, the assumption that prosperity brings political stability has seemed valid. This interconnection can no longer be taken for granted. In fact, we have entered an era in which it is possible that prosperity will prove a major force for continued unrest and political instability.

For one thing, it is how people use their economic gains that gives prosperity its political direction. The blacks pushing out of the slums into better housing and the whites moving to the suburbs combine to aggravate racial conflict in our northern cities.

Prosperity and economic change have also stiffened resistance to effective desegregation in the South; encouraged radicalism among some college students, a hunger for material advancement in others.

Beyond that, how our economy is being managed is undermining the stability of government; both Republican and Democratic economists are committed to continued inflation; nor are we able to—or want to—shift any real part of our productive resources to where they are needed most.

This failure is most evident, of course, in the battling over the allocation of federal tax funds that at times appears to be turning us into a society of claimants, warring and feuding with one another.

The fierce passion with which efforts to "reorder our priorities" are being pressed is usually attributed to the critical nature of urban and other needs neglected during the war. One factor not fully appreciated is how the changed structure of our economy intensifies conflict.

A comparison with how the class struggle between capital and labor was tempered may illustrate the nature of these changes. Antagonisms between workers and bosses were eased partly by giving labor the right to bargain collectively, but more, because productivity increased so greatly that both profits and wages could be raised. Workers and employers were also part of the same company, the same production unit; bargaining over the sharing of production gains could be reconciled directly, although even this took years of bitter, even bloody, strife.

Today's claimant wars are being fought by segmented parts of the economy—the cities, besieged by their suburbs, the defense complex, expanding health and education needs —none of which existed on their present scale a few years ago. Between the First and Second World Wars our defense establishment was largely dismantled. But in a nuclear-missile age it dominates the federal budget. The rest of our economy has not yet managed to adjust to a standing military-industrial complex.

A boost in productivity may ease employer-worker relations, but a boost in nuclear and missile efficiency means new weapons systems which increase rather than decrease the dollar costs that must be paid by society generally. Technological improvements in health care such as lung and kidney machines or heart surgery are also so costly that only society can pay the bills.

Into this struggle over how these new social costs are to be divided is drawn virtually every unresolved conflict that stiff-arms apart the American people. Take the fierceness of the 1969 Senate battle over approval of the ABM missile, which Nixon won by a single vote. Feelings were sufficiently intense over the need to curb military spending to release some billions to attack social problems neglected during the Vietnam war. Whipping these emotions further were fears that deployment of the ABM or continued testing of the MIRV nuclear warheads could touch off a nuclear arms race with the Soviets which could put both nations into possession of the ability to launch a first strike that could destroy the other.

Seven of every ten dollars spent on research has come from the government. Nixon's reductions in those funds cloud the career choices of thousands of graduate students. Other decisions affect the career profits of much of the adult population, whether they be military contractors or educators; also which localities may have to raise taxes because of cuts in federal funds, and which will be able to lower local taxes because they are helped by a new project.

This battling over what is to be given priority also has a symbolic importance far greater than the sums involved. The federal budget-making process has become perhaps the one complex of decisions through which all the interested claimants strike a blow for what *they* think this country should stand for, what purpose this nation should have; also how our changing economy should be restructured or redirected.

With so much seemingly at stake why has so little been accomplished in reallocating the nation's resources? One reason is that the concepts being used to organize our economic thinking do not fit the problems we face. This becomes clearer if we turn back to some exciting dreams built up in those two eventful years that followed the assassination of John F. Kennedy and Johnson's landslide triumph in 1964, two years in which we moved formally into a managed economy.

Early in February of 1965, Johnson called together in the Fish Room of the White House the assistant secretaries in charge of legislation for each agency—about thirty in all. One man who was there recalls Johnson saying somewhat melodramatically: "Here is the program . . . put your back to the wheel . . . don't lose a day in getting these passed. . . . In the 1966 Congressional elections I may lose the power I now have . . . this is the historic moment. . . ."

The Johnson landslide had swept in forty-six additional Democratic congressmen, turning all the old stop signals on Capitol Hill to green. Through the Eighty-ninth Congress was rushed the greatest expansion of social legislation since the early New Deal days—Medicare for nineteen million under Social Security; aid to education; air and water pollution control; plus other projects as varied as aid to Appalachia and highway beautification.

One expert estimate was that the 1965 legislation alone authorized at least $20 to $25 billion in additional social spending. Often programs were begun with only downpayments to get them started in the hope of expectation that more funds would be available in the future.

What was happening could justifiably be described as a bold new adventure in public enterprise.

The need for greater expenditures in the public sector had long been agitated. Adlai Stevenson had spoken of "the contrast between private opulence and public squalor." John Kenneth Galbraith, Harvard's economist-politician, had contended that the satisfaction of public needs would always lag behind what should be done unless basic changes were made in the structure of our economy.

Now Johnson and his aides saw the opportunity to expand permanently the public sector of our economy.

They went about it much as business might search for new markets: by developing new programs, as a manufacturer might bring out new products; by stimulating demand; even by creating new demands to be able to satisfy them. The public's awareness was to be aroused not to halitosis or body odor, but to social neglects and how government money could be obtained to correct them.

Memoranda from the Office of Economic Opportunity emphasized "the culture of the poor," as a realtor might a new subdivision he was developing. Some "poverty" programs like community action were consciously designed to awaken unrest in the slums, so "the poor" would become more active politically.

Puerto Ricans in New York City had generally been easygoing, even indifferent, about their ethnicity. To qualify for a grant from OEO they were told they had to demonstrate a lively consciousness of being a minority group, and had to dig up statistics to show how poverty-afflicted they were. The statistics and militancy were developed.

Once enacted, it was felt the benefits would attract their own constituencies who would demand that these programs be kept and expanded. An Office of Education circular appealed to "the aggressive and enterprising librarian" to realize that "never before" had she "so many benefits to choose from." When President Johnson, in preparing his final budget, cut library funds, the protests from "aggressive and enterprising" ladies astonished the Budget Bureau. Recalled one official, "It reminded me of how the American Legion went after the bonus." The librarians put their anger into telegrams, not letters. From Arkansas to Washington journeyed one gray-haired librarian to protest personally to her congressman, Representative Wilbur Mills, who chaired the House Ways and Means Committee.

It is not fanciful to describe the men who put together some of the Johnsonian programs as a new breed of entrepreneurs—captains of public enterprise—who were trying to enlarge our economy, much as the captains of industry or merchant princes had done in earlier periods.

As with the earlier entrepreneurs, these new captains of public enterprise varied considerably in personality and accomplishment.

At one end smiled Sargent Shriver, a handsome salesman-type whose operations evoked conflicting reactions. Those who thought that the anti-poverty effort had yielded thin scrapings saw Shriver as akin to Samuel Insull, heading a hastily-flung-together holding company that had been organized to make political capital of a headline, the "war on poverty," with a prospectus that would never have passed SEC scrutiny. Others likened Shriver's poverty work to the building of the railroads that crossed the country so rapidly, a feat that was wasteful and reckless but ended with real accomplishment.

In sharp contrast was Wilbur Cohen, whom Johnson rewarded by naming him Secretary of Health, Education, and Welfare, and who, it might be said, did for Medicare and Social Security what John D. Rockefeller did for oil.

In line with accepted Horatio Alger business tradition, Cohen began his career of public enterprise at the bottom of the public ladder. A native of Milwaukee, he had picked up an interest in social security while at the University of Wisconsin, in the days when La Follette progressivism seemed more relevant to the students than black studies. Cohen's first Washington job, with the Committee on Economic Security, in the Depression year of 1934, paid $1,620 "minus 5 per cent." The "minus 5 per cent" was an "economy cut" imposed by Franklin Roosevelt on all federal employees in that fleeting interval when he tried to balance the budget.

Cohen never left the Social Security field, even when out of the government during the Eisenhower Administration. His first Medicare effort—to put the whole population under health insurance—proved too ambitious and was defeated in 1950 after a nine-year battle in Congress. The setback taught Cohen the value of a small step at a time. His next effort limited Medicare to older people on Social Security. To prepare the way almost every other year he brought forward a piecemeal proposal; some were defeated; others were passed, such as disability payments for Social Security pensioners and health insurance for dependents of members of the armed forces. Enactment of Medicare in 1965 represented twenty-seven years of Cohen's labors.

Enterprise thrives on optimism, and this essential liveliness was provided by the "discovery" of a remarkable economic phenomenon suggested by the fact that federal tax receipts actually increased after the $11 billion tax cut of 1964. Christened with the chilling name of "the fiscal dividend," this discovery meant simply that if the economy continued to grow at, say, 4 to 5 per cent a year, tax revenues would increase automatically, perhaps $15 billion or more each year, at income levels then current.

To the advocates of public enterprise, the "fiscal dividend" was like a promise of inheriting royalties from fabulously rich oilfields, out of which would flow regularly billions of dollars to pay for new social programs, and for a constant enlargement of the public sector.

Prospecting for new public enterprise took a leap into the future. After all, the "fiscal dividend," while available for new government programs, could also be returned to the public in tax cuts. The captains of public enterprise were determined to have on hand bright, gleaming social programs ready to be pushed when the fiscal dividend of increased tax receipts rolled in.

Johnson liked to name task forces, usually composed of university professors, to make special studies of varied problems. One instruction given them was "look into what else ought to be done" by the government.

On February 7, 1965, though, Johnson sent the first B-52 bombers over North Vietnam. The fiscal dividends for years to come were exploded on jungled hills and bridges of dubious worth in Vietnam. Some of the angriest attacks against the war came from liberals who had shared such exciting visions of expanding public enterprise.

Johnson fought to keep the dream alive. With the war nearly a year old, the budget he sent to Congress in January 1966 called for an increase of more than $3 billion in Great Society programs. His budget message declared: "The struggle in Vietnam must be supported. The advance toward a Great Society at home must continue unabated.

This budget provides the means for both these goals."

In holding to both guns and butter, Johnson started the deficit spending that was to bring on the inflation that has been undermining governmental stability ever since.

Still, while the war dragged on there was one consolation. When the fighting ended the $30 billion being spent in Vietnam would become available as a "peace dividend" that could be spent for deferred orphaned projects and widowed hopes, or so the public entrepreneurs thought. Through the war years, in fact, these entrepreneurs continued to search American society for faults and ills to be exposed so they could be corrected.

One such exploration, more ambitious than most, headed by Professor Daniel Bell of Columbia University, aimed at developing a set of "social indicators" which would make visible what needed to be done in education, health, crime, etc. A Council of Social Advisors was to be created to do for the social sciences what the Council of Economic Advisors had done for economics.

By early 1968, though, budget experts like Otto Eckstein of Harvard and Charles Schultze, Johnson's budget director, were voicing doubts that the end of the Vietnam war would free much money. The more digging into the Pentagon's plans that was done the clearer it became that the fiscal dividends for years ahead were already spoken for. In testifying before Congress in June 1969, Schultze could list upward of $80 billion worth of nonVietnam weapons that the military had approved and might want to buy—Minuteman, Poseidon, and ABM missiles, replacing the Navy's entire force of interceptor fighter planes, three new nuclear-powered aircraft carriers, a new anti-submarine plane, a new continental air-defense system—and so on.

To drape these figures in mourning, Schultze added the gloomy finding that in the past the final costs of missile systems had averaged 3.2 times the original estimates.

Unless some limit could be imposed on the devouring

appetite of military technology, there would be no tax funds for the cities, rumbling with unrest; for schools; for clear air and water; for low-cost housing and other social needs.

Defense spending had to be slashed. This, the advocates of public enterprise felt, was *the* number-one issue before the country. Into the assault on military spending went much of the emotions and organization that had been stirred by the Vietnam resistances.

That first 1969 assault did not seem too successful. Only a billion dollars or so was cut from the Pentagon's spending. In his 1970 budget message President Nixon proposed reductions of $5 billion, but these savings came mainly from reductions in our Vietnam outlays. Instead of being cheered, the advocates of public spending were made gloomier.

The Council of Economic Advisers had inserted into the President's Economic Report a table which projected receipts and expenditures into 1975. Programs already in existence, including Nixon's new welfare plan, would gulp down nearly all the funds that would become available. Little could be anticipated in the way of new starts for at least five years, and probably longer.

That such a table could be issued was really startling. Five years! What did the government think the term "priorities" meant? If the country was really in trouble, it made no sense to say nothing much could be done about it for at least five years. If the troubles weren't real, then a lot of rethinking had to be done by much of the nation.

## 2. Claimants One and All

In expanding the public-enterprise sector, Johnson and his aides were seeking a better balance of political conflict in the country, with more support for public spending and greater self-awareness and political participation of "the poor." As it turns out, though, a bursting economy stimulates economic self-awareness in all groups, raising the general level of conflict in the country.

One evidence of this heightened sense of self-interest was the quickened pressures for tax reduction and tax reform that brought a $9 billion tax cut in 1969 when, as Joseph A. Pechman of Brookings wrote, the most urgent need was more revenue for social spending. Inflation fed the public's desire for lower taxes, of course, but so did the hungers for more purchasing power to be able to buy goods and services of every kind; also the knowledge that economic growth generates higher tax receipts that can be used to cut taxes.

One might say, in fact, that the battling over the fiscal dividend and other tax funds tends to make claimants of us all, in a highly personalized way.

With a national budget of $200 billion—a fifth of the Gross National Product—there always will be some program that each person can point to and say if "that" wasn't going on "my" taxes could be cut. During 1968 and 1969 "welfare handouts" served as the chief target for many voter resentments. But if it hadn't been that, some other activity would have drawn the fire.

In the future these tax-cut demands would continue to be flung in with the many other competing claims for some share of available tax resources. Funds released by lowered defense spending would not go with certainty for schools, cities and other public spending. After the fight over Pentagon procurement, a second battle would still have to be fought against the numerous requests for government subsidies for shipbuilding, airport expansion and mass transit, as well as demands for tax reductions and many schemes that would be lobbied up for using "tax credits."

The American Medical Association, for example, to block the extension of Medicare for the general population, has urged that a tax credit be given people who buy health insurance. Endless will be the plans brought forward for "tax credits."

The advocates of public enterprise had tried to draw a sharp political line between the public and private sectors, but the "fiscal dividend" remains open combat territory which anyone can invade.

In this struggle, moreover, the economy itself becomes a contender and, as constituted now, throws its weight in favor of private, not public, enterprise. Consumer and industry demands that are generated by the private sector become pressures for their own expansion which fight efforts to divert resources to the public sector.

How the economy has been operating since 1965 seems less what John Maynard Keynes envisioned than a new version of *laissez faire*. By stimulating demand across the entire economy, nearly every economic interest was strengthened to pursue its own profit-making purposes to the extent of its own competitive abilities.

Where the needs of society corresponded with what individuals could do for themselves or with the interests of the stronger segments of the economy, the new *laissez faire* was marvelously effective. On one street in Cleveland, a Negro mechanic had come up from Mississippi ten years before with no skills and an eighth-grade schooling, but he said, "I never missed a day of work." He had just bought a $15,000 home.

Beyond that, though, prosperity plainly did not bring society into better balance. In fact, it worsened old imbalances by piling new stresses on points of weakness and by throwing up new dislocations more rapidly than old ones could be packed down.

One basic fault is that managing the economy by both the Republicans and Democrats has been governed by too single-minded a goal of high employment and more and more production. That goal, as we have seen, is not an adequate basis for social or political stability.

The crusade against pollution points to one concept that should be added to our economic thinking, certainly not original with me, that of social costs. When someone dumps industrial wastes into a lake he causes a social damage, the costs of which have generally been borne by society as a whole.

It is becoming clear that pollution cannot be controlled unless we prevent social damage from occurring, to minimize it at its origin. With air pollution, it makes little sense to produce a million additional cars, as was done between 1967 and 1968, and then try to wash the air clean of the fumes they exhaled. The sensible approach, with which some auto makers seem to agree, would be to manufacture cars that do not pollute the air.

In adopting such a policy we will be breaking with our habitual thinking that production and more production is the dominant criterion.

This concept of "social costs" should be extended through the whole economy. Sometimes when social damage is neglected, the price is modest; at other times, as with the mechanization of cotton, neglect brings a revolutionary upheaval.

The Rust brothers, who invented the first successful cotton picker in 1936, had a sense of social responsibility. Realizing their machine could displace more than one to two million sharecroppers and farm laborers, they proposed creating a foundation to share the profits and help ease the dislocations.

When World War II ended, though, the most efficient cotton pickers were being manufactured by the larger farm implement companies, like International Harvester and John Deere. Their cotton pickers were bought as mechanization spread; these implement makers did nothing about the displaced croppers. Nor did the plantation owners; nor the local communities of the southern states. Most of the Negroes who were displaced became a migrating social cost, which was finally presented for payment in our cities.

Admiral Hyman Rickover has suggested that some tech-

nological inventions, which would cause too much disloca-
tion, should not be put into effect. I would not argue that
the cotton picker should never have been allowed out at
night. In the long run, our country will have been strengthened by the South's being left with a more balanced economy than it has ever had, and by the fact that in moving
North the blacks came into a social arena which, while not
assuring equality, did give them a real chance to fight for
their rights.

Still, a large part of the political struggle over "reordering our priorities" reflects the fact that the social costs let
loose by the South must be paid for by other parts of the
country. Increasing employment, raising the GNP, does not
overcome such problems.

Many other effects of prosperity are unsettling. Economic expansion, particularly if continued for some time,
quickens changes that overwhelm local government; residential movements that weaken our cities, more automobiles
to choke the streets and highways, more social problems of
every kind, and often in forms not anticipated.

In its relation to the general economy, local government
has been not unlike the janitor who has to wait until the
party is over before he can clean up. It is no accident that
the years of prosperity have been years of social breakdown
in our cities. Instead of providing additional financial resources to overcome our urban crisis, the boom dumped
fresh complications over the old neglects.

Put directly, an economy like ours cannot be managed
for long on the basis of economics alone, without adjusting
for the political and social impacts of what is happening.

These dangers were sensed by Walter W. Heller and
other liberal economists. In his Godkin Lectures at Harvard,
Heller emphasized how important it was for the public
sector to correct "the ravages" of rapid growth, such as air
and water pollution. He also urged revenue-sharing with
the states and cities, conceding that Galbraith was correct

in maintaining that "prosperity gives the federal government the revenues, and state and local governments the problems."

But even today we have only a vague appreciation of how large is the burden of social costs that must be shared, of how large a shift of financial resources from the private to the public sector would be needed *after* production and employment are boomed.*

The battling over "priorities" in 1969 was dramatized as a struggle of social needs against defense. Early in 1970, a second offensive was being organized; in addition to reducing defense spending efforts would be pressed to curb some of the many private spending activities which were far less important than either defense or social needs.

Arthur Okun of the Brookings Institution, a one-time member of Johnson's Council on Economic Advisers, gave these statistics to illustrate what was involved. Defense spending took 9 per cent of the GNP, while nondefense federal, state, and local government expenditures took 14 per cent, but this drops to 5 per cent if one looks only at aid to the cities and the poor. But the real heavyweight is private spending, which represents 77 per cent of the total Gross National Product.

There are however only three known ways of extracting money from the individual citizen—through charitable contributions, robbery and by raising taxes.

Since 1960 the median family income has risen from $5,417 a year to $9,280. Why in view of such an increase, should resistances to higher taxes and to new welfare proposals remain so intense?


### 3. Welfare Against Tax Cuts

The day after Robert Kennedy won the Nebraska presidential primary I flew into Omaha for some interviewing.

---

* These needs would not be dented by the $5 billion in revenue-sharing for states that Nixon has promised by 1976.

In checking the vote, it developed that Kennedy had swept not only the Negro wards but had also carried the racially sensitive low-income white workers who come in from rural areas to settle in East Omaha.

Many of these East Omaha workers went for him because "I voted for his brother." With others, though, the chief appeal was the feeling that "he wants to get the colored off welfare."

A woman who drove a taxicab explained, "My husband and I pay taxes. We work hard. Negroes should also work hard."

She had been pleased by Kennedy's talk of encouraging private companies to give Negroes jobs. In speaking of her neighbors in East Omaha, she revealed her own sense of pride, saying, "They aren't as well off as other people. Their houses aren't as expensive—but they want to get ahead through their own personal efforts."

It was intriguing to note how directly welfare was tied in her mind to the taxes that she was paying and how she reasoned that if Negroes worked and shared the burdens of taxpaying her own tax bills would be lightened.

Ordinarily one would not expect a welfare proposal advanced by Richard Nixon to stir the same voter reaction as one put forward by Robert Kennedy. Still, this is pretty much what happened with Nixon's family-assistance plan when it was made public in August 1969.

The feature of Nixon's plan that registered most strongly with the general run of voters was its emphasis on the requirement that people receiving grants would be required to register and be available for work or training. This was widely interpreted as evidence that—to quote a Memphis barber—"Nixon wants them to work."

The family-assistance aspect of the plan, which has been hailed as a beginning step toward a guaranteed annual income, was shrugged off by most people in favor of the belief, or hope, that welfare costs might be reduced. Said a thirty-nine-year-old carman in Cleveland, "If Nixon can get them to work, it would mean a lot less people on welfare."

This reaction was not accidental. Both President Nixon and his urban expert, Daniel Moynihan, in selecting their sales pitch, had described their plan as "one that would encourage people to work." In his message to Congress, the President promised that more than half of the families participating in the new welfare plan in the first year will have one member working or in training.

Actually 12,000,000 to 15,000,000 persons are expected to be added to family assistance roles at a starting cost of more than $4 billion on top of the current federal outlays for welfare. To welfare experts the main attractions of the new plan are that it would end the incentive the present ADC program gives a father to abandon his wife and children so they can get welfare; also the plan would be a start toward a guaranteed minimum income and would make for greater geographic evenness in welfare around the country.

Currently the steam behind the idea is being generated by varied urban groups who see it as a way of lifting the heavy load of welfare costs from our groaning cities.

With New York City accounting for a twelfth of the total welfare load in the nation, one can understand why Governor Rockefeller and Mayor Lindsay agree on one thing, that the whole welfare burden be taken over by the federal government. But this seems some years away. The starting allowances proposed by Nixon are so low that the South would be the section of the country helped most.

Whatever program is finally adopted by Congress, we can be sure that it will generate demands from other citizens for more liberal Social Security benefits, higher pensions, higher wages, and so on. The competition of discontents which is so strong in our private sector operates with government programs as well.

The ordinary person generally reacts to a new economic proposal such as the President's plan by figuring or imagining what the direct impact will be on his own family. When people were asked what they thought about a guaranteed annual income, most of them took the figure given them—$3,000 for a family of four—and compared it with their own situation. Older people on Social Security or nearing retirement then protested, "That's more than I get under Social Security," or "I've worked hard and paid in all that money for Social Security, and I'd get less than someone would for not working."

Others would compare the proposed income grant with their own earnings and, if not far apart, would complain, "Who would keep working for what I make?"

During the 1968 campaign I was struck by how many persons—far more than in any previous year—protested why the benefits they drew were "less than the woman across the street gets."

Complained one widow in Richmond, "A Negro I know showed me a welfare check which is twice what I get under Social Security. Why don't we get as much?"

The tone of her protest was exactly like that of a steel-worker complaining that his wages haven't kept up with those of the auto worker or of the fireman demanding pensions as high as those of school teachers.

This competitive envy among people who feel that they aren't sharing equally in the benefits of government programs is not new. In Southwest Kansas, one farmer talked of a letter he had received shortly before the 1956 voting from a friend in Colorado.

"Those Colorado farmers were getting a better deal than us," he complained. "You know why? The people in Washington weren't sure they would win Colorado. Being solid Republicans like we are in Kansas, they forgot about us.

"I voted for Eisenhower," he continued, "but I went Democratic for governor and Congress. Things have been too one-sided in this state for too long."

Currently the strongest resentments are voiced over the

workings of the Medicare and Medicaid programs.

In Hollywood, Florida, an electrician recalled angrily, "We had a baby and the kid needed blood. They charged me $110.25 for that blood and $90 more for the hospital. What does it cost the coloreds to have a baby? Nothing. Nothing for blood either."

On the main street of Saratoga, in eastern North Carolina, a gray-haired woman was sitting in a car parked outside the local insurance office. She and her husband owned thirty-seven acres of tobacco land, but, she explained, "We've had to rent it out. My husband has cancer.

"What gets me," she protested, "is that these colored girls go into the hospital and have their illegitimate babies paid for. My husband had to pay his own hospital bills—nearly $2,000. He's in town now trying to arrange a loan. We work so hard. Why should we be treated worse than people who won't work?"

Only part of the complaints against welfare came from persons with low earnings. More often the protests were prompted by the many things people wanted to do or buy with their own earnings. This was particularly true with younger voters, who were only beginning their own climb up the economic ladder and felt pressing needs for all the money they earned.

In Columbus, Indiana, the wife of a twenty-three-year-old factory supervisor voiced a typical reaction when she said: "I don't like the idea of giving people money if they don't want to work. We've been planning to buy a house here in the next two years. If we've got to pay our taxes to them, we'll never get our house."

Becoming a homeowner can change the political thinking of even "liberal" persons. A Cleveland couple, when first interviewed, were divided over whether Mayor Carl Stokes should be re-elected.

"I admire him; he has to be almost saintly," declared the wife. "He has had to walk the straight and narrow. If he leans to the colored, the whites don't like him. If he leans too much to the whites the colored don't like him. He's shown white people that a Negro could serve as a mayor and do a good job."

Her twenty-eight-year-old husband favored Stokes's opponent because "he's promised homeowners a break on taxes."

By late October, his wife had shifted against Stokes. She explained, "We were in rent for so long and this is our first house. We used to be liberal in voting for new bond issues. Now we figure out the mills and what it will cost us and we say sure it's needed but we can't afford to pay it."

Then she added, "We also want another child. We saved for this house and have to keep saving. I buy the cheaper meats. We never eat steak; only on birthdays."

At older age levels the pressure for more buying power may come from a son or daughter of college age. Complained one Los Angeles housewife, "We're not rich enough to send our boy through college and we're not poor enough to get him a loan."

A full-employment economy does enable many people to increase their buying power by working for it. More than a third of all married women are now employed—in 1947 the proportion was only one in five. Nearly 4 million workers hold down two jobs.

But full employment also flings heavier burdens onto state and local government, which, of course, shift the cost to the taxpayer. In just three years—from 1965 to 1968—state and local taxes in the country jumped by 40 per cent, with much of the increase falling on homeowners in middle-income brackets.

A systems analyst in Queens, when asked what was the biggest problem before the country, declared, "It's how homeowners can afford to pay taxes for these welfare people."

The wife of an Indiana club manager grumbled: "Something's going to have to be done about all this taxation; we're living below our salaries. I'm against taxing the public to give money to people who aren't working."

The contrast with the public's mood in 1965 is instructive. That year, an almost euphoric trance enveloped the nation. The reduction in federal taxes in 1964 and the burst in employment that followed had left people feeling that no one was paying the cost of any of the "Great Society" programs. All of it seemed to be coming for free.

In Jasper County, Iowa, a farmwife who had voted for Goldwater summed up how most people felt when she recalled: "We were talking the other night about how nearly everyone is getting a government check. I don't think it's right. But I can't see how it's hurting us. I'd vote for Johnson tomorrow."

By 1968, the word "welfare" had become a doghouse label. Still, the same persons who protested against "welfare" in general, when asked, said they favored higher Social Security payments and the extension of Medicare benefits. The next big welfare-state thrust, I would judge, will be for universal health insurance to take care of the rising medical and hospital costs.

Most voters are not so much "conservative" or "liberal" as they are self-centered. They react separately to each specific proposal to expand the public sector, approving those which benefit them personally. Beyond that, their support of public spending in general tends to rise when unemployment increases and living costs and taxes are not climbing rapidly.

High employment does reconcile many people to rising prices largely because they seem to move together. But high employment does not seem to reconcile people to paying mounting taxes.

One overall conclusion to be drawn from all this is that a booming economy stimulates a great deal of selfishness, or economic self-interest, if you prefer that word. We have long had the highest standard of discontent in the world and usually have regarded it as an incentive to work harder and produce more. But strengthening selfishness makes it only more difficult to transfer financial resources from one part of the economy to where they are needed.

This same sense of self-interest that spurs the individual drives each segment of our economy, each of the different sections of the country. Often they reach out for subsidies, investment credits, and other incentives that would enable them to press their economic interests more strongly, while the costs are left for others to pay.

The sections of the country which have profited most from economic change seem most resentful of taxes; they are eager to keep their earnings and reinvest them in further expansion. Prosperity produces some benevolence but also sharpens the struggle for economic power.

The constant cry is for "leadership," but if we dig past personalities we find at least three basic weaknesses in how our economy is being managed.

1. When Walter Heller and his associates inaugurated the "new economics" they had quite strong intentions of taking part of the new wealth that would be created and of applying it to ease our more critical social problems. But those intentions were left out of the programing when the boom started, and no one has been able to get them into the computers since.

This suggests that the fight to include social costs must be made before the boom is given its go-ahead. If we let everyone produce like hell and then try like hell to take some part of it away, for social needs, we can predict who will catch hell.

2. The theory—which now seems taken for granted by both Republican and Democratic technicians—that inflation is needed to maintain high employment should be re-

examined. The economics of inflation always operate to
cause people to try to pass on the costs of inflation to someone else, in higher prices, higher wages, higher profits, or in
lowering their own tax burdens. This kind of transfer of
economic resources fights social purpose. It escalates the
costs of everything the government buys, which in the case
of defense runs to billions; it also weakens those parts of
society that are most burdened with social problems.

3. We cannot continue weakening government at every
level and maintain an orderly society. While breakdown is
most severe at the local level, the stability of the federal
government is also in question.

That may sound like a strange statement to those who
have become accustomed to measuring the strength of government by how much money it spends. But all the leaping
zeroes in the federal budget are evidences of Washington's
inability to reconcile the conflicts loosed by our enormous
productive power. Sometimes it is difficult to determine who
controls the government, those being subsidized or those
who pay the bills. Items of pressing urgency are left out of
the government computers; while others get in because they
are already there or because someone with political power
can put them in there. We can measure the incentive of self-
interest with fine mathematical precision. But what is the
binary-computer equivalent of restraint? Can it come from
the techniques of economic management now employed? Or
can it come from the voters? What has prosperity been
doing to them?


## 4. A New Breed of Voters

Of all the political effects of prosperity, the one which
seems most elusive could prove the most important.

The kind of prosperity we have been having has been
changing the ordinary voter's attitude toward government

and has also been loosening his sense of political tradition and party loyalty.

Prosperity widens the range of personal choice open to the individual. Being more secure in one's job or being able to move more freely to other work, to have two incomes in a family, to be able to buy more varied material possessions —all these things stimulate the individual's sense of self-worth and political independence.

This weakening of party loyalty has helped create a new breed of "free-floating voters" who are capable of quick party shifts from one election to the next, and who come close to holding the balance of voting power in the nation.

That doesn't mean that the loyalties and antagonisms of the New Deal are no longer important. A precinct analysis of the 1968 election reveals that the vote for Nixon and Humphrey structured along much the same income lines in city after city. Nixon's gains came largely in middle- and upper-income neighborhoods, while in worker precincts the economic appeal of the Democratic Party asserted itself with sufficient force for Humphrey to almost win.

This economic cleavage remains probably the strongest single influence in voting, but it no longer structures enough of the vote to give either party a majority. With each election to come, the hold of New Deal memories will loosen, while the weight of the free-floating voters is likely to be felt more strongly.

Age and occupation are two of the more important factors that distinguish these free-floating voters. Age exerts its influence in at least two ways. Younger voters are not pulled, as are older people, by ties of gratitude for Medicare, Social Security, and "good times" that contrast so sharply with recollections of the Depression.

In Los Angeles, an accountant's wife, casting her first vote, recalled vaguely that "my father was a Democrat" but couldn't say why. In hopes of stirring a revealing recollection, I asked, "Did your father ever talk of how hard a time he had during the Depression?"

"When was that?" she replied.

Within the same Democratic families, the younger members did more shifting to Nixon than their parents. Some parents, in fact, found it easier to express their protests by moving halfway to Wallace than by swinging fully to the Republicans.

In Huntington Park, California, the wife of a city employee talked of how "my husband wants to vote for George Wallace but I keep telling him we have to go for Humphrey."

Her twenty-nine-year-old daughter volunteered, "My brother and I are switching to Nixon."

"If you do that," said the mother, "you'll be breaking our family tradition. No one in our family has ever voted Republican."

The daughter answered back: "Wallace wants to end violence with violence. Humphrey thinks he'll end it by giving in to them. I feel Nixon is in between. He'll end the rioting in the right way."

Asked what she saw as the big difference between the Democrats and Republicans, the daughter replied, "I can't say. I don't see any."

Her mother interjected, "You weren't even born when we went through those terrible years that made us Democrats."

Age is also important in a generational sense. Early in this study we noted that only about a fifth of the counties in the country have voted for the same party's candidate for each of the last five presidential elections.

This means that a sizable proportion of parents have been unable to pass on to their children any tradition of loyalty to either the Democratic or Republican Party. The parents themselves may remain torn in their feelings through their lifetimes, not loyal and yet unable to break cleanly.

Their sons and daughters, though, as they become of voting age, are not hampered by previous party ties; they are able to make clear, sharp choices between the parties on the basis of current issues or their current interests. This split-generation effect would become more important if the voting age were lowered to eighteen; also it is particularly significant in the South, where the break from one-party loyalty has widened steadily with each election since 1948.

Younger voters in the South have hardly any image in their minds of the Republican Party. Nixon has the opportunity—and he has been using it—to give them an image that they will be drawn to.

In our interviews with college students we noted how choice of career serves as the carrier of a young person's sense of economic interest and of which party he identified with. Occupation exerts a similar influence upon adults, and currently is swelling the numbers of free-floating voters among older as well as younger people.

This finding emerged fairly dramatically during the 1968 campaign in the responses to the query, "Would a Nixon victory hurt you economically?"

Among the normally Democratic voters interviewed, nearly two-thirds replied, "No." Many, in fact, shared the blithe lack of concern of a welder's wife in Chicago who said, "If Nixon wins only my pride will be hurt."

In comparing those who voiced fears of a Nixon victory with those who did not, occupation turned out to be the main divider.

In two Pittsburgh precincts, for example, most of the Democrats who feared they might suffer under a Republican president were steelworkers. Several recalled, "I was laid off when Eisenhower was president." Others declared, "Republicans have too much money and don't care about working people" or "Every time the Republicans are in labor gets hurt."

Fears of a Nixon victory were also voiced by a widow who was worried because "they say Nixon may cut off Medicare. Old people need that."

In these same Pittsburgh precincts the Democrats who were untroubled about the economic future included a retired life insurance salesman, an auditor, a draftsman, a TV film editor, a city supervisor, an auto repair mechanic, and a policeman's wife.

"The way it looks," said the policeman's wife, "there will always be enough work for my husband. The Republicans may even be the better party for us. At least they like policemen better than some Democrats do.

"But," she added, "my father and father-in-law are union men. They're afraid."

This division of replies corresponds quite closely to a major change that has taken place in the nation's occupational structure. One reason our economy has become less vulnerable to recessions has been the decline in the proportion of factory workers compared with the expansion in steadier fields, such as state and local government or white-collar and service work.

In the ten-year span between 1958 and 1968, the number of persons employed in trade and services increased by 40 per cent; in government by 56 per cent; in manufacturing and construction by only 23 per cent.

In a pioneering study, Victor R. Fuchs of the National Bureau of Economic Research points out that the United States has become the first country in the world with "a service economy," that is, the first nation in which more than half of the employed population does not work in producing food, clothing, automobiles, housing, or other tangible goods.

The political interests of these "service economy" workers are nowhere as deeply involved in the business-labor conflict as are factory workers and those who identify directly with management.

In one respect these free-floating voters are a force for political instability—or at least voter instability. Always in the past the main structuring of any majority coalition has been that of common economic interests. These free-floaters may not be easily brought into a new coalition. And yet until one of the major parties can capture their loyalty, neither party will be able to command a stable and assured majority.

But these free-floating voters can be said to have an extra sensitivity to the issues of a managed society. It is not because they understand the intricacies of fiscal policy or of juggling interest rates, but because they react so much more quickly to any change in the economy—be it good or bad—than do voters with firm party loyalties.

This relative ease with which voters can shift is currently serving as a constant pressure upon the parties to develop manageable means of dealing with our more important conflicts. To this extent the speed with which these voters may react should operate to make the president-manager more responsive to the people.

Nixon, in fact, may be overly sensitive on this score. The story is often told that early in 1960 Arthur Burns, now Chairman of the Federal Reserve Board, warned Nixon of an approaching recession, but that President Eisenhower could not be induced to begin government spending to avert it. This inaction, Nixon believes, cost him the presidency that November.

The economic policies followed by the Nixon Administration would seem to bear out that story. His economic technicians, headed by Paul McCracken, formerly of the University of Michigan, underestimated the strength of the inflationary boom and at the end of a year of effort, anti-inflation controls were only beginning to show results. Although the cost of living was still rising at an annual rate of more than six per cent, the President shifted to "jaw-boning" the Federal Reserve to expand the money supply, which it did, in hopes of stalling off a recession before the November elections.

A political cynic, noting this, would assume the Nixon Administration would also try to time economic affairs for a spectacular upsurge during the presidential year of 1972.

But whether either party—or the party system—will be able to resolve these conflicts that divide the nation still is not certain. On the actual managing of the economy, no wide disagreement seems to separate Republican and Democratic economists.

The changeover from Johnson to Nixon produced no basic shift in management techniques. The economic technicians of both parties seem committed to employing the same techniques of monetary and fiscal policy to maintain high employment. The Republicans talk more about the evils of inflation than the Democrats, but they also appear to be willing to accept a persistent increase in living costs of perhaps 3 per cent each year as the price of keeping unemployment down. Democratic economists would be quicker to expand the public-enterprise sector, while Republicans would favor cutting taxes more.

But if the key to resolving our crisis of unresolved neglects is the ability to shift economic resources to deal with these problems, neither party's approach seems adequate. The extra lift that is likely to be obtained by expanding the public sector or by extending the reach of private enterprise will not provide the resources to overcome the problems we face.

In its political effects, the economy remains organized for continued battle. But how much conflict can this country stand and for how long? How much dissension can we have and still meet the threat of war from abroad? On this score the lesson of Vietnam is anything but reassuring.

# EIGHT

# THE "NEW ISOLATIONISM"

### 1. "Solve Our Own Problems"

THE BITTER FRUSTRATIONS OF Vietnam have left in their wake a new isolationist spirit which seems certain to force far-reaching changes in American foreign policy.

Whether those changes prove beneficial or disastrous will hinge in good part on our understanding how drastically different this "new isolationism" is from that of the past and whether the disunities and mistakes that shaped it can be overcome.

The traditional scold-theme of the State Department has sought to attribute isolationist sentiment in this country to our supposed "immaturity." The American people, so the scolding runs, have never quite grown up to the harsh realities and responsibilities of world power; and so, when the going gets tough, we tend to yearn for "withdrawal" and "isolation."

Somewhat in that vein Dean Rusk, before leaving his post as Secretary of State, pictured the new isolationism as being a rejection of the idea of collective responsibility for safeguarding the peace.

But this explanation hardly fits in with the two main

streams of isolationist sentiment in the country. The angriest resistance to our Vietnam involvement erupted in our universities, in the past always one of the more international-minded sectors of our society. This resistance, so much the result of a mishandling of the draft, has been projected into an almost ideological assault on anything related to the military, especially defense spending, which is digging a deep trench of political conflict between defense and the needs for action on pressing domestic problems.

A second wave of isolationist feeling, reflecting the mood of the general run of voters outside the universities, is neither anti-military nor ideological. These voters do not talk of withdrawing into some Fortress America or of standing apart and alone in a nuclear world.

The dominant note that came through from my interviews with them is the feeling that "we can't be everyone's policeman" and "let's solve our own problems first."

As a retired schoolteacher in Detroit explained, "I'm not an isolationist, but we shouldn't overreach."

Generally these voters were prepared to fight if Western Europe were attacked, but when asked what we should do if Vietnam were settled and "another similar situation developed in Asia," three of every four declared, "Stay out; never again."

The question "What was the big lesson of Vietnam" brought two main responses—"Keep our noses at home" and "If we get in, go in with enough to win it quickly."

This desire to impose some manageable limit upon our role in policing the peace was shared quite generally by Republicans and Democrats, by both critics and supporters of the Vietnam war.

What makes the "new isolationism" so omen-bearing—for good or evil—is that it is a carrier of these mixed pressures, of the desire to reduce our commitments abroad or rely on end-it-quick intervention, plus militant demands that more of our resources be used at home, plus a readiness to project into our foreign policy all of the domestic conflicts and weaknesses we appear unable to resolve.

In this respect the new isolationism raises doubts about our ability to follow through on any effective foreign policy until a greater degree of domestic conciliation can be arrived at.

One other aggravating factor should be noted—how much more difficult it has become to define who or what the "enemy" is. Johnson always pictured us as fighting "the communists" in Vietnam, as has Nixon. But this justification never was convincing to a majority of the voters.

When people were asked during the 1968 campaign why we were in Vietnam, only about a fifth of those interviewed said, "We can't let communism take over" or "If we pull out they'll push farther and then come here" A far larger proportion of the voters replied, "We made a mistake getting involved" or "We're in too deep now." Other reasons cited fairly often were "We must save face "or "We're committed and can't let the South Vietnamese down."

Senator J. William Fulbright has charged that American policy makers still believed in the myth of a world-wide, monolithic communist conspiracy which no longer exists. In actual practice, though, both Johnson and Nixon have drawn sharp distinctions between Soviet Russia and Red China. For a time at least, Johnson seemed to think that the Soviets might help us extricate ourselves from Vietnam, a hope that Nixon also played with for a time.

As for the voters generally, most of them have not believed in a monolithic communist conspiracy for years. A study of mine for the Council on Foreign Relations showed that 60 per cent of those interviewed saw Red China as a bigger threat than Russia and even then, in 1963, more than a fourth felt that Russia would become allied with the

United States in some future war with Red China.

With young people the "communist" spectre is much less credible. My 1965 and 1966 surveys of college students across the country revealed that more than 80 per cent of the students thought China was a bigger threat than Russia.

Generally the students felt that Red China, while "militaristic" and "irrational," still "doesn't have the power to reach us."

What alarmed them most about Red China was not that she was a communist nation but that she might resort to war because "China has nothing to lose"; that she is "overpopulated and needs land to expand"; and that "her leaders don't care about the people."

Of the reasons given by the students as to what they feared most about Red China, only 18 per cent of the mentions were that she was a communist country.

For this new generation, exhortations that "we must stop communism" are not a believable justification for Americans fighting in Asia.

Quite a psychological contest will be fought between the President and the American public before a balance is struck between our foreign commitments and reconciliation at home.

For one thing, the President feels strongly about our remaining the leading Pacific power. Writing about "Asia after Vietnam" in *Foreign Affairs* not long before the 1968 campaign began, he envisioned the United States taking the leadership in containing Red China through the creation of a "Pacific community" in cooperation with Japan, which he wanted to see rearmed. In the article Nixon urged that "we now assign to the strengthening of non-Communist Asia a priority comparable to that which we gave to the strengthening of Western Europe after World War II."

The article does not go into detail on how the area is to be stabilized militarily, but at a televised press conference Nixon talked of ABM missiles protecting the Philippines from "nuclear blackmail" by China.

The remark was reminiscent of the reasoning developed by John Foster Dulles after the Korean War by which we were to place primary reliance on the threat of massive retaliation through nuclear weapons, leaving the ground fighting to be done by the smaller nations.

The idea that we can operate as the dominant Pacific power and maintain a "low profile" militarily is most wisely viewed as an expression of hope. Our allies will not always agree to a division of fighting that suits our convenience; if they get into trouble they will want to involve us more deeply. The spread of the Vietnam war into Laos and Cambodia reaffirmed what we already knew, that a creeping involvement is not easily halted.

Any Asia policy we embark upon will carry a risk of being drawn into "small wars." That will be against our intention, of course, but in much of the region, governments are unstable; insurgencies and insurrections pop and erupt periodically.

The likelihood—at least that must be our expectation—is that sometime during the years ahead this country will be tested again in terms of where and for what we are ready to fight. This test could come over Berlin, the Middle East, in another Asian land; it could rush up at us in a showdown confrontation of our readiness to use nuclear weapons as Kennedy faced in the Cuban missile crisis or, more likely, it could creep in upon us as another limited war.

But will we do any better in fighting a limited war than before? In neither Korea nor Vietnam were we able to develop the right strategic and military policy, and we have yet to learn what needs to be done here at home to wage a limited war abroad successfully.

Our inability to master the problems of limited war seems all the more ominous when we recall what President Kennedy told the nation in 1961 on returning from his

Vienna meeting with Khrushchev. All-out war had become unthinkable, Kennedy explained, since we and the Soviets had enough nuclear power to destroy each other, but, he warned, we did face the threat of limited "wars of liberation."

What is it about a "limited war" that makes it so difficult for this country to fight? Why does it divide us so intensely?

## 2. A Dove Is a Hawk Is an Albatross

Our long, bitter struggle over Vietnam policy was fought as if it were an irreconcilable conflict between doves and hawks. Actually if any bird symbolized American war opinion it was not the dove or the hawk but the albatross, with the vast majority of Americans sharing a fervent drive to shake free of an unwanted burden

The raging debate was really a clash of two impatiences, each seeking to end the war quickly—between those who wanted to pull out and those who wanted to end the war by stepping up the fighting.

The angry passions with which Vietnam policy was fought out during the closing months of 1968 have been attributed to the widespread feeling that it was an "immoral" war and to the intense dislike of Johnson personally and of his "credibility gap."

That overlooks the early public support of his Vietnam action. The first time any voter I interviewed praised Johnson as a "strong" president was during the 1964 campaign when he ordered the retaliatory bombing against the Bay of Tonkin action. Only as it became clear that our bombings of North Vietnam meant a prolonged war of attrition did public opinion turn against Johnson.

Much the same pattern of American behavior appeared during the Korean War, which was always recognized as a "just" war. President Harry Truman was warmly ap-

plauded in Congress when he announced that we would re-
pel the overt aggression by North Korea in invading South
Korea. Our action was also formally authorized by the
United Nations Security Council, with Soviet Russia
strangely absent.

Still, when Communist China intervened on the side of
North Korea and the war settled into a bloody stalemate,
public opinion turned against Truman and the country split
with the same demands of "Let's get out" or "go all out"
that were voiced over Vietnam.

What divided the American nation in both these wars
was the special trickiness that lies concealed in a limited
war. A "small war" looks so much easier to fight than an
all-out struggle such as World War II. Actually, a limited
war is far more difficult to fight—successfully.

The sheer scale of an all-out war serves as its own
unifying force. Hardly anyone escapes the sacrifices required. The goal is always clear and sharp: to win as soon
as possible.

In a limited war the objective cannot be as clear, since
our strategic interest is limited. But what really splits the
public is the uneven impact that a limited war has on the
public, plus the uncertainty over how long the war will
drag on.

It is these two factors that prompt the emergence of two
forms of impatience, each seeking to end the war quickly,
one by prompt withdrawal, the other by escalating the war
to "get it over with."

In both the Korean and Vietnam wars the loudest protests that "this is a senseless war" came from families whose
sons had been drafted or faced the draft. They represented the strongest single pressure for quick withdrawal.

What is not generally realized is how much of the pressure to "step up" the fighting came from parents who wanted
to see the war ended before their sons grew up to draft age.

Quite often people being interviewed said, "We have no

reason to be in Vietnam" but still urged, "Go in and bomb the hell out of them."

Nearly always on questioning it developed that they shared the motivation of a steel finisher in New Haven who explained, "I have an eighteen-year-old son. I want to get the war over before he's drafted."

In Elmont, Long Island, a machine manufacturer, when first interviewed in 1966, urged: "Step up the military action. Do whatever is necessary to win." At that time he explained, "My two sons are seventeen and twenty, and they may have to go in."

Reinterviewed two years later, he wanted to pull out. "Both my sons are in college now," he said, "I'm worried they'll be drafted."

That people will shift their opinions as the likely impact of the war changes should not be surprising. Any setback that seems to lengthen the war's duration increases resistance to it and sharpens the conflict between those who want to pull out and those who would escalate the fighting.

The summer of 1968 was a particularly tense one in this regard. The "peace talks" begun in Paris that spring were getting nowhere. As hopes for a quick settlement ebbed, the feeling built up that further escalation might be needed to force negotiations; estimates of how long the war would drag on became gloomier.

Fears that "this war will last as long as we have sons to go" spread down the age ladder beyond families with sons in Vietnam or facing the draft, down to families with sons in high school and even in elementary school.

An Akron postal clerk voiced a typical reply when he said, "I can see the war lasting until my fifteen-year-old is ready to go."

In Covington, Kentucky, a book bindery worker talked of how "my thirteen-year-old son has nothing to look forward to but a lifetime of war."

Across the river in Cincinnati a machinist remarked: "I'm not one who likes riots, and the police in Chicago did about as good as they could. But I can't blame those young kids for wanting to protest. What lies ahead of them but the prospect of war? I know how my fifteen-year-old boy feels."

Reactions like these emphasize why the old draft, as managed, undermined morale on the home front and swelled opposition to the war. In a limited war the one thing the draft should not do is to increase the uncertainty over who will be drawn into the fighting. The fact that General Hershey and members of Congress balked for so long at changing the draft illustrates how thin has been our understanding of the nature of limited war.

The psychological fallout of this uncertainty about the war's duration also points to what makes it so difficult for a president to wage a limited war According to war-game theory, the aim of limited war is to bring about negotiations. But if a president tries to impress the enemy by declaring, "We will stand fast no matter how long it takes," he increases the opposition to the war among millions of parents who worry that the war will be lengthened and take their sons.

If, on the other hand, a president promises quick victory, he gains favor at first, but this support turns into a credibility gap if the war does not end rapidly.

As long as the voters believe he is moving to end the war, Nixon probably can count on continued public support for his policy of slower-paced withdrawals of American troops. But if Vietnamization seemed to be failing and the prospect of prolonged war reappeared, American impatience would leap alive anew. The pressures would rise to either "pull out at once" or "step up the fighting and finish it." *

On the economic front as well, attitudes toward the war tend to reflect the differing impacts that the war has. Leading the agitation to end the war quickly have been

---

* A volunteer army, being urged by Nixon, would reduce public opposition somewhat to military intervention abroad.

many of our mayors, who badly need the funds being used in Vietnam.

With much of the public the boom seems actually to have reduced the opposition to the war. The wife of a Los Angeles factory worker shrugged off questions on Vietnam by saying: "Anything Johnson does is all right with us. My husband is working overtime."

During the Korean War, quite bitter feelings were expressed about the "blood money" that was going to people who were "profiting from the war." There has been much less of this resentment during the Vietnam ordeal, even though no specific effort has been made to "take the profit out of war through an excess-profits tax or stiff renegotiation of military contracts.*

The adverse economic effects of the war weren't really felt until after the 1968 election, when living costs were spiraling upward.

In farm areas, opposition to Vietnam for economic reasons was stronger than in the cities because farmers, unable to raise their prices, are hurt more quickly by inflation than workers. In some rural communities the cleavage over the war aligned those with draft-age sons against those who objected to the cost of the war.

Near Dyersville, Iowa, I reinterviewed ten families I had talked with back in 1952, during the Korean War. I went into this area because it exemplified so well the ethnic nature of much of isolationist feeling in the past. Overwhelmingly Catholic and German-American, this community broke violently with its Democratic heritage in opposition to both world wars. It swung back to vote for Truman in 1948 only to break sharply for Dwight D. Eisenhower in 1952 because of the Korean War.

During the summer of 1968 I found that the war attitudes of these farmers were being shaped this time not by their ethnic background but primarily by each family's vul-

---

* Not since the Spanish-American War have we been so indifferent to war profits.

nerability to the draft and, as a conflicting influence, by economic considerations.

Four of the ten farmers wanted to "pull out." All but one had sons who were in the reserves or who faced being drafted if the war were escalated.

Five other farmers, with no sons of draft age, argued, "If we just walk out, they'll come back in some other place." Three of these, who complained, "This war is bankrupting the country," wanted to "step up the fighting to end it."

The tenth farmer proved to be the angriest of them all. He protested: "My son has just finished high school. He has the brains to go to college but doesn't like school. I can give you the names of farmers around here who put their sons into college just to avoid the draft. Why isn't my son as good as theirs? They should all be taken.

"Either pull out or get out," he stormed. "If we have to, we might as well use the nuclear bomb now as next year."

One of these ten farmers held a special interest for me. In 1952, when I visited the Recker farm, I stumbled onto a family reunion celebrating the return from Korea of one of the six Recker sons.

The father angrily told his son, "Show the man your legs." The boy, still in uniform, lifted his trousers, baring an ugly black scar on each leg.

At that time all of the Reckers wanted to pull out of Korea. In 1968, none of the Reckers wanted to get out of Vietnam.

About forty, the son who had been wounded in Korea still limped as we walked from the pigpen to the house. Several times he seemed to be trying to avoid saying directly what he thought, repeating, "I know how I felt when I was in Korea" or "I wouldn't want to be making the decision."

Finally he said: "I can't see how we can pull out. We've got to do what is needed to win."

As I drove off I thought how a man's views can change

when someone else's sons are doing the fighting.

That is not said with any sense of cynicism but merely to stress this essential point—that how people feel about a limited war is shaped quite directly by the impact the war is having on their lives.

Public opinion on Vietnam has always been remarkably fluid, and consistent. Newsmen and the public opinion polls tried to divide the country neatly into two columns sharply labeled hawks and doves or as supporting or opposing the President. But at all times in my Vietnam interviewing I found the mass of people were torn by the albatross feeling, that we had stumbled into the war and didn't know how to get out. Remarked one housewife, "I want to get out but I don't want to give in."

Nor was the line between a dove and a hawk sharply defined. Often the first replies of a person would be "Pull out" to be followed later in the interview by a shift to "Step up the fighting" (or vice versa). The Dubuque policeman who drove me around the Dyersville area on his day off was a case in point.

"My family are Democrats, but we need a change," he told me at breakfast. "Maybe Nixon will have a different approach and won't drag the war out forever. Besides, I'd like to see some changes in the Supreme Court."

Later that afternoon he was troubled by second thoughts. "If the war gets bigger," he reasoned, "they'll take me I'm only twenty-eight. It's better to pull out."

Many other voters echoed the comment that was heard so often during the last months of the Korean War: "I don't care which we do, but let's go in to win or let's get out."

Similarly, remarks like "Bomb the hell out of them until they quit" sound warlike, but when one probed more deeply and asked what specific actions this country should take, the bark generally proved more belligerent than the bite.

In the summer of 1968, more than half of the persons who

urged that the war be stepped up balked at sending more American troops to Vietnam. The action favored most frequently was to intensify the bombing of North Vietnam. How effective bombing had proven to be was beside the point—which was that the public's emotions were searching for some substitute military action which they hoped would mean "we won't lose so many of our boys."

A hawk is a dove is an albatross.

This desire was also reflected in the eagerness with which people leaped on the suggestion that the war be "de-Americanized" by having the South Vietnamese take over the fighting.

Many voters who endorsed this thought later talked of how "corrupt" the South Vietnamese government was. Certainly it was no confidence in Saigon that spurred support for Vietnamizing the war.

Three-fourths balked at using nuclear weapons (with another 15 per cent undecided), saying, "That would bring on World War III."

Among the one in ten who would use the weapons, the general explanation was: "We wouldn't have to. If we told them we'd do it they would quit."

After the election my interviews showed a rise in the number of people who replied yes to the question "In any settlement, should there be a coalition government in Saigon with some communists in it?" Further questioning usually revealed that these people wanted to get out so badly they didn't really care about South Vietnam.

Some concern has been expressed whether the American people would accept a Vietnam outcome that looked like open defeat or whether such a defeat would bring a right-wing hunt for a political scapegoat and a feeling that our fighting men were "stabbed in the back" by a lack of home support.

Nixon's refusal to agree to a quick withdrawal has negated such a prospect, I believe. Still the divisions over

Vietnam will fester for years. One runs into voters who protest, "They won't let our men win" or "we've never really fought that war right." But all my interviewing disclosed little sense of any feeling that Vietnam was worth a "showdown" war with either Red China or Russia.

Further evidence of this lack of any real belligerence among the American people was demonstrated in the public's reaction to the Soviet invasion of Czechoslovakia.

When Soviet tanks rumbled into Prague, some observers predicted that a surge of anti-communist feeling would be unloosed in this country, stiffening popular support for fighting on in Vietnam.

This reaction never surfaced, even in the first days when the Soviets were most unyielding in their repressions.

Almost everyone interviewed in those days seemed deliberately to want to avoid linking the Russia-Czechoslovakia problem with ours in Vietnam. Even indignant Soviet critics, avowed anti-communists said, "Let's get out of one fire before we take on anything else."

To sum up: first, I believe the conclusion is justified that the American people were never as deeply divided over Vietnam as the bitter debate in Washington made them appear to be. The depth of our division was exaggerated by the impatience with which both the hawks and doves tried to end the war quickly, even while disagreeing on how to do so.

Second, for this country every limited war we are drawn into becomes a major test of our ability to remain united. In Korea and Vietnam the direct threat to our interests was not great enough to impose unity upon ourselves, and we seem too impatient with war to restrain ourselves for long.

Whether the American people can actually fight a prolonged limited war remains open to question. Usually we have considered war as an interruption of our normal living and have fought to end that interruption as quickly as possible. That same impatience can be seen in how quickly, once a war bogs down into attrition, we throw off the restraints of a limited war and demand "a pull-out or go-all-out" solution

If we are forced to fight another limited war, the lesson of Vietnam and Korea would seem clear: such a war would require an extraordinary effort to keep united. Every internal weakness can be expected to rise to complicate matters. A far more conscious effort to minimize these weaknesses will be needed, with more thorough preparations in advance of any such conflict.

### 3. Moonlighting a War

During World War II, while in Washington as chief aide to Bernard M. Baruch, it seemed to me that the nation had finally learned, after much painful trial and error, that our ability to wage any war was shaped by everything done at home.

An all-out war would require different preparations than a limited war; a booming economy would have to be handled differently than a slack one. Still, there is an essential continuity in moving from peace to war that has to be reconciled, and needed adjustments cannot be ignored without paying a serious price for disruption.

This was forgotten, though, with our involvement in Vietnam.

The bombing of North Vietnam seems to have been begun with little, if any, thinking about what it might lead to, or of how the economy would be affected if escalation deepened the war.

By the summer of 1965 we were clearly in a war. Still, in preparing the 1966 budget the Council of Economic Advisers, then headed by Gardner Ackley, calculated that Vietnam would take only 7.6 per cent of the Gross National Product. So small a war, it was felt, could be managed with ease, as if it were a part-time, moonlighting job.

The excuse has been offered that the estimates of what Vietnam would cost were misjudged. But that is only part of the story. The fact is that the Johnson Administration avoided making the troop and other projections which would have cast doubt on the butter-plus-guns policy the President wanted to pursue.

By law the Office of Emergency Planning was charged with studying the likely impact of war demands on the economy. Its staff could not obtain hard and fast troop estimates from the Pentagon. When the issue was taken up to the White House, the Pentagon was upheld. In the spring of 1966 the Defense Department's chief budget officer told me he had been instructed not to project war costs beyond that June.

Actually, to take a booming economy into a war requires the most sensitive preparations. This point should be underscored in thinking ahead to the future. The higher the rate of economic growth and prosperity, the more vulnerable our society becomes to economic disruptions if faced with the threat of even a small war.

When Hitler began World War II, and again when South Korea was invaded, there was considerable slack in our economy. Mobilization could move more slowly and the costs of delay were not excessive.

With an economy running at full employment, the inflationary impacts of a shift to war would be felt immediately. Even the threat of war could touch off far-reaching repercussions.

In this regard the Nixon Administration's record in trying to check inflation is alarming. Little consideration seems to have been given to the possibility that the Vietnam troubles might worsen and spread to Laos and Cambodia, or the Middle East might explode into war, risks which would have suggested more effective controls more quickly. After a year's reliance on orthodox measures of tightening credit and money, the consumer price index was still mounting 6 per cent a year. In any future war threat, the need would be for more drastic, quicker action—which we might be unprepared to take.

Even more important, in the event of another limited war, whoever was president at that time would face the immensely difficult task of trying to keep the country from splitting into warring factions, as happened over Korea and Vietnam.

If little or nothing had been done *before* the outbreak of war, it might be too late. If the measures taken are to be effective, the problems of unifying the nation must be dealt with in advance of any war threat.

The sound strategy, in fact, would be to make unifying the country a consciously thought-through undertaking in peacetime. We know now where some of our more perilous disunities and weaknesses lie growling, and should be acting to quiet these dissensions in any case. This seems the most important single point in all the discussion about "reordering our priorities."

Priority should be given to overcoming the problems that might weaken us in any possible war crisis, and these are the same problems that divide the nation today.

The economic resources that might be necessary for this effort are as important for our national defense as are the resources being spent on some weapons.

What kind of foreign policy can this country pursue if racial turmoil continues to divide and polarize our cities? Who will do the fighting if our universities remain centers of anti-war resistance which can be plunged into disorder so readily?

If reason and debate hold the key we seem to have lost the ability to use them. If economic strength is the answer to unifying the nation we plainly have not yet learned how to apply it.

# NINE

# THE CONSCIOUS
# STATE

## *1. The Nixon Coalition*

THE PASSAGE FROM Richard Nixon's inaugural address that I
remember best was his request to "lower our voices . . .
until we speak quietly enough so that our words can be
heard. . . ." We had indeed been pounding on our universities, the police, the draft, our political parties as if they
were tables that would make our shouting louder.

Still, these angers and impatiences in the country were
projections of the conflicts on the run which divide us and
which, while not as noisy at this writing, may even be
intensifying. To lower our voices and regain our balance as
a nation, we must somehow find a basis of ending or reconciling these conflicts.

What is needed, I believe, is a *consciously* thought-
through effort to reunite the nation.

The word *consciously* is italicized because I see no other
way to recover our lost capacity for self-government. We
cannot do it by simply booming our economy, reasserting
traditional values, or leaving things alone. Nor are there any
computers that can be programmed to perform the task of
unification for us. Much that we have taken for granted in

the past will have to be thought through and made conscious.

In summing up where we stand, it may be helpful to examine the unusual nature of the party realignment now going on.

The new Nixon coalition is still not fully formed, and its staying power with the voters has to be tested in 1972. But for the sake of analysis let us assume that the Republicans will emerge as the new majority party in the country.

As it is now taking shape, the Nixon coalition is a startling, almost radical departure from the traditional nature of American political parties. Its base of conflict seems too narrow and excluding to be able to unify this divided nation.

The potential unifying reach of any coalition will be found in its ability to attract and hold clashing political elements. Why this is so is explained in what has come to be known as the Sun-Moon theory of political parties which was first advanced in my book *The Future of American Politics*.

Only rarely have we had two parties of equally competing strength. Usually there has been one dominant majority party (the Sun), which served as the arena in which the issues of the period were fought out, and a minority party (the Moon), whose radiance reflected the frictions and conflicts going on in the majority Sun.

The fact that the majority coalition is constantly threatened with being torn apart generates powerful incentives on the coalition leaders to search for policies and candidates that will hold these clashing political elements together. This necessity for compromise and reconciliation has placed a high premium on middle-of-the-road politics. Enlarging the voting elements drawn into the majority coalition widens its potential as a unifying force.

A narrow-based coalition can win elections and hold

power, but its ability to conciliate conflict would be limited, and it might even intensify the divisions in the country.

How crucial this distinction is can be seen by the contrasting framework in which racial conflict would be dealt with in the new Nixon coalition as against that of the Roosevelt coalition.

Under the New Deal, white southerners and Negroes were brought together in the same party for the first time. For both, the racial issue was a life-and-death political struggle, which the Democratic leaders had to try to reconcile or the party could break apart.

In turning Republican, the white southerners move into a coalition in which they are almost the only element with a mortal stake in racial conflict. "Liberal" Republicans who are sensitive to the problems of the northern cities are troubled, but most of the other elements in the Nixon coalition at least for a time can ignore or be indifferent to the issue—rural Republicans who never see a Negro except on TV; suburbanites who live as far away from ghetto slums as they can manage; the businessmen who, unlike white workers, do not compete with blacks for jobs and housing.

This detachment could prove a good thing if it enables the Republicans to develop sensible policies which the more emotionally disturbed Democrats are not able to put together.

But a lack of involvement can also lead to the shrug-off attitude of "let the southerners do their own thing." This, of course, would please many white southerners who want to belong to a party that controls the government in Washington and yet leaves them alone.

Until Nixon has his majority on the Supreme Court, the full effects of his racial policies will not be felt. Public opinion or the outcome of the 1970 elections could also bring shifts in policy.* However, the makeup of the Nixon coalition

---

* If Nixon has to deal with a somewhat critical Senate we will get a stronger Court and a more balanced racial policy.

thus far is such that it could turn its back and accept any degree of segregation.

Political bargaining is always total bargaining, and the racial approach of the new Nixon coalition will become interlocked with its policies on economics and war and peace.

In this regard the "piece of the action" which reveals a good deal about the Nixon coalition was the 1969 Senate approval of the ABM missiles. The ABM battle showed first of all an "iron" determination on Nixon's part to hold to a high defense and missile capacity despite the most intense public pressures to reduce military spending in favor of urgent domestic needs.

The Senate vote also disclosed fairly clearly where Nixon would find the readiest congressional support for his defense and foreign policy. Of fifty Senators who voted for the ABM, eighteen came from the South, (fourteen of them nominal Democrats) while another ten were from the southwest and mountain states of Arizona, Colorado, Wyoming, Utah, Idaho, Nevada, and New Mexico. These two areas, in fact, were the only regions in the country where a majority of the Senators voted for ABM.

The "sun belt" from Florida to Southern California and the mountain states have been pointed to as two regions of new and growing Republican strength. They also happen to rely heavily on military and missile installations.

Plenty of sunshine and economic prosperity, some might think, would make for a relaxed, benevolent politics. Actually the economic conditions in these two regions stimulate a drive for acquisitive gains and even a pulling back to *laissez faire* economics.

Much of the South, in emerging from past poverty, as with the younger Wallace supporters, is spurred by a hunger for economic advance, and by anti-tax, anti-government, and anti-welfare feelings. Also, although the South now has a more balanced economy than ever before, a good deal of its profit-making still rests on low-paid labor.

The acquisitive drive also flourishes in areas where fortunes can be made from natural resources such as oil and gas, or through real estate and other enterprises that boom with a rapidly growing population. In such regions the prevailing attitude becomes "We don't need the government." People feel, "I could keep more of my profits if taxes weren't so high" or "if the government didn't spend so much."

Government spending on defense, space, and aircraft, which benefits these regions greatly, is defended as "patriotic" enterprise which is different from welfare.

Among these western and southwestern newcomers to the Republican party, one also finds a "westward ho" feeling and dreams of building up a thriving economic empire in Asia across the Pacific.

One western Republican leader remarked to me, "The Republicans should develop a Pacific policy. That's where the future lies. That's where the people are."

Asked about financial aid to the northern cities, he replied, "I don't see how the Republicans can get any real support in the cities. You can't spend money there and make any difference. That money would be wasted. If you tore down all the slums and put people into high-rise apartments, in six weeks they would be turned into slums."

One of the more ironic contradictions of our time may be developing: that some Republicans may fight to deny aid to our northern cities even while being prepared to take up the white man's burden in Asia.

The newcomer voting elements in the South and West who are being drawn into the Nixon coalition, in short, represent a rising power that is bursting with oil and vinegar. To the extent that their influence makes itself felt, the Nixon coalition would tend to become a fairly permissive coalition—as permissive perhaps towards business and race relations, as university professors have been towards their students.

From where in the Nixon coalition would the liberalizing and restraining influences come? Here again the ABM vote is revealing. Of the fourteen Republican senators who went against ABM, seven come from the eastern states, while three others are especially sensitive to the racial problems of the northern cities.

That the economic views of the South and Southwest should differ so markedly from the East and urban Midwest, is hardly surprising. These latter regions hold many of our older industries; also strong labor unions; they rely more heavily on the use of capital and have problems finding enough unskilled jobs for the available labor; incomes are higher and so are welfare payments. In foreign policy they have looked across the Atlantic, not the Pacific. Perhaps most important currently, here are the cities into which Negroes from the rural South moved and which now groan and writhe under impossible burdens of welfare and other social costs. In the eastern states Republican voting strength has been declining for years.

Can the Nixon coalition temper this conflict between Republicans in the urban North, and the South and the Southwest? On the plus side, Nixon's family-assistance plan would lift welfare payments in the South. Senator Goldwater no longer wants the eastern states cut off from the mainland and allowed to drift out to sea as he suggested in 1964. But younger conservatives like Kevin Phillips in *The Emerging Republican Majority* continue to picture "Yankee liberalism" and "The eastern establishment" as the villains of the new GOP coalition.

The changes in the squeeze of power that have developed within the Republican Party can be seen in Table 11 which gives the proportion of Republican-held seats in Congress by sections of the country from 1936 through 1968.

Over this thirty-two year period, two dramatic shifts are evident—the greatly lessened Republican dependence on the eastern states and the abrupt GOP upsurge in the South.

TABLE 11

*Proportion of Total Republican Seats in House of Representatives Held by Each Region* [a]
*(Selected years, 1936–1968)*

|  | 1936 | 1946 | 1952 | 1958 | 1962 | 1964 | 1966 | 1968 |
|---|---|---|---|---|---|---|---|---|
| East | 52% | 37% | 34% | 37% | 30% | 27% | 23% | 23% |
| South | 2 | 1 | 3 | 5 | 6 | 12 | 13 | 14 |
| Midwest | 38 | 41 | 41 | 39 | 43 | 41 | 42 | 41 |
| Pacific | 6 | 9 | 13 | 14 | 12 | 12 | 11 | 11 |
| Border | 2 | 8 | 5 | 3 | 4 | 5 | 6 | 6 |
| Mountain & Southwest | 0 | 4 | 4 | 3 | 4 | 3 | 5 | 6 |
| TOTAL % [b] | 100% | 100% | 100% | 100% | 100% | 100% | 100% | 100% |
| TOTAL NO. REPUBLICAN SEATS | 89 | 246 | 221 | 153 | 178 | 140 | 187 | 191 |

[a] To insure comparability, seats in Hawaii and Alaska are *not* included. The states in each region are: *East*—N.Y., N.J., Pa., Me., N.H., Vt., R.I., Mass., Conn.; *South*—Ala., Ark., Fla., Ga., La., Miss., N.C., S.C., Tenn., Tex., Va.; *Midwest*—Ohio, Ill., Ind., Mich., Iowa, Minn., Wisc., N.D., Neb., Kan.; *Pacific*—Call., Ore., Wash.; *Border*—Del., Ky., Md., Mo., Okla., W. Va.; *Mountain and Southwest*—Colo., Nev., Wyo., Mont., Id., Utah, Ariz., N.M.

[b] Figures for each region have been rounded to the nearest whole per cent, so totals may vary from 99 to 101 per cent.

In 1968 only 23 per cent of all the congressional seats held by the Republicans were in the East. Back in 1936, the eastern states provided more than half of the total GOP representation in Congress. This was the year of Franklin Roosevelt's greatest triumph, which plummeted Republican representation in Congress to its lowest point in history; but the GOP held up best in the East.

Some of this change since 1936 reflects the loss of fourteen Congressional seats because of population decline in the East. But the Democrats in 1968 held 60 per cent of the eastern seats, reflecting a long-term trend of realignment which has been making the East more Democratic.

No real southern defection developed until after Franklin Roosevelt's death. While isolationist voters in the North and Midwest turned against Roosevelt in 1940, the South, which has always supported a strong military policy, stood firm. Before 1952, the South sent only two Republican congressmen to Washington, both from eastern Tennessee, which had refused to secede during the Civil War. Eisenhower's 1952 landslide increased the GOP's southern strength to six seats; but the really dramatic surge came with Goldwater's candidacy in 1964. By 1968, the twenty-six congressmen from the South accounted for 14 per cent of all Republican seats in Congress, a higher percentage than the West Coast states with their population jump.

Since 1962, in fact, the Democrats have held more than a majority of all the California seats. The pro-Republican trend in California is not overwhelming.

Through this whole period the Midwest held roughly the same proportion of seats; the Mountain and Southwest states have registered a gain in influence.

That the East and South should have been realigning in conflicting directions for so many years furnishes some intriguing insights into the rhythms of conflict that characterize coalition politics. My study of these changes suggests an elaboration of my Sun-Moon theory of political parties in three respects: why the conflict which ultimately breaks apart a majority coalition is present at the very inception of the coalition; how conflict is transferred from one coalition to another; why the forces which overwhelm a coalition are usually powerful social changes which develop for years until they become unmanageable.

Inside each coalition, it would seem, are old-timer and newcomer voting elements. The old-timers are those born into a party by way of parental loyalty and family tradition; the newcomers are the angry, disturbing spear-carriers of realignment. The coming together of these two elements, each reflecting a different political era, generates antagonisms and strains inside the majority coalition which are never outgrown.

Once the majority coalition is established, the strongest defections tend to come from those old-timer elements who were unsympathetic to the realignment that formed the majority coalition. Thus the pre-New Deal Democratic Party consisted largely of white Protestant workers and farmers in the South and Catholics in the North. Since the New Deal began as a worker coalition, business-minded Catholics and business-minded southerners would be expected to break first, even on small political provocation; the workers in the South, and even more so in the North, would be slower to defect and might even prefer a third party to turning Republican.

When the dissident old-timers switch parties, they become the newcomer elements in the new majority coalition, and come into conflict with those old-timer elements which have been loyal to the party by tradition. In the new Nixon coalition the zealots in battling liberalism are the defecting Democratic elements like the better-income Irish Catholics in New York's Conservative Party and the more conservative southerners. Some old-timer Republican elements, on the other hand, have learned to live with liberalism and may even like it.

And so, in a fascinating rhythm of history, one finds that the voting elements which were old-time Democrats and old-time Republicans when the New Deal coalition was formed would become the principal antagonists in any Republican coalition that replaced the Democrats as the majority party.

The breakup of a majority coalition is sometimes attributed to accidents of personalities, such as the feud between Lyndon Johnson and Robert Kennedy, or to some critical event, as the Vietnam war. But the forces which upset the equilibrium of conflict within a coalition must be ones which require at least a generation to grow up. With the New Deal, the strongest single breakup force would be the changed relationship of white southerners and Negroes, largely the result of the economic revolution which transformed southern agriculture. In the process the northward migration of blacks was swelled to proportions that upset the big-city voting balance; while the South, having shifted the social costs of a burdensome Negro population onto the North, was able to assert a new economic and political independence.

The influence of two other forces should also be noted: 1) the build-up of new economic power among elements largely outside of the coalition through war technology in the Southwest and the strengthened bargaining power of business, reflecting primarily its job-creating powers at a time when record numbers of youth were coming of working age; 2) the groping for new political identifications of this new generation.

If this elaboration of my Sun-Moon theory proves valid, it follows that the areas of vulnerability in the Nixon coalition could spread far beyond the eastern states. *Any state or locality where Republican loyalty rests primarily on tradition* may be realigned to swing Democratic, if hurt by the impact of current issues.

If the emotions stirred by racial conflict prove sufficiently strong, a "liberal" Republican bolt might reshuffle both parties in 1972. The Nixon coalition would either die abortive, or it could emerge with a clear majority. Generally, though, the adhesive power of a new coalition is strongest at the outset when even the zealots curb their impulses so as not to divide the party just when it finally seems triumphant.

Once a president is re-elected, the struggle for succession

and control of the party breaks out, and all the latent conflicts choose sides to do battle with each other. Under Eisenhower, the war for GOP succession came into the open in 1958, the year the John Birch Society was formed and right-to-work laws were pressed in such key states as California and Ohio. This effort to turn the Republican Party to the right was washed out by the economic recession of 1958 which swung the voters back to the Democrats.

This new Republican coalition is not fully formed, of course, and if Nixon gains new strength its unifying potential would be widened. Still, certain striking differences with the New Deal coalition would be likely to remain.

The thrust of the Roosevelt coalition was unifying and nationalizing in nature, supported by direct governmental benefits to many in the nation. The Nixon coalition seems organized almost as a sectional alliance. Sectionalism, like states' rights, is usually less a cause in itself than an effort to restructure *the way* in which critical conflicts are fought. The Nixon Republicans are not seeking *national* solutions to the conflicts that divide the nation, but are trying to ignore some of these conflicts and shunt others off on sectional sidings away from Washington. In the past sectionalism has also enabled varied business interests to take advantage of state and local economic differences.

But this new sectionalism of the Nixon coalition also raises some puzzling and quite disturbing questions. The coalition seems organized for a spreading political conquest. Nixon's 1968 strategy was designed to elect him, if need be, without the support of more than one or two big-city states. After his thin victory this strategy was not abandoned but was redirected to gaining control of all three branches of the government with even the slimmest of presidential margins.

The House of Representatives is already controlled by an alliance of southerners and northern Republicans. The 1970 battle for the Senate sought less Republican control of the chamber than defeat of enough opponents of ABM and of Haynsworth's confirmation so Nixon could be sure of having his Supreme Court appointments confirmed. If this were won, a favorable Court would follow. All three branches of the government could be won without the presidential backing of New York, Pennsylvania, Michigan, plus all of New England. *

The excluding base of this new Nixon coalition bears some marked resemblances to the Republican Party that emerged right after the Civil War. Then the radical Republicans exercised a virtual one-party monopoly, while the South remained a conquered province, quarantined from political activity. For the Nixon Republicans, the by-passed provinces are the big northern cities defeated by the loss of industry, the suburban exodus of better-income whites, and by the need to provide an array of governmental services to so many blacks on a shrinking tax base.

The aim of the radical Republicans was to rule and get on with the job of spanning the continent. Nixon and his people have also been determined to rule. Some of them mutter over their memos about the dangers of a possible revolution; they have been committing the nation as rapidly as they can to the policies they want to pursue, perhaps too rapidly.

The decision to be able to rule the country was certainly the only one any president could take. The anti-war demonstrators seemed eager to topple Nixon as they had Lyndon Johnson; sufficient uncertainties lay ahead for him to feel that he needed to establish support for his policies quickly. In doing so, though, he invited being swept along by the South which was prepared to back him fully and immediately, while other voting elements were holding back to see how his war and economic policies would work out.

* With sixteen senators, the eight Mountain-Southwestern states have a smaller population (8 million plus) than any one big-city state.

To this was added another harsh political fact of life. To gain a clear majority Nixon had to break apart the unifying structure of the New Deal. This meant dividing more deeply not only the Democrats but the whole country.

Where does a coalition of this nature leave the Democrats?

Perhaps the main asset of the Democratic Party is the simple fact that it exists. After Goldwater's defeat the Republican Party seemed wrecked and was almost up for bids as salvage. Yet four years later it was the Democrats who seemed all Humpty Dumptyed with no one able even to pay off the debt on the pieces and try to put them together again.

With party loyalties so lightly held, a failure in performance by the Republican president-manager would return the Democrats to the White House.

Even were this to happen, there does not seem much chance of re-establishing the New Deal coalition in its old form. The inability to resolve the conflicts dividing the nation is producing a new alignment of two incomplete, narrow-based coalitions, polarized against each other. The hopeful aspect is that both parties must still compete for the rest of the national electorate. In doing so, each party could be forced to tame its own strongest supporters. Only the mainstays of a party can prevent it from developing the policies required to gain a full and decisive majority. Inside each coalition its strengths can prove its chief vulnerability.

With the Democrats, their major vulnerability is near-unanimous Negro support. The militancy of the blacks, even though strengthened by numbers and concentration inside our spreading Black Cities, has to be reconciled with the interests of white Democrats.

A Democrat returned to the presidency would make more money available for the cities, but money is no assurance of conciliation. The torturing fact facing the Demo-

crats is that there is no quick way of stabilizing the dis-
organized conditions under which so many Negroes live; nor
of developing quickly a pattern of neighborhood life through
which whites and blacks can dwell in racial peace. A vocal
minority of black militants may refuse to refrain from violence even while Negro progress continues.

The Republicans, in pushing so strongly for the South,
are becoming as racially vulnerable as the Democrats. It
would be intriguing to know how President Nixon and Attorney General Mitchell reacted when they learned that two
school buses with Negro children had been overturned by
angry whites in semi-rural Lamar, South Carolina. Did the
President grasp the significance of that incident?

It meant that *what white southerners do* will determine
the ultimate verdict of the American people on Nixon's
school policies. All of the President's political skills, the legal
talents of Mitchell and Chief Justice Burger, the pugnacious
oratory of Agnew will be unavailing if in the years to come
white southerners repress the Negroes, fail to lift their educational opportunities, and more blacks migrate to the North
and West. The white South can wreck the Nixon coalition
if it makes racial peace impossible in the country as a whole.

Suburbia, currently the source of the heaviest Republican
pluralities, can also prove racially vulnerable. In his un-
collected but freely distributed White House memoranda,
Daniel Moynihan contends that the Negro problem is one
of social class rather than race. The Democrats used to
argue it was a problem of poverty not race. Both poverty
and social class are parts of a conflict that *is* racial; the main
carriers of this conflict today, as Cleveland and other polarized cities can testify, are the population pressures of blacks
on the move.

Continued prosperity will enable increasing numbers of
blacks to move into the suburbs, which will find themselves
grappling with many of the same problems that frustrate
the cities. If "benign neglect" by the Republicans in power

fails to bring *racial peace,* suburban voters will divide, some more intensely anti-Negro, but others demanding more effective urban action than the Nixon Administration has taken. Over the years most white voters in the North, to repeat a point made earlier, will shift toward what promises racial peace.

At some point in the future a major Republican bid for the Negro vote is certain. Nixon, of course, has repeatedly invited blacks into his coalition, but thus far Negro leaders have felt their standing would be little better than being able to send in a note to the Boss.

Still, some specific Nixon-made benefits will reach the blacks when the family assistance plan goes into effect. Republicans will also help Negroes get jobs, particularly where that brings them into conflict with the labor unions.

Some inner-city business leaders will want to use the Negro to lend strength to their requests for federal aid to the cities. Other employers may try to play blacks off against white workers to divide the unions. This was the practice before the New Deal. It could return.

Another gleaming hope and vulnerability for the Democrats is the swelling numbers of younger voters. They were the wave of the future dreamed of by Robert Kennedy and his partisans; 14 million not old enough to vote in 1968, but who will be in 1972; another 15 million new voters by 1976. Giving eighteen-year-olds the vote would add nearly 12 million more whenever the age change is made.

Two cautions should be noted. Census estimates show that only about half of the eligible young actually vote; also since they divide party-wise primarily by careers, many would be Republican-inclined. Still, this new generation does share a particularly strong aversion to war, especially in Asia.

To capitalize on this sentiment, though, the Democrats would have to be able to square the circle of being militantly against war and still stand for a constructive foreign policy which meets the real security needs of the country. Nixon's vision of an American-dominated Pacific community can be expected to increase the currently small U.S. investments in Asia, and will carry a continuing risk of becoming involved militarily, particularly in small wars. Still, violent student demonstrations against participating in the development of Asian countries could backfire.

Much may depend on how the war issue becomes visible. Unkempt beards and disorderly dress are part of the image of "new left" disruptions in the minds of many voters, an image which has become a considerable Republican asset. Of course, if this younger generation were to shave their beards, it would be an omen of a Democratic landslide.

The proposal for a volunteer army of up to 3 million men places another tricky temptation before young voters and the Democrats. Naturally the idea will be attractive to young people. If adopted, though, whoever is president would have a sizable force in being, which might make him somewhat readier to intervene abroad militarily than if intervention had to be supported quite quickly by higher draft calls.

A third critical vulnerability and asset, shared by both parties, is the management of the tremendous productive power our economy can generate. It is difficult to restrain this power without trouble; it will prove as difficult to let it run free without trouble.

Thus far neither the Democratic nor Republican economists have been able to achieve a satisfactory economic or political balance between unemployment and inflation. Nor are the economists of either party likely to succeed in stabilizing our society until they widen their objectives beyond high employment and more production.

It may be Nixon's good political fortune that the pollution issue was raised so early in his administration since it points to one neglected factor in the management of our society—how social costs are to be shared and whether they cannot be prevented or minimized before serious social damage is done.

One crucial testing the Nixon Republicans face is their ability to do what President Johnson never did, curb the mounting costs of the military-industrial complex which distort and upset the whole economy. Presumably a business-oriented coalition can command the skills needed to establish effective cost control. Whether it has the will to discipline its own political supporters remains to be demonstrated.

The immediate years ahead, in short, may be the most critical political years this nation has faced since the Civil War period. The Nixon Republicans will be driving hard for power, and it may take several elections to turn the party competition toward restraint. The decisive influence may be the millions of free-floating voters who have been shifting between the parties with ease. If they can force both parties toward restraint, then the revolt of the voters described earlier would be coming at precisely the right historical moment to show our political leaders the way to national unity.

But there is also the possibility that presidential voting may be indecisive, as it was in 1968, and that whoever is in the White House will use the powers of the presidency in such a way as to commit this country deeply and irrevocably to conditions which may have to be accepted because they cannot be changed.

On this score much of the old stability in American politics is gone. Abrupt changes in government through a single election are possible. Franklin Roosevelt, after his landslide sweep of every state but Maine and Vermont, was still subject to strong limits on his power. The Supreme Court was a check, though its make-up changed. Two lasting restraints were the balance inside the Democratic Party with the southerners so much more conservative, and the separation of political and economic control since the economy was run by businessmen, mainly Republican.

Both of these old limits on power are being swept aside. Nixon heads a business-oriented party at a time when a managed economy, the creation of the Democrats, has all but erased the line separating the economy and government. With the South split off, the liberal Democrats might find all three branches of government under Republican control, along with the seats of private economic power.\*

That it is even possible to concentrate so much power so quickly in a president elected with only 43.7 per cent of the vote is startling. We've always assumed that the American government is indestructible and that no man could move too far without encountering effective resistance. But with so much unreconciled conflict in the country, the doctrine of limited powers is likely to be pushed aside. If the Nixon coalition gains control of all three branches of government, there is no telling now where a line of effective resistance could be drawn.

### 2. The Future Before It Happens

When the tombstone on the Great Society is finally carved, the appropriate epitaph might read:

"Here lies political power which sought to change so much so quickly, but was toppled because of the changes it overlooked."

One Johnson oversight was the birth statistics that foretold that starting with 1965, the year of the Vietnam escalation, nearly 4 million young men and women would reach their eighteenth birthday each year.

A second blind spot was that despite all that he and his aides tried to do to speed the Negro advance, they did not understand what was happening inside our cities. This failure can be seen in the long list of new programs that were enacted in 1965 when Congress was ready to approve any

\* How much of the vitality of the separation of powers has reflected the historical accident of the South being Democratic we do not know.

spending request Johnson made. The riots in Watts were to explode within the year and make clear that new urban approaches were needed but this was not anticipated in the Great Society legislation.

James Sundquist of Brookings has explained why. In his excellent study *Politics and Policy*, he points out that the programs which were sent up to Congress were primarily ideas which varied Democrats had developed for many years previously and were on hand when the Johnson landslide opened the spending floodgates.

Perhaps it is not so surprising that the newest currents of change were not sensed until they exploded. People who want to change things themselves are often so intent in their belief that they can remold the future that they can be insensitive to changes that run against their desires.

As a nation, we need, a continuing watch of the processes of change, so that we can build a basis of conscious and confident judgment on how change should be dealt with, when or what should be slowed, when or what should be quickened.

Rapid change does more than move the same things along faster; often it gives a problem an entirely new quality, exposing us to vulnerabilities for which we are unprepared. This point was made rather well in a *Wall Street Journal* editorial on the predicament of a pilot and crew when confronted by a man hijacking an airplane. Aloft, the pilot and passengers are helpless in their vulnerability. If the hijacker were on some earthbound form of transportation he would not pose much of a threat.

In similar fashion, once a nation or an institution gets pushed off balance, the swift pace of additional change can bring on a truly revolutionary crisis. Stability can be lost in a political instant. The momentum of past neglects is like a tailwind pushing us faster than we would like to go. A wrong decision can be devastating in its consequences, and yet a time-shortened world requires quicker decisions.

One way of easing that dilemma is to set about systematically to anticipate change and act on it before it becomes unmanageable.

As a specific suggestion, an Early Warning Service on emerging change should be established. In addition to alerting the nation to serious dislocations that threaten, the Service should study change in its broadest frame—to try really to anticipate the future before it happens.

Many agencies monitor change in their own fields quite well. This Early Warning Service would study the interaction of changes in varied fields as they move through society, how they relate to one another, new vulnerabilities being created, whether unifying institutions are available to overcome them.

Such a Service could be set up in the White House or Congress, or privately. In any case it should report regularly to the people.

If such a group had been in existence, I would like to think it would have spotted the early rises in the welfare rolls and acted before their numbers swelled so heavily.

Also when it was first realized that an enormous nuclear-missile–space complex was being created, I hope this group would have appreciated that something entirely new to our national experience was building up, and would have begun reporting its implications.

If that had been done, we might know by now what adjustments are needed in our system of checks and balances to fit a managed society.

In some cases the evidence is clear that institutions and habits which helped preserve our national balance in the past now aggravate our troubles.

For example, one vital need that emerges from our study is to be able to end some of the conflicts that divide us. But bringing conflicts to a head is particularly difficult for this country. Our habit has been to let them wear themselves out.

Through our history, we have used the abundance of land and mobility, space, and wealth to escape unpleasant decisions by moving on, usually westward.

Today space and mobility remain the means by which the Supreme Court's desegregation decision is being nullified. The Court allowed ample time for adjustment. But the time was not used to test varied ways of complying with the law. The multiplicity of governments we encourage was employed to aggravate the conflict by fighting the Court through state and local governments.

Eisenhower, Kennedy, Johnson, and now Nixon, four presidents have faced the problem of enforcing the Court's decision. And the resisters seem now to be waiting to outlive the present justices, hoping that a changed Court will yield to their opposition.

In that time the bitter flour-sack struggle of blacks and whites in the old rural South got packed into suitcases and was taken to the cities, both North and South. Currently it is being transported in ranch-wagons into the suburbs—and still without any resolution.

Eleven years of spreading racial conflict, from 1954 to 1965, and Johnson plunged into war; he apparently had no appreciation that there was a limit to the amount of un-reconciled conflict that even this country could stand.

Once again we face the possibility that the separation of powers could prove a tragic trap. In this case it threatens a constitutional crisis with a chain-reaction effect.

For years to come the nomination of each new justice to the Supreme Court will be regarded as aiding one side or the other in the raging racial conflict. To change or preserve the balance in the Court could determine who will be elected president. The legitimacy of the Court itself may remain gerrymandered until we reach racial conciliation.

In the 1880's a "solution" could be imposed which Negroes had to accept. Living in the isolated, rural South they could be forgotten. But the black migration out of the South has created a new vulnerability in all of our urban areas.

There are also grave doubts whether we can continue to deal with population shifts as we have in the past. Statistics on population changes are readily available. Many businesses, in fact, use these figures in planning plant expansion and investment, and in projecting patterns of consumer demand.

But it has been no one's business to do a comparable job for society as a whole.

We have seen that some of the greatest disruptions arose from the entry problems created by the abrupt emergence of large numbers of young blacks and college students. Those population figures could have been translated quite readily into a new draft law.

Similarly, it has long been known that arrests are highest among youths between eighteen and twenty-five. Yet little was done to prepare for the rise in crime that would come with the increase of youngsters in this age group.

Population mobility is another carrier of change that can stand constant analysis. It was fitting even if ironic that Nixon chose his March 1970 statement on desegregation policy to declare that "economic, educational, social mobility . . . are essential elements of the open society." Residential mobility as we have noted has been restructuring our racial crisis into a territorial struggle. The President's words invite the question—how can mobility be kept from disrupting our society?

Of the 10,700,000 Negroes estimated to be living outside of the South, roughly 3 million represent the numbers added since 1950 as a result of the mechanization of southern agriculture. They are either Negroes who migrated themselves or children born to these migrants. Much of our urban agony reflects the fact that school integration and opportunity for southern Negroes did not precede but actually lagged behind the mechanical cotton picker.

In 1954 when the school desegregation decision was announced only 22 per cent of the cotton crop was being harvested by pickers; in Mississippi only 11 per cent. Three years later mechanization had spread to a third of the cotton crop, but only a tenth of 1 per cent of the black children in the South were going to schools with whites, and none in Mississippi. In 1964, when the first 57 blacks were mixed with whites in Mississippi schools, mechanization covered 68 per cent of the state's crop.

By 1968, machines were picking virtually all of the cotton crop. The proportion of black children in school with whites was 20 per cent in the South; only 7 per cent in Mississippi.

TABLE 12

| YEAR | % COTTON MECHANIZED ALL SOUTH | MISSISSIPPI | % BLACK CHILDREN IN MIXED SCHOOLS ALL SOUTH | MISSISSIPPI |
|---|---|---|---|---|
| 1954 | 22 | 11 | 0 | 0 |
| 1957 | 32 | 17 | .15 | 0 |
| 1963 | 70 | 58 | .45 | 0 |
| 1964 | 78 | 68 | 2.25 | 0 * |
| 1965 | 85 | 76 | 6.1 | .6 |
| 1968 | 96 | 93 | 20.0 | 7.1 |

* Less than .5 per cent, or 57 Negro children.

Our economic system has been bitterly criticized because of the living conditions in Negro residential areas in the North. We ought to be specific about our indictment. The fact that our economic system did absorb successfully so many blacks from the rural South, with no education, no training, no familiarity with city life, is no small achievement.

Even with inevitable racial tensions, how much more impressive would the record have been if southern Negroes had received some education and training before they were pushed off the land? During these same years, agriculture was mechanized in Iowa, but there were no troubles in the cities into which the Iowans who left the land moved. They had the necessary education to fit readily into new conditions.

But the mechanization of agriculture in the South has almost torn the country apart because we didn't consciously face up to what we really knew, that the South's yesterday would become the North's tomorrow.

Negro displacement from the rural South still continues at a rate of roughly 100,000 a year, nearly half of it from the cotton belt of Mississippi, Alabama, Arkansas, and Louisiana—and then there is the prospect of a tobacco harvester which could displace another 500,000. Can we remain one nation in which all people are able to move about freely unless there is school integration or its aims are realized in some other way?

Finally, a continuing study of change is indispensible in a highly managed society, if only as a check against what the computers leave out and the tendency to move towards "automated" decisions, writing into law that certain actions will be taken as soon as unemployment reaches 4.5 per cent or some other figure.

But the relationships which may have justified one statistical formula will no longer mean the same thing several years later. In Detroit, for example, when auto workers are laid off they draw almost their full pay. Should we rush to inflate the economy because they raise the unemployment rate?

Studies of change should focus on its impact on people. A managed society seems to pressure constantly for techniques of control that can be broadly applied relatively quickly, ignoring the wiggles below. But the wiggles below are the people.

## 3. Real Priority Thinking

The budget for $200 billion submitted to Congress in January 1970 was the first one prepared from start to finish by Nixon and his aides. In their briefings of newsmen the budgeteers pointed with special pride to a "five-year look ahead", of how much in taxes would be collected each year and how little would be left even if no new programs were begun beyond those already contemplated. The "look ahead" was developed, it was explained, to contribute to more informed discussion on "reordering our priorities."

Drawing up budget estimates for five years in advance is of some small value, but it makes no real contribution to our understanding priorities. As the term has come to be used, it has been robbed of its essential meaning. It lacks both a sense of urgency and any clear principles that can be used to determine why one use of tax money is favored over another.

For those principles we would do well to go back to our wartime experience with "priorities," when the term first came into general use.

Probably no American gave more thought to the meaning of "priorities" than Baruch, who first applied the concept in World War I as chairman of the War Industries Board and again in World War II as an adviser to the president and varied agencies when I worked with him. Some of the principles he liked to reiterate would enable us to use priorities far more effectively today:

(1) Everything the military wants is not of the same order of urgency; some civilian needs will contribute more to our security than some military needs.

(2) Since time is of the essence in priorities, what is postponable should be rated lower than what cannot be postponed.

(3) When faced with competing demands, one should not declare that anything is simply not essential; always it is that some things are more essential than others.

If we pause to think over those principles, it becomes evident that "priorities" lose their essential meaning if considered primarily in terms of money alone. A special sensitivity to time needs to be added, not merely as a spur of urgency but as a means of organizing what is to be done in specific and conscious detail.

Wartime controls would not be needed; applying these three principles would enable us to compare the relative urgency of our more critical domestic problems with defense and other needs—which are least costly for the nation to postpone. We certainly should be able to maintain a "sufficiency" in defense and still meet the *truly urgent* domestic needs.

For example, we have watched with horror the spreading social disintegration in our cities, from slums, through more parts of the cities, out into the suburbs; also down the age ladder, from youths in college to those in high school, and even to elementary school children.

Halting this social breakdown would contribute more to our national security than going ahead with an improved tank or some other weapon that can be deferred for a few years.

Accordingly, we might take several particularly critical aspects of social breakdown—like the traffic in drugs, crime, poor reading skills—and organize a thoroughly thought-through attack on them.

This would not be done by merely allocating "X" dollars to the effort. But, drawing again on our wartime priorities experience, each program should call for:

*specific performance goals, just what is to be done by a specified time;*

*a detailed analysis of the resources of manpower, ma-*

*terials, facilities—whatever is needed—to meet the goals
on time;*

*synchronization of what is undertaken with related ef-
forts to avoid waste.*

If all related efforts are reduced to time schedules,
priorities can be employed to move everything along as part
of one unified operation. That, of course, was how wartime
priorities were used; guns and ammunition, planes and
bombs, ships and troops—all were synchronized to be where
they were needed on D Day.

This time-priority approach should not be confused with
the "crash" programs that have been pressed at varied
times in the past. The essence of time-priority thinking is
to think through what needs to be done to meet a set goal.
At the end of the effort the evaluation is there in whether
the goal was met or failed and why.

With social problems, what will work is not always
known with certainty. In such situations the best available
knowledge should be applied, performance goals set and
tested in action.

This same active sense of priorities should guide other
economic policies. "Cooling the economy" to curb inflation
does not require slowing production where serious shortages
exist. Yet this happened with housing, where an already
severe shortage was made worse by higher interest rates
which shut off mortgage money. Investment funds for more
housing could have been assured while other uses of bank
credit were held down. Andrew F. Brimmer, a governor of
the Federal Reserve Board, has proposed, for example, that
loans for housing be exempted from credit curbs; also that
special preference be given to local and state governments,
which also are vulnerable to inflation.

The expansion of facilities for training doctors was also
slowed in some cases by credit curbs, despite the fact that
medical and hospital costs are rising so rapidly. Similarly

with a growing population, gas, electric, and telephone util-
ities must expand their capacity. Raising to 9 per cent the
interest they must pay for the money they borrow means
higher utility rates in the future. In the name of halting inflation, more inflation is built permanently into the price
level.

The argument will be raised that there should be a "minimum of interference with normal business decisions and the
economic force of the marketplace." The debate on that point
should be joined clearly. Replacing the marketplace is not
at issue. The essential question is can the workings of the
market economy remedy the really serious deficiencies and
weaknesses in our society in a reasonable period of time?
Where the market clearly falls short, not to use the priority
power is mismanaging the economy, particularly when we
are at war. Both Korea and Vietnam showed that in any
limited war the sources of disunity in the country have to
be eased. This lesson has to be incorporated in the managing of our economy if we are to strengthen support for our
foreign policy and be able to meet the threat of another
limited war in the future.

During World War II the use of priorities operated as a
great unifying influence. Today the battle to "reorder our
priorities" has become a powerful divisive force which
weakens public support for our foreign policy and has produced an almost ideological cleavage between advocates of
defense and social needs.

One cannot expect to recapture completely the sense of
wartime unity but at least three actions might be taken.

(1) Setting basic priority policies and major allocations
should be made by a nonpartisan group directly responsible
to the President and Congress.

Priority decisions became part of the budget-making
process simply because, like Topsy, things just grew up that
way. As tax collections rise with the growth of the economy,

stupendous sums are drawn into Washington, $200 billion a year and still growing, which then must be redistributed around the country.

These sums are entirely too large to be distributed by political partisans. Priorities and allocations should be set and administered in an atmosphere similar to that which prevailed in wartime, with basic principles known to all and clearly in the national interest; no special advantages to anyone.

(2) Constructive use should be made of the frictions that unavoidably accompany priority decisions.

During the war all the varied requests for, say, steel were reviewed by representatives of agencies which needed steel themselves. The theory, which worked out quite well, was that no one would be more vigilant against wasteful or needless uses of steel than men who wanted that steel badly for their programs. Whoever was turned down also had the satisfaction of having made his case and of knowing why other programs were deemed more important.

An equivalent arrangement for the major claimant areas would be valuable in handling peacetime priorities. Both government and civilian groups should face the discipline of justifying their requirements before vigilant critics. The end result would be greater public confidence and understanding of the whole priority process as well as a reduction in overbargaining and waste.*

(3) A conscious effort should be made to apply part of our economic resources toward our unreconciled conflicts. The main advantage would be to make conciliation an organized effort, which would also yield a keener understanding of the disunities to be overcome.

With young whites and blacks, for example, the central need is to speed their entry into society, which hinges largely on the career opportunities open to them. An eco-

---

* When a commission asks for billions to "rebuild our cities," how the money is to be spent should be specified; similarly with defense requests.

nomic policy that narrows the career-creating potential in the public sector could deny many young people the opportunity to work with what they feel are our most serious problems, as with urban difficulties. Many youths are not likely to take jobs in the private economy without fighting back politically and becoming more embittered against "the system."

If a president is to unify the country, his sense of priorities cannot be drastically different from that of sizable segments of the people. The ability to create jobs and careers, like all forms of economic power, carries with it political power. Democrat or Republican, a president should make priority decisions on the basis of national interest, not to favor his own political supporters or some ideology.

Differences in judgment over how to define the national interest will not be reconciled by ignoring the conflicts that divide us; they can be moderated by specific programs of time-priority action, paced over several years, which show why only so much can be done now and what must wait until later, what government cannot do, what individuals must do.

In short, we must begin consciously to come to terms among ourselves. Letting things run on in hope that they will somehow fall into place is only polarizing us further apart.

## 4. The Crisis of Authority

Pope Paul has talked of a crisis of authority in the whole of western civilization. Perhaps we can be a little more precise. When men believed in God, this belief lodged in them some inner restraints on their own behavior. Now that real belief in God is fairly uncommon, particularly among younger people, these restraints are being lost. At the same time, though, we are turning in part at least to government as a virtual substitute for God.

This could prove the most critical aspect of our governmental crisis, that just when we expect and demand so much from government, the sense of personal responsibility and inner restraint is declining and can no longer be relied on.

Actually we demand more of government than was asked of God. The Bible and sermons assured us that God, as the Over-all Manager, was all-wise, all-powerful and all-knowing, even to being able to account for every swallow's whereabouts. Still, He was not expected to perform His miracles until the afterworld. Today we demand that government deliver on sight.

When people believed in "God's will" they were prepared to accept some hardship as inevitable since, it was felt, there were limits to how much of living could be changed. Today many feel that only some man's will or some man's institution stands in the way of what they want to see done.

People turn to government not because they trust it, as they had faith in God, but because it is the only tool that seems powerful enough to speed change. It is the only stick that reaches far enough to change people's thinking, to change the relationship between the slums and suburbs, to gain tax resources for varied needs.

Others would use government to frustrate and prevent even the most needed change. Still others, particularly among some of the young, feel left without God or government as a substitute.

We are constantly sermonized to lower our expectations of government. But whose expectations are to be abandoned? Those of the black man that he will be treated as an equal or of the waitress in Wilson, North Carolina, who declared, "I have the right to send my child to any school I pick;" of the many families like the Menefees in Guthrie County, Iowa, who did not want a second son sent to Vietnam or of the Cincinnati housewife who said "I want to get out but I don't want to give in"; of the Rutgers senior, going into research, who felt, "Spending is what the government is for" or of the western politician who thought, "the future is in the Pacific . . . that's where the people are."

It is the government, of course, that will decide which of these clashing expectations are to be fulfilled. Will one side or the other be favored, or can the government act in a manner that both sides feel is fair and just?

Perhaps we need to drop the pretense that government is a substitute for God, and face up to the real crisis of authority, which is that of self-government. There are no gods among us; only men who must learn to govern themselves.

If that is so, a large part of our crisis is the need to make government believable. Can that be done in times like these, with so much unreconciled conflict, a war not ended, such clashing expectations, spreading distrusts?

The blunt fact is that the old formulas that we took for granted have been lost, and we now must consciously determine what mixture of fear and hope, restraint and freedom, competition and subsidy, the market or priorities, will gain public trust. At some point there may be too much government; at other points we may have to test new governmental mechanisms.

From all of this can we guide ourselves so that we enunciate a set of principles that people will accept voluntarily as being pretty fair to all?

Acting on the basis of principle is made more difficult by two other influences—that we are in the midst of ideological war among ourselves, and that the turbulence of recent years has caused a loss of confidence in each other.

Some actions of the Nixon Administration indicate that it shares this mistrust of at least some of the American people. And yet if the people lose confidence in themselves they cannot have confidence in their government, their institutions or their president.

Each president has to operate within the frame of his own temperament. President Nixon thinks of himself as a "centrist." While Eisenhower was president and Mr. Nixon his vice-president, he was often given the chore of conciliating the more conservative Republican members of Congress and the Senate who might be angry that the White House was too liberal. Usually Nixon would adopt the tactic of saying "It's a lot better having Ike in there than a New Deal radical like ———," and he would name a man whom this senator or congressman disliked intensely.

President Nixon is highly skilled at this technique of playing off one side against the other, remaining, himself, in the middle. This is no trivial skill. It can often achieve more constructive results than confrontation. As I once wrote, in politics a straight line is almost never the shortest distance between two points. Still, the President needs to recognize that his technique can deepen distrust and fear in the nation; also that manipulation all too easily destroys principle.

The war of ideologies represents the distortion of two American traditions. We live in a psychological age that has stimulated our self-awareness which, in turn, spurs conflicting drives for self-fulfillment.

Those who distort the "liberal" tradition seem to seek greater social freedoms by using the government to change anything and everything, certainly in part as a means of avoiding the need to discipline themselves.

Those who distort the "conservative" tradition contend that they should be free to satisfy their hungers for material gain by letting the economy run free; they would weaken government and demand that people steel themselves to be satisfied with what they get.

In a curious way each camp would use one of our major parties for its purposes, the Democrats to justify social permissiveness, the Republicans to justify economic permissiveness.

The mass of Americans would not trust either form of permissiveness to be running loose. The nation needs restraint in both the economy and social relations.

Still the influence of these men of impatience on both sides is enhanced by the fact that this country is now passing through that most critical of political periods, when one majority coalition is being torn apart and both political parties are struggling over what kind of new majority coalition is to emerge.

At the same time, though, we are moving into the politics of a polarizing society, still clinging to the luxuries and irresponsibilities of the old politics of stability. In coalition politics the prevailing attitude is to push for power while one has the chance—"I've got the ball and I'll run with it until I'm tackled." But if a polarizing society is not to be wrenched apart, restraints must be developed within the groups in conflict.

Self-restraint has been so rare in our politics as to seem almost un-American. Talked of endlessly, it is always to be applied to the other fellow; what is really sought is power— to rearrange other people.

Is that what self-government requires? Perhaps that is the riddle put to us by the nuclear sphinx, for which no one knows the sure answer. My own judgment is that the dangers we face here at home are not so great that we do not have time for patience and conciliation. The dangers that threaten from abroad demand that we use the time we have to overcome the worst of our differences, to unite this country.

There is a greatness in the American people that neither the social scientist nor the businessman recognizes. There is no reason why that greatness should be reduced to the stature of either party, of any political leader or any ideology.

That greatness is, first, that the American people are unashamed in their sense of self-interest. They also are a highly pragmatic people who will adjust to changing events and changing times. Finally, although their sense of freedom is colored by their sense of self-interest, they will accept disciplines and restraints and even higher taxes to keep this country from being torn apart.

For myself, personally, I do not think this is a time to lower our voices to whispers of distrust. This is the time to raise our voices in confidence and to demand orderly and meaningful debate on all the issues that concern us so we can reconcile at least some of our differences. Our need is not to be manipulated, but to govern ourselves.

# *ACKNOWLEDGMENTS*

SINCE THIS BOOK has been in the thinking for so many years, it would be impossible to thank all the many individuals who contributed to it.

My debt is particularly heavy to Evan Thomas, who displayed a patience greater than Job's in editing successive drafts of the manuscript, and to Walter B. Everett, Director of the American Press Institute, who read each version as it developed. William B. Harrison of the *Washington Star* also made valuable editorial suggestions.

I also want to thank Tom Boardman, the editor, and Herb Kamm, associate editor, of the *Cleveland Press,* for inviting me into Cleveland to do a survey of the re-election chances of Mayor Carl B. Stokes. Dick Maher and Hilbert Black were invaluable in helping organize the survey. Interviewing with me were three Press reporters—Marge Banks, Barbara Mann, and Russ Musarra. Five intensive weeks of interviewing gave me some understanding of what the politics of racial polarization are really like. The Cleveland experience, with all its tensions and police feuding, as I have observed, seems a hopeful beginning toward stabilizing white-black relations in our northern cities.

In addition to the grant that made possible the later phases of my youth interviewing, the Ford Foundation has given me a travel and study grant to prepare a book on my methodology, which is not yet completed. This display of confidence is appreciated all the more because there still are some Foundation and University people who have argued that journalists should leave the kind of thing I do to the social scientists.

My methodology relies heavily on an intensive analysis of the voting results after each election. To use election returns most sensitively one should work with them in the smallest available unit—the precinct. With the Wallace vote, every precinct in fourteen northern cities was percentaged and mapped in relation to the movement of Negro population over several elections. The result was to make dramatically clear that our racial crisis had taken on a new territorial form.

More than 10,000 individual precincts were handled. Collecting these returns and identifying the racial makeup of these precincts could not have been done without the help of Frank Angelo of the *Detroit Free Press;* Charles Egger of the *Columbus Citizen-Journal;* Ben Maidenburg of the *Akron Beacon-Journal;* Andrew Stasiuk of the *Newark Star-Ledger;* Jack Colwell and John Powers of the *South Bend Tribune;* Terrence O'Rourke of the *Post Tribune* in Gary; Dick Thornburg of the *Cincinnati Post and Times Star;* John Troan of the *Pittsburg Press;* and Frank Crane of the *Indianapolis News.*

Jack Welsh, voter registration supervisor, supplied the necessary Philadelphia returns. The Baltimore precinct vote was furnished by Loyal Randolph of the Board of Elections there.

A similar precinct analysis of the Wallace vote in southern cities was made possible by Duard Le Grand of the *Birmingham Post-Herald;* Everett D. Collier of the *Houston Chronicle;* George W. Healy, Jr., of the *Times-Picayune* in New Orleans; J. Edward Grimsley of the *Richmond Times-Dispatch;* Tom Fesperman of the *Charlotte Observer;* Ed Topp and Charles Schneider of the *Memphis Press-Scimitar;* Sam Ragan, while with the *News and Observer* in Raleigh; Robert J. Haiman of the *St. Petersburg Times;* Jack Wentworth of the *Hollywood* (Florida) *Sun Tattler;* Robert Hollingsworth of the *Dallas Times-Herald;* Ben Bowers of the *Greensboro Record;* William Workman of the *State-Record* in Columbia, South Carolina; John Walters of the *Florida Times-Union* in Jacksonville; James Clendinen and Bob Turner of the *Tampa Tribune.*

Ross Beiler of the University of Miami helped out with the Miami votes. In Houston, Bob Turrentine of the Board of Elections has been invaluable.

Heading the list of other editors to whom I have a special sense of obligation are Walker Stone, formerly editor-in-chief of the Scripps-Howard newspapers, who helped make possible all my campaign reports since 1952, and Earl Richert, present editor-in-chief of the Scripps-Howard papers. I am also appreciative of the other editors who consistently supported my approach to election reporting, particularly Lee Hills of the Knight newspapers; Paul Miller and Vincent Jones of the Gannett chain; Nelson Poynter of the *St. Petersburg Times;* Nick Williams and James Bassett of the *Los Angeles Times;* the successive editors of the *Chicago Daily News;* John Leard of the *Richmond Times-Dispatch;* Bill Dickenson of the *Philadelphia Bulletin;* Kenneth MacDonald and Frank Eyerly of the *Des Moines Register-Tribune;* John Colburn of the *Wichita Eagle;* Ed Murray of the *Phoenix Republican.* Henry Gilburt of United Features has been an effective syndicate advocate.

Joseph Shoquist of the *Milwaukee Journal* was particularly helpful with post-election material; I am also grateful to Otto Zausmer of the *Boston Globe,* for battling official red tape, albeit in vain, on my behalf.

Assisting me in my interviewing of college students were Susan Weiss Gross, Henry Scarupa, now with the Dayton newspapers, Pamela Mendelsohn Herr, Jane McGuire, and my son, Bernard, while he was at Columbia; during the 1968 election campaign, Michael Maidenburg, now with the *Detroit Free Press,* Barbara Lewis Treckler and Patrick Murphy.

Others who have helped me with the collection of voting returns are Pierre Purvis, who does the finest job of keeping congressional districts up to date; Lance Torrance, while with the Republican National Committee; Marvin Wall of the Voter Education Project; T. S. Holman, a COPE analyst, with a remarkable sense of New Jersey voting; and John Steinke, whose specialty is Wisconsin.

I am also indebted to many friends for varied assistances, from voting returns to arranging for drivers to take me through a state. In Iowa it has been my good fortune to be chauffeured by none other than Wallace Ogg, a highly perceptive Extension Service economist, which is like having a driving (not walking) encyclopedia to consult with between interviews.

James G. Maddox, professor of economics at North Carolina State University, assembled his staff to give me a thorough briefing on the economic changes going on in Eastern North Carolina before I went into that stretch of "Wallace country."

For a better understanding of the urban crisis I am enormously indebted to Paul Ylvisaker; also in Chicago, to Pierre DeVise; and in Detroit, to Irving J. Rubin, director of TALUS, and Merle Henrickson of the Detroit Public Schools; in New York, to Don Elliott of the Planning Commission, Maude Craig of the Youth Board, Henry Cohen of the New School for Social Research; also to Wallace Sayre, Eli Ginzberg, and John Fischer, who served with me on the university committee that drafted a report on Columbia University's urban-minority program; also to Dave Starr of the *Long Island Press;* and George Killenberg of the *St. Louis Globe-Democrat.*

In Washington I have become particularly obligated to that curious outfit known as "The Brookings Institution"—notably to Joseph A. Pechman, Charles Schultze, Arthur Okun, James L. Sundquist and Alice Rivlin, who responded to my many queries with good humor and patience. Brookings at present can perhaps be understood best as a kind of economic government in exile, awaiting the return of a Democratic president. Many of its extremely able staff members occupied key posts in the Johnson Administration, and at Brookings they simulate many of the government's economic operations.

William Butler of Chase Manhattan has been good enough to give me periodic briefings; also Martin Gainsbrugh of the National Industrial Conference Board.

Of the many government officials who responded to research inquiries in their departments, I can mention only a few—Joseph Loftus of the Labor Department; Henry B. Schechter of the Department of Housing and Urban Development; Lloyd Henderson of the Civil Rights Division at HEW; Joseph Laitin, who began by being wonderfully cooperative and then became unavailable; John Baker of the Bureau of the Census, who displayed remarkable skill and versatility in feeding me Census statistics on the many problems covered in this book; Henry D. Sheldon, also of the Census, who provided the special projection of how much more rapid would be the increase of Negroes over whites among the youths in our largest nonsouthern cities by 1975.

As for the tables, Calvin Beale of the Department of Agriculture provided the statistics on the yearly progress in the mechanization of cotton picking in the South; also the estimate that nearly a third of the 10,700,000 Negroes now living outside the South are either migrants since 1950 or born to migrants.

In Table 5, the 1969 vote for mayor in New York City is based on unofficial returns for each assembly district.

The vote totals of the twelve largest nonsouthern cities and their suburbs in Table 2 cover the same ones used in my other books—New York, Philadelphia, St. Louis, Chicago, Baltimore, Boston, Los Angeles, San Francisco, Pittsburgh, Milwaukee, Detroit, and Cleveland. To insure comparability over the years, the District of Columbia was not included.

The southern urban counties included in Table 6 are the same ones used in "Revolt of the Moderates," and cover these cities: Birmingham, Mobile, and Montgomery in Alabama; Little Rock and Fort Smith in Arkansas; Miami, Jacksonville, Tampa, St. Petersburg, Orlando, and West Palm Beach in Florida; Atlanta, Augusta, Savannah, Macon, Columbus, Brunswick, and Decatur in Georgia; New Orleans, Baton Rouge, and Shreveport in Louisiana; Jackson and Meridian in Mississippi; Charlotte, Greensboro, Raleigh, Durham, Wilmington, Winston-Salem, and Asheville in North Carolina; Charleston, Columbia, and Green-

ville in South Carolina; Memphis, Nashville, Knoxville, and
Chattanooga in Tennessee; Dallas, Houston, Fort Worth, and
San Antonio in Texas; Richmond, Norfolk, Alexandria, Roanoke,
Lynchburg, and Portsmouth in Virginia.

In this book the words Negro and black are often used inter-
changeably. I appreciate the desire of the militants to label their
cause so it will seem different from the past, but I also know how
Marcus Garvey fought to have Negro capitalized. No disrespect
is intended in the use of either word.

Finally, it is really difficult to express the many ways in
which my assistant, Juyne Kaupp, contributed to this book. She
has been a remarkably effective interviewer, demonstrating anew
that shy people are often the most sensitive to other people's
feelings; her talent for drawing election maps is brilliant; she
also has a fine analytic mind. Something of her must be im-
printed on every other page of this book.

My son Walter helped with some voting analyses; my wife,
Helen Sopot Lubell, did her usual Poo-Bah chores from typing
and proofreading to feeding, also managing to put up with the
extra tribulations of moving from New York to Washington in
mid-book.